ROYAL HORTICULTURAL SOCIETY

THE RHS COMPANION TO
# WILDLIFE
# GARDENING

ROYAL HORTICULTURAL SOCIETY

# COMPANION TO
# WILDLIFE GARDENING

## CHRIS BAINES

*Revised edition of How to Make a Wildlife Garden*

FRANCES
LINCOLN

# CONTENTS

PART I
**WHY MAKE A WILDLIFE GARDEN?**

10  WHY WILDLIFE?

24  A SPECIAL ROLE FOR GARDENS

34  PLANNING THE GARDEN AS A HABITAT
    FOR YOU AND YOUR WILDLIFE

PART II
**CREATING NEW HABITATS**

50  THE WOODLAND EDGE HABITAT

76  HEDGEROWS AND CLIMBER-
    COVERED SCREENS

92  LIVE-IN LAWNS AND WILDFLOWER
    MEADOWS

114  GARDEN PONDS AND OTHER
     'WETLANDS'

# PART III
## SUPPLEMENTING THE HABITATS

142 COTTAGE GARDEN SERVICE STATION

178 A WILD KITCHEN GARDEN

188 BOOSTING WILDLIFE HABITATS

208 PROPAGATING NATIVE PLANTS

220 A RICH TAPESTRY OF WILDLIFE

232 STUDYING GARDEN WILDLIFE

246 OVER THE GARDEN WALL

# PART IV
260 USEFUL ADDRESSES
262 INDEXES
271 ACKNOWLEDGMENTS
272 PICTURE CREDITS

Frances Lincoln Limited
74–77 White Lion Street, London N1 9PF

*RHS Companion to Wildlife Gardening*
Copyright © Frances Lincoln Limited 2016
Text © Chris Baines
Photographs © see page 272
First Frances Lincoln edition 2016

All rights reserved.
No part of this publication may be reproduced,
stored in a retrieval system, or transmitted, in any
form, or by any means, electronic, mechanical,
photocopying, recording or otherwise without the
prior written permission of the publisher or a licence
permitting restricted copying. In the United Kingdom
such licences are issued by the Copyright Licensing
Agency, Saffron House, 6–10 Kirby Street, London
EC1N 8TS.

A catalogue record for this book is available from
the British Library.

ISBN 978-0-7112-3791-9
Designed by Arianna Osti

Printed and bound in China

1 2 3 4 5 6 7 8 9

Quarto is the authority on a wide range of topics.

Quarto educates, entertains and enriches the lives of
our readers – enthusiasts and lovers of hands-on living.

www.QuartoKnows.com

# INTRODUCTION

GARDENING AND WILDLIFE make perfect partners. So many people are discovering that by choosing the right plants for nectar and fruit, providing some shelter and safety, a little extra food and water, and a nest box or two, any garden, balcony or backyard can be dramatically brought to life.

Now, many of the keenest gardeners are as proud of their nesting songbirds and the bees and butterflies in their flower border as they are of their productive fruit and vegetable plots. Others are discovering that more birdsong and a few more bumblebees and wildflowers on their doorstep simply makes it more enjoyable to be outdoors. Firstly, it really works! Hang up a fat bar or a feeder filled with sunflower seeds and wild birds will appear from nowhere. Plant colourful flowers with perfume and plenty of pollen, and when the sun shines the bees and butterflies will bring the garden to life. Provide a pond, no matter how small, and the effect is nothing short of miraculous. In no time at all pond skaters and damselflies will arrive and take up residence; newts and frogs often spawn in the very first spring, and in no time at all there will be the living proof.

Wildlife gardens can be very beautiful. There is an important difference between relaxed informality and untidy neglect. It is true that a wildlife gardener needs to make space for some undisturbed decay, but the hedgehogs, beetles and fungi that benefit are perfectly satisfied with a neatly stacked pile of logs or a carefully collected heap of autumn leaves. Pollinating insects are best attracted to simple, colourful flowers with an attractive perfume. A patch of water with a fringe of pretty wetland wildflowers will give endless pleasure and reflect the changing seasons.

## CLOSE OBSERVATION

Much of my own pleasure comes from the detailed observations that wildlife on the doorstep has to offer. I am always thrilled to discover the perfect circles, snipped from the leaves of my rose bushes by leaf cutter bees. The pecking order on the bird feeders is a daily distraction, made all the more dramatic by the occasional smash-and-grab arrival of a sparrow hawk. I can spend hours watching dragonflies emerging from the pond, and slowly stretching their wings until they are fit to fly, and a torch-lit safari reveals a whole amazing world of night creatures in the flower beds and the water's edge. My garden has given me many more close encounters with the natural world than any other landscape, and all just a moment away from my desk, my bed or my next cup of tea.

Gardening with wildlife makes a very positive difference, and that has great appeal for many of us. Our gardens are one little patch of land where we can start to turn the tide against the seemingly endless gloomy news of melting icecaps, polluted seas and world-wide habitat loss. In the UK alone there are more than 400,000 hectares of domestic gardens – a much greater area than all the nation's nature reserves. Add to that the

**OPPOSITE** A hawker dragonfly takes quite a while to emerge and a garden pond is the ideal place to witness the astonishing transformation.

**ABOVE** The view from my window. Pond, wildflowers, sheltered surroundings and glorious birdsong give me my daily dose of nature.

public parks, the school grounds and the open spaces around offices, hotels and hospitals and it is clear that wildlife gardening can make a massive contribution to creative nature conservation – indeed, it already has. Some of my wintering garden birds nest in northern Norway or Siberia, my flowers feed moths and butterflies from southern Spain, and my dawn chorus includes songbirds that have crossed the continent of Africa to join me for the summer. The way I garden makes a very real contribution to the lives all of them live – and it most certainly makes my own life more enjoyable. I hope this book will help you to share in that pleasure.

# WHY MAKE A WILDLIFE GARDEN?

This painted lady butterfly
may have flown more than
2,000 kilometres to feed on
the nectar in my garden.

# WHY WILDLIFE?

Most people have an instinctive love of nature. You can see it in the way children rush to feed the ducks in the park. You can feel it in the thrill of seeing an urban fox streaking through the beam of your car's headlights. When a butterfly is trapped in the house, you automatically open a window and carefully guide it back to freedom.

Contact with nature seems to be essential if we are to cope with the stress of modern living, and for most people, the garden or the local park is the natural place to enjoy wildlife close to home. Just a few minutes of quiet relaxation among trees, with bird song and bumblebees for entertainment, and even the most exhausted of city workers is ready for anything. Certainly a quiet five-minute stroll through my own small patch first thing in the morning, with dew still wet on the grass, and a mug of tea in my hand, seems to make the perfect start to a working day. There is something magical, too, about the feeling that you are sharing your landscape with a whole host of wild creatures. Some are obvious. Town blackbirds will hop just a safe few feet ahead of you, stopping every now and then for a sideways glance in your direction, and a quick jab at some poor unfortunate snack. Many

of the larger creatures, particularly the mammals, avoid confrontation by operating under cover of darkness. Take the trouble to join them in the late evening twilight, and a minute or two of silent waiting may be rewarded with the swoop of a bat overhead or the snuffles, scuffles and grunts of hedgehogs, field mice and the various other night visitors that share your landscape.

## SMALLER WILDLIFE

The large creatures that you can spot at fifty metres are fascinating to watch, and comforting to have around, but for most people the variety of large animals and birds they are likely to see on their doorstep is fairly limited. The real excitement lies in the far greater variety of wildlife living in the scaled-down world of tangled grasses, bramble leaves and rotting logs. Choose a leafy spot, sit quietly for five minutes and watch this mini-jungle carefully. As your eyes become accustomed to the new scale you will begin to see more and more amazing creatures, all making a secret living right under your nose. If you want to spend a totally absorbing half hour 'on safari', just run a piece of string through a patch of mini-jungle,

get down on your hands and knees, and with the help of a magnifying glass, work your way slowly along your portable nature trail.

Needless to say, all of this nature is important for much more than its entertainment value. It's not too fanciful to suppose that a landscape that is healthy for mini-beasts is also healthy for us – and of course the reverse is also true. Landscapes that are hostile to wildlife must be unhealthy for humans to live in. It is frightening, therefore, to discover just how unfriendly to wildlife our environment has become in recent times. In my lifetime of just two or three generations we have devastated the natural world with chemical pollution, urban expansion, land drainage, road construction and industrialised forestry and farming. I have witnessed the disappearance of a relatively rich landscape, where cowslips and primroses were commonplace, woodland was within walking distance for most people, and butterflies were still part of the standard entertainment on sunny summer days. Those times are just a fond memory now.

The best of our surviving wildlife has been locked away for safe keeping in green museums that we call nature reserves. So far as the preservation of individual species is concerned, that policy might work tolerably well. Put a fence around a bluebell wood, and so long as you continue to manage it positively, cutting the coppice hazel regularly every few years, and controlling the amount of browsing that goes on, there should be bluebells to visit indefinitely. Unfortunately, not all wildlife is as obliging as the bluebell. Dragonflies which breed in nature reserve ponds have a dangerous habit of flying over the fence to hunt their insect prey. All too often the midges beyond the boundary will have been 'got at' by some chemical or another. The dragonfly snaps up a few hundred each day, and by the end of the summer, that's one more spectacular insect that fails to make it back to base. British species of dragonfly have become extinct at an alarming rate since the Second World War. The numbers of half our species of native butterflies are in very steep decline. Hedgehogs, bats, water voles and many other species are now in very serious trouble and it has become all too clear that conservation based on isolated sanctuaries, set in a sterile surrounding landscape, simply doesn't work.

LEFT Our ancient bluebell woods look spectacular, and their glades filled with wildflowers and birdsong are a great inspiration for wildlife gardeners.

BELOW 'Ratty' the water vole is hanging on in a surprising number of urban waterways.

RIGHT This is a buff-tipped moth, perfectly camouflaged to look exactly like a broken birch twig.

RIGHT BELOW A great tit in a hawthorn tree.

## MISSING LANDSCAPE LINKS

In the half century, despite our great national love of nature, we have destroyed 98 per cent of our wildflower meadows, half our ancient lowland woods, 60 per cent of our lowland heaths, 80 per cent of our downland sheepwalks, and the majority of our lowland fens and mires – and despite this scale of loss we are still continuing to destroy some of the surviving special places. Many of these precious habitats are special because they are ancient and can never be replaced. To grub out an 8,000-year-old bluebell wood, just to build a new industrial estate, or grow a few more tons of wheat to add to the surplus mountain is as stupid as demolishing Canterbury Cathedral or Stonehenge to build a multi-storey car park, and yet that is exactly what we have been doing.

To make matters worse, we have also seen the linkages in the landscape disappear. Through the 1970s and 80s many thousands of miles of hedgerows were grubbed out of the farming countryside, stream banks were sterilised by drainage engineers, and as more and more pockets of wetland, woodland and wild grassland were removed or de-natured, the natural networks in the landscape became fragmented. Losing these natural linkages has been disastrous for wildlife. Many species, both plants and animals, need extended territories. They need to travel around the landscape in sheltered safety to search for food or a potential mate. As the landscape has become more disjointed, survival for much of our wildlife has become increasingly difficult.

## ACTION PLAN

So what can we do about it? How can we reverse the trend, and provide future generations with more

wildlife rather than less? When I was writing the first edition of this book, back in the 1980s, the prospect seemed daunting. Since then we have seen some surprising progress. The wild otter is a case in point. In 1980 these wonderful creatures had completely disappeared from all but the most remote westerly and northerly fringes of Britain. Hunting and pesticide pollution had undoubtedly taken their toll, but it was the loss of wild green linkages in the landscape that had proved fatal. Otters need long stretches of unpolluted stream and river, with well-wooded banks. Sadly, towards the end of the last century that combination had all but disappeared. Less than thirty years later there are wild otters back in every single county, right across the country. Close and creative collaboration between conservationists and the water companies restored the habitat links, removed much of the worst water pollution, and revived the otters' fortunes.

Otter conservation is not the only success. In that same period we have seen salmon returning to the Thames, the Tyne and the Mersey. There are red kites and ospreys in the skies again, and one or two of our most endangered butterflies have been brought back

from the brink. These may be exceptions, but they are important, because they show that it is possible to make a positive difference. With skill and commitment we can start to rebuild living landscapes, link the surviving habitats back together and look forward to the slow return of much of our once-familiar wildlife.

We must cling desperately to those fragments of rich, ancient habitat that survive. We need to value the irreplaceable nature of these places, when considering short-life alternative land uses. A new out-of-town shopping centre with an economic life expectancy of twenty to thirty years should never be allowed to replace a precious, green wildlife habitat with a potential life expectancy of – forever!

## TRADITIONAL HABITATS

Almost all our wildlife habitats need managing since we have very little true wilderness in Britain. Where traditional farming practice has produced the habitats, as is the case with water meadows, cornfield wildflowers and hay meadows, then we need to find ways of persuading farmers to continue to manage them along traditional lines. Legislation and financial

OPPOSITE Cornfield weeds or colourful wildflowers? Disturbed brownfield sites now offer some of the best displays.

LEFT In the 1980s the otter was almost lost, but it has made a remarkable recovery, in towns as well as the rural countryside. Nevertheless they are extremely secretive and hard to spot.

## BRILLIANT BEES

Bees have long been fondly regarded as a familiar part of the British countryside. Their value to the natural world and the maintenance of healthy ecosystems is immeasurable, but so is their economic value to the farming industry. A significant 84 percent of food crops grown in Europe rely on bees and other insects to pollinate them. Insect pollination is estimated to contribute €14.2 billion to Europe's economy, with bumblebees our most important pollinators. However, despite their evident worth to us, within the last century bees have suffered the extinction of two species and a major decline in population. It is estimated that a quarter of the 250 different species left are now at risk of extinction. These dramatic losses are attributed to a number of different factors including climate change, intensive farming practices, the use of pesticides, and a loss of habitat. Many species, particularly bumblebees and solitary bees, only collect pollen and nectar from a small number of specific plants, often wildflowers. The tragic loss of our wildflower meadows has contributed significantly to their decline, and your little patch of bee-friendly oasis is a great place to start as we try to undo the damage done to these miraculous creatures.

incentives have helped to bring some positive changes in recent years. Major crises such as foot and mouth disease and mad cow disease, bovine encephalopathy, have helped to raise awareness of the important role that public access to nature plays in the rural economy, and a number of farmers and foresters have pioneered more imaginative ways of combining food and timber production with nature conservation.

Around the turn of the century an important change in conservation thinking occurred. A group of leading lights from the conservation charities and the government's environmental agencies worked together to develop new thinking about the scope for rebuilding biodiversity – bringing back wildlife on a grand scale. The resulting strategy had two strands. The first was to approach habitat restoration on a much bigger and more integrated scale. The Wildlife Trusts adopting a *Living Landscapes* campaign and the RSPB's *Futurescapes* programme embraced much the same joined-up approach to land management. Most importantly, there was a realisation that all landscapes and all landowners must play a part if whole landscapes were to be restored. The very special conservation sites would provide the jewels in the crown, but habitat restoration and more careful management would give even the most degraded landscape elements a positive role to play in restoring landscape integrity and improving the long term prospects for wildlife.

## NATURAL LANDSCAPES

The second important strand revolved around the function of the landscape. Conservationists realised that a more natural landscape had important and valuable roles to play alongside nature conservation. A soft shoreline of living salt marsh could protect the coast from erosion and flooding, heather moorland and peat bog in the hills could store and purify drinking water, and the green spaces in and around towns could heal the scars of industry, clean the air and improve public health. By building these additional benefits into the equation it has proved increasingly easy to justify a more sustainable and wildlife friendly approach to the management of entire living landscapes.

## PEOPLE POWER

Grand strategies are all very well, and they are undoubtedly producing results, but they can leave individuals feeling intimidated and relatively powerless. I'm glad to say that, in my experience at least, that certainly doesn't need to be the case! You can have enormous influence simply by writing a positive letter to the right decision-maker at the right time, since all too often councillors and others are forced to make decisions with only one side of the argument presented to them. It is true that most personal lobbying is triggered by some very local issue, and is often dismissed as NIMBYism – 'not in my back yard' – but it is entirely reasonable for people to care most passionately about their most familiar and accessible places. Remaining silent in such circumstances is a sure way of giving the green light to further habitat loss. To win such arguments it helps to offer NIMBY- *plus!* In the 1990s I campaigned to protect street trees from the root damage caused by cable TV trenching. Success was mixed, but there were two extra elements that helped the cause considerably. The first was linking the value of the street trees to other issues of public concern such as improved air quality and reduction in childhood asthma. The second was to work with the more enlightened trenching companies to adopt techniques

OPPOSITE Some dragonfly species hunt over extensive territories. Dig a pond, and common hawkers like this will quickly find your garden.

LEFT Pipistrelle bats hunt over my inner city garden on warm summer's evenings, but in more than 25 years I have yet to discover the tiny holes in which they shelter through the day, or where they hibernate each winter.

OVERLEAF Linkages through the landscape are vital for wildlife. Canals like this one, railways, streams and street trees all help to bring more creatures into contact with your wildlife garden.

that explored innovative ways of laying cables beneath the tree roots. An unholy alliance of conservationists and contractors proved particularly persuasive.

## LARGER WILDLIFE

For the big, ambitious campaigning issues, perhaps the most important thing you can do, though, is to lend your support to your local environmental group. Throughout the UK there are Wildlife Trusts, local RSPB groups and others. They all depend on the support of individual members, and a few minutes online will put you in touch. At one time they would have been preoccupied with monitoring rare species and preserving nature reserves in wild and remote places. How things have changed in thirty years! The national conservation bodies have become powerful campaigning organisations, consulted by local authorities when planning decisions have to be made, influencing policy at national and international level, and working hard to provide more and better places for wildlife. If you aren't a member of your County Wildlife Trust already, then you certainly should be. They need your support, and in return you can rely on them to help you fight your battles in support of the local wildlife.

## POSITIVE APPROACH

The picture I have painted so far is pretty gloomy — a desperately urgent need to cling to the few remaining fragments of our once-rich natural heritage. So far as the ancient habitats in our farming countryside are concerned, I'm afraid that is absolutely true. Most of the rural landscape has been turned into a hostile green desert for wildlife, and ancient meadows, bogs and woodlands cannot be re-created, no matter how much field-corner tree planting farmers do. There is, however, a silver lining to this big black cloud.

In our villages, towns and cities there is a vast amount of land that no one expects to be intensively farmed or highly productive. The average metropolitan conurbation may seem at first glance to be a pretty hostile concrete jungle with noisy traffic, polluting chimneys and sterile glass and concrete dominating the scene.

In fact, the view from the street is very misleading. Climb to the top of a tall building in London, Manchester, Birmingham or any other UK town or city

and you will see what I mean. Even the most congested conurbation is likely to be more green than grey and the green space in towns is all available for nature conservation – no productivity targets to satisfy here!

## URBAN LANDSCAPE

My most familiar urban area is the West Midlands, but I know from my childhood in Sheffield that the story in South Yorkshire is much the same. While the main roads are flanked by buildings, they simply screen a fantastic mosaic of greenery – an urban living landscape. The railway lines, canals, road verges and river valleys provide a continuous network of rich green ecological corridors - ideal for wildlife to move along. Most people are familiar with the kestrels that hunt for small mammals and large insects along the verges of the urban clearways, and in recent years they have been joined by buzzards, and even red kites in some of urban Britain. Many people are familiar with the foxes that clear up the debris of chip papers and dropped ice creams in the city centre after the last bus has left, and we know that they travel in from the leafy suburbs along the commuter railway lines.

Kingfishers have followed the canals, and now nest deep in the heart of the city, presumably enjoying the sticklebacks which live in the unpolluted water, and undoubtedly benefiting from the slightly warmer winter temperatures which mean less ice to cope with. Tawny owls provide a night-time soundtrack for much of the urban forest; lime hawkmoths lay their eggs on the leaves of street lime trees; swifts scream above the rooftops and trawl for insects over parks and city gardens. There are definite advantages to town life for a great many of our wild creatures.

## WILDLIFE CORRIDORS

Interlinked networks of wild green habitat are vitally important if wildlife is to move around. Certainly there is plenty of evidence of a move into the towns for the more spectacular large predators. By the mid 1980s, foxes, stoats, hedgehogs, kestrels, herons and kingfishers were among the more spectacular creatures that had travelled along the wildlife corridors to establish new territories in the grasslands, woodlands and lakes of our public parks, in our overgrown Victorian cemeteries and in our suburban

gardens. Ecological corridors play an equally important role in the lives of less spectacular wildlife. This is obvious if you think about it, since the predators rely on the rich pickings provided by the smaller creatures, and they, in turn, all depend directly or indirectly on the availability of a rich diversity of plant life.

Stand by a railway line in late August and you will see how successfully the clouds of rosebay willowherb and thistle seed hitch a lift in the slipstream of the trains. The birds and animals that move along the corridor will inevitably transport the sticky, hooked fruit of species such as burdock and goosegrass (cleavers) a little further into town – just take a look at your socks and trousers after five minutes of jungle-bashing. The ease of movement along green corridors is also the main reason why some of our most invasive and unwelcome species have colonised so successfully. The American mink that are wiping out the endangered water vole have swept along canals and streams to occupy most of the country, and Japanese knotweed and Himalayan balsam are just two of the invasive aliens that have made effective use of the green network.

Many non-invasive plants are also surprisingly good at moving around. You can plot the progress of large plants quite easily, particularly where a new corridor is created, for example on the embankments of the latest section of the ring road. Provided the soil isn't too rich, and the gangmowers are kept at bay, saplings of those trees and shrubs that have windborne seed spring up almost immediately. Silver birch and goat willow are the classic first colonisers, silver birch having a very light, flat seed case, and goat willow floating along with a little cotton-wool cloud in much the same style as a dandelion parachute. Because their seeds are very small, these two tree species can travel over long distances, but they need to germinate in open ground, since they don't contain enough of an energy reserve to grow a seedling that can penetrate through other vegetation. A sand pit or a pile of fresh rubble is ideal. You may also have the winged seed of ash and sycamore spinning in and germinating. Their reserves are greater so that they can colonise established grassland and other mature plant communities.

Within five or six years the front line of pioneer trees will themselves be mature enough to produce seed of their own, and so blow a little further along the wildlife corridor.

## FIRST VISITORS

Once the pioneers have produced a branch or two, birds will roost there. Inevitably the fruit-eaters, such as blackbirds and thrushes, will leave behind a sprinkling of hawthorn, elder, rose and other shrub seeds – all conveniently stripped of their juicy outer fruit and specially prepared for instant germination. Within a year or two the initial tree colonisers will be surrounded by a thicket of bramble, wild briar and May blossom. A year or two later, this scrub will be generating blackberries and rose hips of its own, to feed the birds that carry the seed to the next patch of open ground.

Of course the green corridors are only a part of the wildlife resource in towns, but they have the advantage of being easy to identify and appreciate. In planning terms these networks of canals, streams, road verges and railway embankments are now being used as the basis for green infrastructure strategies – official plans that recognise the importance for people and for wildlife of keeping the habitat network intact.

Take a look at your neighbourhood on the aerial photos available on Google Earth and you will see that the corridors link together a great number of 'green bulges'. Sometimes the bulge may be no bigger than a traffic island or a quarter-hectare building plot, but there are huge bulges too. Some are unofficial landscapes such as quarries, railway sidings, overgrown demolition sites and cemeteries. Others such as the parks, school playing fields and hospital grounds make up the more official greenspace network.

## URBAN GREENSPACE

Together all of this land adds up to a vast area; hundreds of thousands of hectares of land that has no need to be sprayed with chemicals. This land should be used as creatively as possible, to help in compensating for the loss of wildlife habitat in the countryside. Urban greenspace has the added advantage that almost nine-tenths of our population live in towns and so the wildlife of the canal, the quarry, the refuse tip and the public park is accessible and familiar to almost everyone.

Generally speaking, the unofficial wasteland sites are much richer in wildlife than the official public open

## HOW GREEN IS THE WORLD?

Half the people in the world now live in towns and cities, and by 2050 the urban population is expected to reach 70 per cent. In much of Western Europe the proportion is already much higher than that. In Britain, nine out of every ten people live an urban life. Such a crowded, stressful existence makes access to green spaces all the more important, and in many places new ways are being explored of bringing more of the natural world into our daily lives. Gardens, balconies and courtyards all play their part at a personal level, but there are also a great many more school grounds where nature conservation and wildlife gardening are encouraged. In the most densely built up areas every available surface offers opportunities for new habitats, and green walls and green roofs are beginning to become commonplace.

OPPOSITE An industrial past is no barrier to a wildlife-friendly future. Worn out sand and gravel pits are among our most important wetland habitats.

spaces. Derelict wasteland is particularly good for coarse weed species such as thistles, docks and teasels, and these attract clouds of butterflies in the summer and large flocks of seed-eating finches in the winter. There is often a drainage problem on wasteland sites. Water collects in compacted hollows, or fills up old basements, and permanent pools are quickly adopted as breeding habitat for amphibians and aquatic insects. Temporary winter wetlands provide an important resting point for the migrant ducks, geese and waders that fly to Britain from the frozen north each year.

EXCESSIVE TIDINESS

By contrast, most public parks and playing fields tend to be neat and tidy, and the traditional landscape of closely mown grass and parkland trees is a relatively poor habitat for wildlife. It does have tremendous capabilities though. Some parkland grass is full of wildflowers, chopped off by the mower blades week after week. A number of the trees are exceedingly old, perhaps dating back to a time long before nineteenth century parks, when the local landscape was woods and fields. The parks offer tremendous potential for habitat

creation. A change in the mowing pattern can produce wildflower meadows almost instantly. An underplanting of hazel, holly, foxgloves and primroses can turn the lonely specimen trees into the top canopy of rich new woodland within a season or two. There is scope for converting redundant boating lakes to marsh and reed bed, flooding the badly drained sports pitch to provide wildfowl habitat, and generally 'roughing up the place' in the interest of wildlife.

Many people would find more reason to visit the park if there were more birds and butterflies around, if the grassland was sprinkled with cowslips in the spring, and if there were brambles and hazelnuts to harvest in the autumn. If that kind of park appeals to you, tell your local authority. There is plenty of scope for creative conservation as well as formal sports provision. If even 10 per cent of the close-mown grass was allowed to flower and was cut for hay, then we would soon hear skylarks in our cities, and there would be far more numerous butterflies for town-dwellers to enjoy.

When you apply the same ideas to school grounds, hospital landscapes, airports, power stations and all the other official green landscapes we pay people to

manage, then you can see what tremendous scope there is for helping wildlife, and making our life in towns more colourful and interesting.

## SIGNIFICANT GARDENS

A major part of the green space in villages, towns and cities is provided by private gardens. Your garden or mine may seem small and insignificant on its own, but when you add all the garden space together it covers a huge area, and often a row of leafy gardens can provide a vital wildlife corridor link in itself. Gardens are relatively quiet, generally sheltered, and they often follow the line of much older landscape features. If you have a hawthorn hedge, a line of trees or a ditch running along the back edge of your garden, then the odds are that it is a relic of the rural landscape that existed before the houses were built. That may mean it dates back hundreds of years, and therefore the habitat will have the added bonus of a long history, in which the wildlife will have had the chance to build up into a complex community.

If you adopt the accepted practices of twenty-first century gardening, then you will be planting exotic shrubs and flowers, and generally putting the local wildlife

ABOVE This is the wildlife garden I created for the RHS Chelsea Flower Show in 1985. It caused a stir with the horticultural establishment, but the gardening public and the wildlife seemed to love it.

RIGHT Thirty years later, the RHS has embraced the whole idea, with research and demonstration gardens such as this *Plants for Bugs* trial plot at RHS Garden Wisley.

under exactly the same kind of hostile pressure that has done so much harm in the farming countryside. It is true that many garden plants are beneficial to pollinating insects, and some may produce heavy crops of fruits and seeds which can also benefit wildlife. However they squeeze out the native plants and suppress the native invertebrates that need to feed on their leaves. The RHS has been studying the relationship between garden plants and garden invertebrates very closely for a number of years, and their *Plants for Bugs* research has added greatly to our knowledge of the subject.

Try a more sensitive approach. See how many things you can persuade to live in your garden, instead of notching up more and more things to kill. Even the smallest of town gardens can provide a rich and valuable sanctuary for a whole host of wildlife. Nobble your neighbours. Persuade them to plant a hedge, use less pesticide, dig a pond or simply stop burning the autumn leaves, and in no time at all you will notice an increase in bird life, a boost in butterflies, and your garden will start to look, smell and sound different. You will have a garden with life in it, and you will be playing a part in the whole business of saving a safe place for nature.

## WILDLIFE PIONEERS

I'm proud to have been the first person brave enough to create a wildlife garden for the RHS Chelsea Flower Show – back in 1985. At that time this was such a novelty for the horticultural establishment that my medal from the RHS was mistakenly inscribed, "To Chris Baines, for a wildfire garden". Linking the words 'wildlife' and 'garden' did not seem to make sense. Most of the wildlife advice at that time on BBC Radio 4's Gardeners' Question Time and in gardening magazines was about how to get rid of the wildlife in your garden. I'm pleased to say, though, that the opposite is now the case. This book has become a bestseller, and there are now wildflowers in almost every Chelsea show garden. Encouraging garden wildlife is a mainstream issue, and a great many more people are managing to bring songbirds, butterflies, hedgehogs and frogs much closer to home.

# 2

# A SPECIAL ROLE FOR GARDENS

THERE ARE around 400,000 hectares of private gardens in Britain and, together, they occupy much more land than all the official nature reserves combined. In many of our cities, our gardens make up almost a quarter of the greenspace. The intricate mosaic of different habitats that they offer and the way that they connect to other open spaces such as parks and school grounds makes this the most important conservation resource for many of the country's wild plants and animals. It should come as no surprise to find that since the turn of the century the value of gardens for wildlife has begun to be taken much more seriously. While even the wildest of gardens cannot hope to provide a habitat for the osprey or the otter, our gardens can make an enormous difference to the well-being of a huge variety of less demanding plants and animals.

Much of Britain used to be covered with deciduous woodland before humans began clearing the land for farming. There would have been the occasional glade where a large tree had collapsed, or wild deer had cropped the tree seedlings, and along the stream and river courses there would have been patches of disturbed ground where collapsed river cliffs and shingle beaches would have provided habitat for colourful wildflowers. When people began digging the soil, these opportunist plants were quickly labelled 'weeds of cultivation'. These 'weeds' became the cornfield wildflowers — poppies, cornflowers, corn marigolds — and while farmers could only control them through cultivation they remained extremely common. With the arrival of chemical weedkillers, particularly after the Second World War, weed control became much more effective and indiscriminate, and many of our agricultural wildflowers began to disappear at an alarming rate. Since woodland was the major habitat in Britain for so long, many of our native plants and animals have continued to be most at home in the dappled shade of the woodland edge, or on disturbed ground — and these are the two basic types of habitat which the average garden offers. This is why garden birds such as the blackbird and the dunnock are so obviously at home here. They scratch around among the fallen leaves of your shrub bed in just the same way as their ancestors must have done among the leaf litter of the primeval forest.

This woodland glade environment is our own natural primitive habitat too. We feel comfortably protected in

a sheltered leafy glade, so a garden that suits us as a place to live in is bound to suit a great many of our favourite wild plants and animals.

Left to its own devices, nature has a great ability to settle into a balanced state. The natural woodland plant communities develop on several layers, with each canopy soaking up a little more of the light until the woodland wildflowers at carpet level have just enough sunshine to flower in early spring, before the upper canopies come into leaf. In a similarly balanced way, there will be just enough predators around to eat up most of the plant-eating creepy-crawlies, and so prevent them from destroying the habitat itself.

## NATURAL BALANCE

By gardening, we automatically disturb that balance in many ways, and the secret of a successful wildlife garden depends on understanding the way in which our various gardening activities will distort that natural balance. The greater the diversity of wildlife, the more enjoyment you will have, but many orthodox modern gardening practices disturb the balance in a negative way, and reduce the range of wildlife that can survive.

**BELOW** Model your planting on natural woodland with multiple layers of vegetation from tree-tops down to carpets of spring flowers.

**RIGHT** Fallen leaves, rotting logs and a little untidiness all help to make hedgehogs and other shy woodland creatures feel at home.

**BELOW RIGHT** It is natural for blackbirds and many other garden species to forage for food among the fallen leaves.

'Live and let live' should be the maxim. Think long and hard before you kill anything, or tidy anything away – and if that sounds like an open invitation to relax in the garden, then you are getting the message.

There are lots of ways in which you can give your garden the woodland edge structure mentioned earlier, but the real key to rich wildlife depends on the way you manage your patch. First of all, minimise disturbance. If your planting develops as a series of layers, with plants tightly packed together, there will be no spare light filtering through to stimulate 'weeds' to grow, and less need for you to crash around in the undergrowth pulling them out. The more timid wild creatures – the hedgehogs, dunnocks and wrens – will be able to move around unmolested.

## INSECT COMMUNITY

A rich wildlife garden will be particularly good for insects: you will notice how many more hoverflies, bumblebees and ladybirds there are around. Left to their own devices these also form a balanced community, but modern chemical gardening can play havoc with the interrelationship between 'pests' and predators. When

BELOW Lavender fills the summer garden with perfume – and with pollinating insects.

RIGHT Native ladybirds – the adults and their larvae – have a huge appetite for blackfly.

OPPOSITE The commercial bird food industry has greatly increased the range of products available and the diversity of garden birds has responded dramatically.

the aphids appear in the spring, and start to suck the sap from your prized broad beans, it is tempting to whack them with the latest chemical spray. Look carefully before you take the plunge. Within days of the blackfly appearing, you will find strange wrinkled grey creatures, about a centimetre long and looking for all the world like miniature dragons, wriggling along the same stems wiping out hundreds of blackfly with the efficiency of tiny vacuum cleaners. These are the larvae of ladybirds, and the familiar adults are just as efficient at snapping up aphids. Spray the pest, and you are more than likely to kill the natural predator. What is more, the pest, in this case the blackfly, is able to return and multiply far more quickly than its predator, the ladybird, so hey presto, with one squirt of your killer spray you have set up the next generation of aphids for a relatively predator-free life of luxury, and goodness knows what special ingredients you have added to your future Sunday lunch.

## RICHER HABITATS

The exciting thing about gardening for wildlife is that you can begin to distort the balance in favour of wildlife. Your semi-detached woodland glade can provide a richer, safer habitat than any that ever existed in nature, because you can boost the habitat. You may be doing that already. Your flower borders provide a surplus of nectar and pollen which brings butterflies and bees from miles around. The food on your bird table helps to keep dozens of local bluetits alive through the long, hard winter and you may well have a nest box or two, providing a safe alternative nesting site for the small birds that would more naturally choose to build in a hollow log or a rotting branch.

In the next few chapters I will show you how you can improve the rich habitats in your garden, or create them from scratch if you are just starting, so that a wide variety of plants and animals will move in permanently. But it is also important to realise the potential for habitat extras: the winter bird food, the banks of perfumed flowers, the bowl of drinking water – these all help to improve your garden as a 'service station' for passing wildlife; the wild animals that need a bigger territory than you can provide. Some of these service station visitors may travel a long way, too. In summer, you could have painted lady butterflies from North Africa and garden warblers from south of the Sahara.

LEFT Provide a variety of different food to attract a wider range of garden birds. Hard nuts and seeds from a feeder and soft windfalls from an apple tree are a great combination.

RIGHT Many bird species, including this garden warbler, will migrate between your summer garden and their wintering grounds as far away as Africa.

BELOW Some butterflies migrate too. This is a painted lady, freshly arrived from the Mediterranean to feed on the nectar of northern Europe's garden flowers.

In the winter months you will almost certainly have starlings from Scandinavia squabbling over the scraps, you may have Swedish siskins enjoying the sunflower seeds in your feeders, and redwings and fieldfares from as far away as northern Russia stripping your shrubs of berries. It is exciting to think that your little wildlife garden can make a significant contribution to international nature conservation.

KEEN OBSERVATION

Another important reason why garden wildlife needs to be taken more seriously: it is so accessible. From a purely scientific point of view, most of the great discoveries of the natural world have been made by patient and continuous observation. Where better to study wildlife than right outside your home? Oddly enough, most naturalists of the past seem to have preferred less convenient places for their study. They may have had a need to stand up to their waist in mud for weeks on end, or to be half eaten by insects, in order to give their work scientific credibility. As a consequence the supposedly common and familiar wildlife you can expect to attract into your garden is often less understood than the more

BELOW The first redwings usually arrive on a blast of cold weather from Scandinavia or northern Russia – perfect timing for our garden windfalls and ornamental berries.

RIGHT Most siskins arrive in autumn from the chilly north. Alder seed is their natural preference, but they have become a common site on garden feeders.

OPPOSITE Make space for rotting logs in quiet corners of the garden. They will provide a slow release of nutrients and habitat for a wealth of the small creatures that are the basis of a successful wildlife garden food chain.

THE TOP TEN INGREDIENTS FOR A SUCCESSFUL WILDLIFE GARDEN

1. Shelter and shade
2. Layers of plants, from tree canopy down to carpeting groundcover
3. Flowers, fruits and seeds the whole year round
4. A reliable supply of water
5. Room for decay, with mulches, composting and rotting logs
6. Freedom from poisonous pesticides
7. A bird-feeding station
8. Extra artificial sites for nesting and roosting
9. Green links to the surrounding neighbourhood
10. A secluded seat for maximum enjoyment

celebrated rare species of the tropical swamp or the frozen tundra.

The house sparrow is a case in point. These seemingly irrepressible little birds, which everyone took for granted, crashed in numbers around the end of the twentieth century and nobody could explain why. Naturalists, with their preference in rarities, had simply overlooked the dear old 'spadger'. Now there is a huge increase in citizen science, with many thousands of individuals taking part in annual surveys of birds, butterflies, bumblebees and other garden creatures. The various wildlife charities that coordinate these mass scientific studies find the resulting increased understanding invaluable in monitoring population trends, identifying the effect of changing weather patterns and monitoring the impact of climate change.

Of course, I do not expect everyone to be interested in years of careful monitoring of snail movement, or the feeding preference of the cabbage white butterfly. For most of us, the great joy of the accessibility which garden wildlife offers is that we can become familiar with the plants and animals living on our doorsteps. We can see how they change from season to season, and the closer we look, and the more familiar we become, the deeper will be our commitment to helping nature to survive into the future. Garden wildlife is there to be enjoyed, certainly, but it also has an important job to do. As people learn to love the wild plants and animals in our own gardens, they are bound to demand much greater care for our more rare and precious wildlife.

## 3

Relax. Close your eyes and be transported to sounds and smells of a countryside which has almost disappeared.

# PLANNING THE GARDEN AS A HABITAT FOR YOU AND YOUR WILDLIFE

DO NOT IMAGINE you need a two-hectare country estate before you can begin to plan for wildlife. Even a window box can provide a welcome resting place for passing butterflies if you grow the right flowers, and every tower block has its high-rise nature lovers, tempting bluetits up to the tenth storey with bags of peanuts and lumps of fat. A friend of mine in Holland has a sand dune, a chalk grassland and an acid bog, each full of appropriate wildflowers, and all on a terrace just a metre square. He has created exactly the right soil and drainage conditions for each community – in a set of concrete plant tubs. Every July he looks forward to the mammoth task of harvesting his hay meadow with a pair of kitchen scissors.

Do not feel either, that you can only start wildlife gardening if you are able to begin with a virgin plot. There is scope for a little more wildlife habitat in the most mature of gardens. A garden that I transformed for the BBC TV programme *Bluetits and Bumblebees* in 1988 was first laid out in 1907, and the lawn had been mown to within an inch of its life throughout every summer for the next seventy years. When I moved in, I decided to leave half the grass uncut for the first summer just to see what happened. Within weeks there were sheets of wildflowers blooming. Lady's smock, or the cuckoo flower, popped up everywhere, its delicate pink flowers pulling in lots of spring butterflies. I was thrilled to see handsome orange tips feeding on the nectar, mating and then laying their eggs on the leaves of this lovely wildflower – all within a month or two of this change of management.

## DESIGNING A WILDLIFE GARDEN

Let us suppose for a minute, though, that yours is a brand new garden in a new development. Every plot in the development will vary – with different aspects, climates and soils – and you and your family will have different needs from your neighbours. The most important thing about garden design is to begin by getting it right for you. Sort out the spaces you need, and then wildlife can be encouraged by building, planting and managing those spaces in sympathetic ways.

I always find it is helpful to imagine the new garden first of all as a solid block, or in our case a solid patch of woodland. What you must then do is think about the spaces; the clearings you want to carve out of the solid. Ideally, if you have room, it is a good plan to imagine leaving a belt of solid woodland around the edge of

BELOW Every little helps.
Even a window box or a
hanging basket filled with
nectar flowers will make
a difference and provide
a close view of nature
through the window.

to be, you can begin to think about carving out some bigger spaces. With a small town garden you may be left with just enough room for one central open space. Having tucked a patio into the sunniest corner, and a bench under the shrubbery facing towards the west, you will want to carve out a 'clearing' to look into. If the garden is bigger you might be able to carve out two or more central spaces, and these glades can perhaps be put to different uses.

The one nearest the house might simply be a formal velvet lawn, neat, tidy and pretty to look at, useful for sitting on, but not much good for wildlife. You may then need another lawn-filled glade where the children can kick a ball about: rougher grass, scope for dandelions, starlings and daddy-long-legs, but a bit too much activity for the more timid wild creatures. A third space might be devoted to vegetable growing, screened from the house but open to the sun, and a fourth glade could be developed specifically as a wildlife habitat, with the 'lawn' managed as a wildflower meadow, a pool in the centre for frogs and dragonflies, and plenty of native wildflowers and rotting leaves to help encourage the mini-beasts.

your garden, to provide shelter, to screen you from the neighbours, and to give the more timid wildlife a secluded access route around, in and out of your garden. You will almost certainly want to carve out a space in which you can sit and enjoy the sunshine, and if that can be close to the house then so much the better – you will be able to eat outside, too. That space probably needs to be the size of an average kitchen. Any bigger and it will be draughty and you will begin to feel uncomfortable. For times when the weather is hot, it is nice to have a place in the garden where you can sit in the shade too. This can be a tiny space just big enough for a bench. If it is tucked under the canopy of your enclosing solid 'woodland', then it will also provide you with the ideal spot for sitting quietly and watching wildlife. Here the solid bank of imaginary trees and shrubs will help with your camouflage, and after a couple of minutes the birds you are watching will forget all about you.

## OUTDOOR ROOMS

Once you've sorted out your sitting spaces, and you've worked out how big, or rather how small, they need

RIGHT TOP Daisies deserve
to be part of everybody's
childhood. Ease up on the
lawn mowing for a couple
of weeks and up they come.

RIGHT BELOW Hedgehogs
are having a very tough time,
but a source of clean and
accessible drinking water will
certainly help if they are still
living in your neighbourhood.

OVERLEAF LEFT If you have
space, then wildlife habitats
such as ponds and hedgerows
blend very well with all
the other elements of
a varied garden.

OVERLEAFT RIGHT A
simple mown path makes
Pam Lewis's magnificent
wildflower meadow at her
Sticky Wicket garden in
Dorset accessible and easier
to appreciate.

If you think about the garden as a series of outdoor rooms, enclosed by banks of shrubbery and woodland edge, then as your family's demands change, the use of the spaces can be adjusted. When the children grow out of the football phase, the goalposts can be removed and meadow flowers can be planted. If the structure of the garden is right, and the various glades are comfortable, then your garden will be adaptable and the structure itself can form the bulk of your garden wildlife habitat.

Now let's think specifically about that wildlife glade, and remember if you are as keen as I am on wildlife in the garden, there is nothing to stop you devoting several 'glades' to habitat creation. Again the emphasis needs to be on you and your enjoyment of wildlife.

## ACTIVITY CENTRES

One sure way of providing plenty of activity in your wildlife glade all year round is to incorporate some water. If you can possibly manage it, invest in a big, shallow-edged pond. The wet margin could provide you with ideal growing conditions for a mass of beautiful wildflowers, the water surface itself will reflect every subtle change in the weather, and within and around the pond there will be a constant buzz of activity. You will have flocks of starlings enjoying noisy January bathing parties, amorous frogs singing away on moonlit March evenings, spectacular dragonflies darting jerkily from one corner to another, and foxes, hedgehogs and all the other passing wildlife dropping in for a late-night drink. Try to make sure that part of the pond can be seen from the house. From my desk I can look across the patio and my flower garden and lawn to the water's edge, and whenever I glance up I am rewarded with some wildlife spectacle or another.

The other wildlife activity centre which you need to place in full view is the bird table. This needs to be out in the open to reduce the risk from pouncing cats, and if you feed regularly, especially through the winter, you can attract a terrific variety of beautiful wild creatures to entertain you just a metre from your window.

## LAWNS AND MEADOWS

The rest of the open space within your 'glade' is likely to be lawn. Britain has a marvellous climate for growing grasslands. The traditional close-mown sward is okay for a few wildlife species. Daisies and plantains love it, for

instance. Starlings and thrushes are happy hunting over it for the leatherjackets that feed on the grass roots, or the earthworms that tunnel away just below the surface. To increase the amount of wildlife it is well worth managing some of your lawn as a meadow. If it is big enough you may even arrange to have a spring flower meadow full of cowslips and lady's smock, which you mow as normal from July onwards, and a taller hay meadow coloured with lady's bedstraw, knapweed and scabious which you harvest in September. Do make sure that you keep some of your grassland mown neatly though. A closely cropped path through the meadow will help you get close to the wildlife without trampling down the taller plants, and a nice crisp edge to the rather unorthodox 'hayfield' reassures your friends and neighbours. They are much more likely to accept your argument that "it's meant to look like that!"

The bank of vegetation – all that is left of your original solid mass – which surrounds the glade should be made of a mixture of woodland edge habitat and service station flower garden. Keep the southern enclosure fairly low, to allow in plenty of sunshine, and give yourself wide enough borders to be able to stack up the planting in a series of layers. Research by the RHS has shown how significant it is to provide as much height as possible, and to design the planting to form a series of different layers, Unless your garden is exceptionally big, beware of planting trees that will grow into giants. It is always a painful decision when they have to come out later, and for most small gardens it is probably better to go for species such as hawthorn, crab apple and field maple instead. Build a space into your woodland edge where you can hide the compost heap. It may be marvellous for wildlife but it is not likely to look pretty, and it can smell in the summer. If you do not have enough room for a 'woodland edge' border around the whole of your glade, then shuffle the whole thing over and use a hedge to form one of the boundaries – perhaps the southern or eastern one. This will let the sun in, give you space on the opposite edge for a more generous bank of shrubs, and will give you yet another slightly different habitat.

## SOIL FERTILITY

Sometimes when taking on a brand new garden you arrive before the topsoil. Sometimes the topsoil will never arrive. If you do have a choice, then it is worth

LEFT Bats need safe places in which to spend each day, raise young and hibernate through the winter. Simple boxes like this increase their options.

BELOW Colourful cornfield annuals like these have almost disappeared from farmland, but with a little annual cultivation they can brighten up the summer wildlife garden year after year at next-to-no cost.

OPPOSITE A shallow source of clean water will be used by garden birds for drinking and bathing the whole year round.

thinking about soil fertility in relation to your garden layout. Ideally you want maximum growth in the vegetable patch where you are hoping to grow crops, and along the lines of structure planting – the woodland edge and shrub borders – where you are hoping for rapid growth to provide shelter. Use up the topsoil in these areas. Your formal lawns and flower beds will benefit from a few inches of topsoil to keep them looking green through the summer, but your meadow will perform best on poor soil. The ideal material for the centre of your glade is fast-draining sandy subsoil. If your meadow is on deep, rich topsoil then the grasses will romp away, and most of the more colourful meadow wildflowers will be swamped out of existence. One of the most inspiring wildlife gardens created in recent years is Sticky Wicket, in Dorset. Here the owner Pam Lewis cleared all the fertile surface soil from the middle of the garden, used it to create mounds and flower borders around the boundary, and created a spectacular low fertility wildflower meadow as the centrepiece.

If you have a choice, go for a garden plot with a variety of levels. Basically you are aiming to attract a wide and interesting diversity of wildlife. That will be easiest

if your garden contains subtly different variations on the habitat theme, and a garden with sloping banks, damp hollows and well-drained plateaux will automatically provide that diversity.

Most of us take on gardens that already have a history. I expect that for most people wildlife gardening will simply be a new phase in the life of a garden they have been living with for years. If that is the situation you are in, then you will be looking for painless ways of improving the wildlife habitat without any dramatic, radical upheaval. Again, as a first principle I repeat my plea to relax. There is a host of ways in which you can subtly change the management of your garden to benefit wildlife. Raise the lawnmower blades a centimetre higher and your formal lawn will improve dramatically as a habitat for insects and creeping wildflowers. Accumulate a stockpile of dead logs, prunings and fallen leaves, and small mammals will thrive. Leave flower heads to run to seed and flocks of finches will feed there through the winter. Have faith in the balance of nature instead of relying on chemical poison to tackle the garden pests – in no time at all you will have lacewings, ladybirds, ground beetles and other natural predators galore.

## SERVICE STATIONS

Once you've adopted the right, relaxed, 'ecologically sympathetic' attitude and learned to love a little untidiness, you can begin building up the wildlife service station aspect of your garden. This can be done gradually and cheaply. Erect a bird table and put out food regularly. Put up a few well-sited nesting boxes for the small birds and perhaps a bat box or two. Introduce more and more garden flowers which are good pollen-, nectar- and seed-producers, and add some native plants to the shrub and flower border.

Grow climbers up the fences and walls, choosing natives such as honeysuckle in preference to 'exotics', and allow the existing shrubberies to grow up and provide the sheltering canopy for lower-growing layers of groundcover and shade-loving wildflowers. Gradually, as the emphasis in the garden changes, you will be rewarded with more and more wildlife visitors.

Once the popularity of your service station wildlife garden is established, you will have a regular stream of summer butterflies dropping in from the local railway embankment to top up with nectar. The birds from neighbouring parks and gardens will fly in to make

use of your boosted food supply and, if you are lucky, you may have the local hedgehog family paying nightly summer visits to feast on your chemical-free slugs and earthworms.

## SETTING UP HABITATS

Once the service station is working successfully it is time to think about rich habitat gardening – providing complete habitats that allow wild plants and animals to set up permanent homes in your garden. Some lucky people have gardens big enough to accommodate a badger sett, or breeding sparrowhawks, but for most of us the scale of habitat our garden offers will be much more modest. Even the smallest outdoor spaces offer scope for supporting whole life-cycles of some special creatures. I sometimes work in an office block in central London which has one small outdoor terrace on the third floor. By cladding one entire wall with a bug hotel of hollow tubes and other tiny hiding places, an extraordinary variety of bees, wasps spiders and other diminutive creatures have taken up residence and are using the wall as hibernation and egg-laying habitat. In another small balcony a friend has created a small pond

in an old stone sink. There is no scope for frogs and toads to reach it, but this mini-wetland does attract diving beetles, damselflies and pond-skaters; it supports a colony of pond snails, and it still has room for a tightly controlled clump of lesser spearwort, some water mint and water forget-me-not.

## WILD WETLAND

If you are wondering where to start with your garden makeover, then I would go for the wetland habitat first. It is the most exciting for me, and it shows thrilling results almost instantly. I have created a few ponds over the years, beginning with the one I helped my dad to dig when I was about four years old. In all but the coldest of weather, within a couple of hours of filling with water, pond skaters and whirligig beetles have flown in to investigate. Damsel and dragonflies have turned up out of the blue when the sunny days of the first summer arrive, and as if by magic, common newts have colonised every one of them within a year. If you have small children, you may feel you need to delay because a pond can be hazardous, although there is a school of thought which suggests that the best way

OPPOSITE Even a pond as tiny as this recycled sink will astonish you with the variety of wildlife it supports.

BELOW Pond snails are natural pond cleaners, and you can't have too many of them. Look for their blobs of eggs beneath the floating leaves of water lilies.

installed a pond for Prime Minister Tony Blair and his young family at 10 Downing Street in the 1990s.

Another way of introducing water safely to the garden is to create a bubbler fountain. I have one splashing away immediately outside my office window. By sinking a water tank into the ground, installing a very small electric pump, and topping off the tank with a supportive metal mesh and a layer of large stones it is possible to provide the pleasure of a gurgling mini-fountain for the family and for the local wildlife, without any risk to small children. Of course a bubble fountain does not offer the kind of habitat that supports pond life, but nevertheless, in icy winters and hot dry summers the water supply is likely to bring birds and other thirsty creatures very close to where you can watch them.

Another alternative is to create a different kind of wetland entirely. Dig a pond, line it and fill it in again to make a wetland marsh. You'll still be able to grow wonderful plants such as ragged robin and marsh marigold, and when the family is ready for a real pond you can simply dig a hole in the middle of your nicely established marsh. In fact, that is a good way of making use of any old leaking concrete pond you may inherit.

## WILDFLOWER MEADOWS

There are a whole range of different detailed habitats to have a go at once you get the bug. You can plant more and more wildflowers into your developing meadow, stack piles of logs in your woodland edge, and if you want a real splash of summer colour, one of the most instantaneous habitats you can create is a cultivated 'weed' patch. Many of our more spectacular wildflowers are short-lived annuals. Flowers like the poppy, cornflower, corncockle, corn marigold, heartsease and mayweed are adapted to grow best in disturbed ground. Remember their original habitat would have been on river shingle, or collapsed stream cliffs. For generations they competed with farmers' crops, and produced the chocolate-box country landscapes we dream about. Nowadays modern herbicides have made it easy to wipe out the cornfield wildflowers. Corncockle is virtually extinct in Britain, though many of the other, more adaptable species have side-stepped from farmland on to the disturbed ground of motorway construction sites and building excavations. The seeds of all these species germinate easily in spring. The flowers bloom right through the summer, and it only

to teach children to respect water is to have them grow up with it. A wildlife-gardener friend of mine in Switzerland stood casually on one side while his two-year-old son took stock of their new pond. Inevitably the infant rushed straight down into the shallow water, got the shock of his life and was whisked to safety by his dad. He has treated water with great caution ever since. If, however, you are not too keen on amateur child psychology, then I suggest you put up a temporary fence, and make the pond child-safe. This is how the Wildlife Trusts overcame the problem when they takes a little light raking of the soil surface at the end of the summer for their crop of fresh seed to germinate to give you a repeat performance the following year. The blaze of colour produced by even the smallest patch of cornfield weeds will excite all those who visit your garden, and this will probably be the aspect of wildlife gardening they find most immediately understandable.

Now, if you are sitting there thinking none of this applies to you, because you only have a tiny garden, a small courtyard, a terrace or a balcony, take heart. There is still plenty of scope for enjoying wildlife. Concentrate on making the view from within your home as interesting as possible. It is usually still possible to provide some living green enclosure by growing plants up the vertical surfaces. By changing the planting from season to season, for instance by swapping spring bulbs for summer annuals and growing a few autumn-flowering climbers and fruiting wall shrubs, it is possible to make the smallest of spaces much more wildlife friendly. You may have no room for a pond, but a shallow dish of clean water will still attract bathing birds all year round. A nest box is often rather more successful on a wall than on a tree, since it is more difficult for predators to reach

**BELOW** What could be more beautiful than a patch of wild poppies flowering in your own back yard?

BELOW TOP Each spring
my garden pond provides my
local pair of song thrushes
with mud to line their nest,
but next door's lawn provides
the worms.

BELOW BOTTOM With cats
and magpies to contend with,
the safest place for a nesting
box is a shady wall.

RIGHT Even the smallest pond
is likely to attract damselflies.
Adults are delicate beauties
but the larvae are lethal
underwater predators.

and even bird feeders fixed to the window will attract visitors from the wider surrounding neighbourhood.

## BROADER LANDSCAPE

There is one more important consideration when designing or redesigning your garden to attract more wildlife. Have a good look at your neighbourhood. The animal life you are able to attract into your garden will be influenced a great deal by the broader landscape in which you live. The richer the wildlife is in the surrounding area, the more passing trade you can expect to attract into your service station. If you do live next door to a large patch of urban wildscape – an old demolition site or a gravel pit for example – then you will have far more chance of attracting clouds of butterflies to your buddleia than those wildlife gardeners who live on the edge of a rural village, with a plot which backs on to acres of chemically managed arable crops. The reason my pond was colonised so quickly, I imagine, had a great deal to do with the number of relatively unpolluted ponds and canals in my neighbourhood.

If you have a wood or a mature town park nearby, then your bird table may attract the attention of such spectacular creatures as spotted woodpeckers and nuthatches as well as a constant stream of dozens of individual bluetits, coal tits, great tits and other small woodland birds. The gardens of your nearby neighbours are also an important source of wildlife, and as more and more families have turned to wildlife gardening the network of supporting habitats has become much richer. Millions of garden ponds have been incorporated into domestic gardens since flexible waterproof liners made it so easy. A survey by Sheffield University estimated that in 2010 there were 25,000 garden ponds in that city alone, so it is easy to see why newts and dragonflies

ABOVE Sometimes the beauty of garden wildlife can take your breath away. Here a fritillary butterfly has settled on the flowers of ragged robin.

will probably be on hand to colonise your own new pond. Even more recently, towns and cities have begun to tackle the threat of stormwater flooding by creating shallow ditches and temporary wetlands alongside roads and in parks and other public landscapes. This approach, known as sustainable urban drainage, offers even more scope for wetland species to colonise new wildlife gardens.

You may be tempted to create a habitat which is completely alien to your particular area in the belief that this will diversify the wildlife of the neighbourhood.

LEFT Corncockle is such an elegant cornfield annual, but beware – its large black seeds are poisonous.

LEFT BELOW Water forget-me-not is one of the easiest marginal pond plants to grow, and it flowers for weeks on end.

There is nothing to stop you creating an acid peat bog community, or an alkaline sand dune if you want to, although watering your sand dune with salty water every couple of days can pall after a while. It is much better to go for garden habitats which complement the local wildlife community. For one thing, an isolated island of peat bog in the heart of suburbia is never likely to be anything more than a collection of introduced plants. The appropriate animal life will simply not be around to colonise it. Conversely, if you create a mini-habitat typical of the area, you are much more likely to succeed in attracting wildlife to join you. Create a small patch of 'chalk downland' in your back garden now, while there are still a few hectares up the road, or dig a pond and plant up a marsh while the local millpond is still full of water. The meadow butterfly population will quickly expand to adopt your mini-downland. The diving beetles and dragonflies will drop into your mini-wetland in no time, and who knows, in a year or two's time the original habitat may be destroyed, leaving you with the only facility in the area capable of sustaining the local wildlife. This may seem fanciful but it has certainly been the case with amphibians such as frogs and newts.

Populations have been virtually wiped out in many rural counties, but garden ponds have provided a viable substitute for the lost farm ponds and ditches.

It is not just existing local habitats that you need to think about either. Most of us have a park or some other 'official open space' close to where we live. Imagine how much more successful your mini-meadow is likely to be if you can persuade the local park-keepers to adopt the same kind of wildlife management on a few acres of their municipal greenery. Use a bit of gentle persuasion and you could have lots of local authority butterflies paying visits to your wildlife garden.

# PART II

# CREATING NEW HABITATS

## 4

Wild foxgloves thrive in the dappled shade of woodland glades. With care a small garden can recreate quite similar characteristics.

# THE WOODLAND EDGE HABITAT

SHRUBBERIES HAVE been a feature of modern gardens ever since the end of the nineteenth century. They provide shelter, screen unsightly corners and make an attractive backdrop for the garden flowers. Your wildlife garden needs all these things, too. This, remember, is the sheltering enclosure that has been left behind after you have carved out your garden 'rooms'. With a little adjustment, you can turn your traditional garden shrubbery into a valuable wildlife habitat. If you have the space, then try to include a tree or two. The layer-upon-layer effect of trees above shrubs above ground cover provides the maximum opportunity for the greatest variety of garden wildlife, and trees also make an obvious contribution to the wider living landscape of the urban forest. If the space you are dealing with is tiny, then growing climbing plants on walls and fences creates a similar multi-layered effect on a much smaller scale, with the trees in the street, the park or in neighbouring gardens providing the taller elements of the important woodland edge around your garden glade.

## LOSS OF HABITAT

I have already explained that many of our favourite garden wildlife species originally lived in the forests. Ever since the ancient Britons started farming we have been chopping down our trees, grubbing up our woodlands, and generally reducing woodland habitat. In recent years the rate of destruction has been greater than ever. We destroyed more of our ancient woodlands in the second half of the twentieth century than our ancestors managed to wipe out in the previous four hundred years. In that same fifty years it is true that we have also planted a great many new trees, but the vast majority of those were exotic, sombre conifers, and you only need to walk from the song-filled, dappled shade of a deciduous copse into the silent gloom of a softwood plantation to know immediately that, in wildlife terms, conifers are comparatively lifeless.

Much of the woodland wildlife that thrived in our oak and beech woods up to the end of the nineteenth century has suffered too, because there has been a dramatic change in the woodland habitat. The trees may still be there, but the sheets of primroses and the clouds of butterflies that used to share your woodland walk have gone. They relied on regular management of the wood. Coppicing in particular produced a rich habitat for wildlife. While the tall trees may have grown unhindered for hundreds of years, local people would

cut down the understorey – perhaps hazel, hornbeam or lime – every ten or fifteen years. That practice continued for centuries, providing firewood, fence posts, hedging stakes and small roundwood poles for every possible local use. At the same time coppicing created an extremely rich habitat for a wide variety of plants and animals. In just two generations this intensive management almost disappeared and for a long time it only survived as a quaint country craft around the odd folk museum or in special nature reserves. Most of our surviving fragments of ancient woodland developed a tangle of bramble, overgrown or collapsed coppice shrubs, and a forest of light-trapping sycamore seedlings. The wrens and the blackbirds still thrived, but the nightingale missed the light openness of the hazel coppice, and primroses became rare.

More recently, thanks to more enlightened conservation management by professional foresters, and the enthusiastic efforts of organisations such as the Woodland Trust and the Wildlife Trusts, coppicing is being revived in many of our best broad-leafed woodlands. Where modern plantations of conifers were established on the site of ancient woodlands, there are programmes of sensitive evergreen removal, the light is beginning to reach the woodland floor once again, and in the best examples the whole woodland ecosystem is being re-established.

A similar revolution is slowly taking place in the urban forest. Inspired by successful habitat restoration in the countryside, woodland shrubs and wildflowers are being reintroduced beneath the canopy of trees in some of our city parks, and the birds, butterflies, beetles and other woodland creatures are gradually bringing life back to inner city open spaces.

## YOUR LOCAL WOODLAND HABITATS

You should take inspiration for your own wildlife garden from these more extensive wooded landscapes. If you are lucky enough to have a good wood which still survives in your area, and the local County Wildlife Trust will almost certainly be taking care of one or two, go along and have a wander through it. In fact you should go along several times in the course of a year, and see just how excitingly it changes from season to season. As you become familiar with your woodland community you will pick up a good many clues about

LEFT For centuries, the shrub layer in broad-leaved woodland was coppiced regularly to promote new growth and allow in the sunlight. This provided ideal conditions for a huge variety of wild plants and animals, and it is a useful model for our wildlife gardens.

BELOW The woodland edge is a rich mixture of wildflowers, shrubs and climbing plants, all sheltered by overhanging trees. Here, silver birch provides an ideal woodland setting on a garden scale.

how the habitat works. Perhaps the most encouraging thing you will notice is how important the edges are. Where the trees and shrubs end and the sunlight breaks through, you find more species of plant and animals than anywhere else in the wood. It is not surprising if you think about it. You have a chance of seeing species which live deep in the shade of the wood, and species that prefer the open sunlight but perhaps cling to the woodland edge for protection. There is also a host of special plants and animals that like the half-shade best of all. The posh word for this ecological boundary line is an 'ecotone', but I like to think of it as a wildlife bonus zone.

Hardly anyone has room in their garden for a complete woodland, though there are a few lucky people who live on the edge of a real one. But even in a small garden you can have a go at creating the richest bit of the woodland habitat: the bonus zone. Of course without the whole of the wood to back it up you are not likely to have badger cubs crashing out of the bramble patch to gambol in your meadow, or a startled deer blinking at you in the sunshine. You can grow all the woodland edge wildflowers, though, and you'll

certainly have lots of small mammals and songbirds moving into the habitat once it becomes established. Woodland edge is particularly good for butterflies, too. I remember cycling along on a holiday in France one year, with woodland down to the road on each side. At ten o'clock each morning the sun came up over the tree-tops, the ditch full of wildflowers was suddenly bathed in light, and within a few warming minutes the whole habitat was alive with dancing butterflies. In my garden there are three species of butterfly that seem to enjoy the woodland edge best. Speckled woods are perfectly camouflaged in the dappled shade. Commas sunbathe happily with orange wings outstretched on the bramble leaves, until you get too close, when they snap shut and the dull, camouflaged underside of their wings makes them disappear. Gatekeeper, or wall-brown butterflies are the third species and they presumably got their country name because they so often flutter around the hawthorn and honeysuckle growing where the field-gate punctures the darkness on the edge of the wood.

Our butterflies have struggled to survive in recent years. A combination of agricultural pesticides, loss of suitable breeding habitat and changing weather patterns has driven most of them into steep decline. When I first started wildlife gardening in the 1970s, it was normal to see a couple of dozen butterflies feeding together on a single buddleia bush or a patch of Michaelmas daisies. Small tortoiseshells, peacocks, commas, skippers and red admirals were just some of the more familiar garden visitors. I still see all these species at some point in most years, and occasionally the seasons provide a weather sequence that seems to suit them perfectly and we enjoy a butterfly boom. When this does happen it is clear that flowery garden glades, set in the shelter of the urban forest, have become essential to their continuing survival.

## WOODLAND LAYERS

There are three simple principles you need to adopt if you are going to create a successful woodland edge habitat. You must develop several layers of plants one above the other; you must include a good range of native plants, from trees down to carpeting wildflowers; and you must build up a rich layer of dead and decaying material, from big logs to fine leaf mould. The multiple-canopy idea is a good one to adopt, even if you are simply growing exotic plants in your

**BELOW** Managing blackberries in a garden is a challenge, but with luck the rewards can be sweet autumn fruits for you and for the comma butterflies.

**RIGHT** In harsh winter weather a heavy crop of fruits and berries can attract some spectacular visitors – and none more colourful than waxwings like these.

garden. Apart from the ecological value, it helps you to fit more plants into a given space. Each of the layers will provide a home for different species of wildlife. If you watch closely you will see that your garden birds are specific about the layer in which they operate. The song thrush, the wood pigeon and the long-tailed tits tend to stick to the treetops. The finches and the robins seem to prefer the shrub layer, and wrens, dunnocks and blackbirds spend most of their time among the leaf litter or in the low vegetation.

In a real wood, each canopy of plants helps create the particular climatic conditions which the plants in the layer below enjoy best. When you are starting from scratch you have to concertina the process, and choose the plants that will thrive in their particular canopy layer. The choice becomes more and more critical, the nearer you get to ground level and the less light there is available. The other problem, of course, is that it takes time for the various trees, shrubs and flowers to grow into their respective layers, and you may well be able to grow sun-loving shrubs such as broom and gorse in your woodland edge for several years, until the trees eventually grow up and overshadow them.

## TOP OF THE CANOPY

Even in the smallest garden it is important to grow at least one tree if you possibly can. If your space is too tiny, then a tall growing shrub or wall climber will still make a significant difference. Trees presumably help to let birds and insects know that yours is a green service station garden, and there is something special about planting a sapling which will live longer than us, and grow much taller.

If you have plenty of room, plant lots of trees. Plant them small since very young specimens tend to transplant much more successfully than bigger ones. They cost less, and they will usually grow more rapidly. I have known many cases where small saplings, less than a metre tall, have grown to outstrip far bigger and much more expensive specimens within a couple of seasons. Plant your young trees about 3m apart. This allows you plenty of space for planting the other layers, but at the same time, the trees will be close enough together to force one another up and produce a canopy of leaves and branches on most soils within three or four years. Look for a good, healthy, fibrous root system, and it is also most important to choose trees which have a

## NATIVE TREES FOR THE SMALL TO MEDIUM-SIZED GARDEN

**Alder** (*Alnus glutinosa*) (above) Grown best in wet soils, where it produces a tall, slender, rather dark tree up to 15m tall. It is a nitrogen-fixer, and purple catkins in spring produce clouds of pollen and fertilise the cone-like female flowers. A popular seed-source for siskins, redpolls and other small birds in the autumn and winter. Tolerant of air pollution. It supports 90 associated insect species.

**Silver birch** (*Betula pendula*) (right) A pretty tree with small leaves, weeping branches, silvery bark and casting a light shade. A rough texture on the young shoots usually indicates good bark colour to follow. Prefers well-drained open conditions – poor soil if possible. Should grow rapidly to an ultimate height of at least 20m, and have a healthy life span of 50–60 years. Old trees good for bracket fungi and attractive to woodpeckers. Propagate from seed. Supports 229 associated insect species.

**Hawthorn** (*Crataegus monogyna*) Well worth growing as a specimen for its display of white May blossom and the rich crop of bright red berries. It is thorny and tough, though not always easy to establish at first. Good protective cover for nesting birds. Supports 149 associated insect species.

**Crab apple** (*Malus sylvestris*) Pink blossom, green or golden fruit and a spreading, characterful habit. There are lots of exotic species and hybrids, but do opt for the native crab. This may be one to try propagating for yourself by striking a cutting from a local hedgerow specimen, although that isn't as easy as you might think. More than 90 associated insect species and also a possible host for establishing some parasitic mistletoe

once the crab apple is mature.

**Downy birch** (*Betula pubescens*) A darker tree, with downy twigs, but growing better where soil is moist to wet. More than 200 associated insect species.

**Rowan** (*Sorbus aucuparia*) Bunches of white blossom in spring, and a mass of orange berries from August onwards make this a decorative tree. It grows well in exposed positions and will reach 15m in height. Supports 28 species of associated insects.

**Aspen poplar** (*Populus tremula*) (opposite page, top left) A lovely small tree with constantly fluttering and

rustling leaves which turn brilliant gold in the autumn. Prefers a moist, neutral to acid soil but will grow in the most exposed of positions. Supports more than 90 associated insect species.

The following forest-size trees are too tall for small to medium-sized gardens, but they can all be grown as coppiced specimens, or incorporated into a mixed hedge.
**Oaks** (*Quercus robur* and *Q. petraea*) have 284 species of associated insects.
**Beech** (*Fagus sylvatica*) supports 64 species.
**Ash** (*Fraxinus excelsior*) supports 41 species.
**White willow** (*Salix alba*) (below left) supports more than 200 species.
**Elm** (*Ulmus procera*) supports 80 species.
**Small leaved lime** (*Tilia cordata*) supports 31 species.
**Hornbeam** (*Carpinus betulus*) supports 28 species.
**Wild cherry** or **gean** (*Prunus avium*) (above) is also excellent, though figures are not available for associated insect populations.

TREES LESS SUITABLE FOR THE WILDLIFE GARDEN
Please note that popular species such as:
**Sycamore** (*Acer pseudoplatanus*)
**Norway maple** (*Acer platanoides*)
**Horse chestnut** (*Aesculus hippocastanum*)
**Sweet chestnut** (*Castanea sativa*)
**The Tree of Heaven** (*Ailanthus altissima*) and
**Japanese cherries** (*Prunus japonica*) are none of them native and they support few different species of insect, though as decorative specimens in the right setting, each of them can be magnificent. It is hard to imagine a childhood without conkers, or an exposed farm in the windswept uplands or a coastal cliff top without its sheltering clump of sycamore trees.

good central shoot growing vigorously upwards. All too often the trees in nurseries and garden centres have had the growing tip, or central leader, cut out. The grower does this to encourage the sapling to produce a bunch of side shoots. This may give the young plant a more tree-like shape at this early stage but it can prevent it from growing up to form a natural shape in the longer term. Mature trees in the wild rarely have their branches starting only 2m up the trunk.

Eventually, trees planted 3m apart will become overcrowded, and you will have to cut some of them down, but I think this is better than waiting years and years for the tree canopy to develop. Little trees are cheap and some of them are surprisingly easy to grow from seed. They do not need staking. In fact there is plenty of evidence to show that young trees establish more successfully if the stem and roots are exposed to some gentle movement in the early years. They grow so fast that normally young seedlings and saplings will overtake the much more expensive standard trees within the second year. I planted a group of silver birch in my last garden. They went in at just over 1m tall, and five years later they were as high as a two-storey house.

Once the trees have been planted – and the best times of year to plant most woody species are either late autumn, just after leaf-fall, or early spring, just before budburst – you can think about interplanting with the shrubs. These will form the second layer down. If you've lots of room you may even be able to fit in a range of species which will give you a two-tier shrub layer. In fact in some good, old woodlands you can find three layers of shrubs below the high tree canopy.

A lovely wood near where I live has some tall, multi-stemmed lime and rowan trees reaching up to the lower branches of the oaks, with hazel and bird cherry below that, and a bottom layer of bramble and wild rose. At woodland floor level there is a sheet of spring flowers. Bluebells, primroses and the rest all flower early enough to be fertilised by the insects and produce ripe seed before the shrubs and trees above them cut out all the sun. I like to plant shrubs at about 1m spacings, and then cut them back hard. Chop them down to a fifth of their original height if you can bring yourself to do it. This encourages them to produce dense low growth and form a shrub layer more quickly.

OPPOSITE The light, dappled
shade of silver birch will still
allow the wildflowers to
thrive beneath.

BELOW A few decaying logs
will improve the woodland
edge for nature conservation
and bracket fungi can be a
beautiful result.

base of each plant will suppress the weeds and keep the
soil moisture up around the roots. Old carpet is another
very useful artificial mulch material, although it can make
the garden look very messy, and there is a risk that the
glues and dyes involved may contaminate the surface
of the soil. There are a lot of finer textured materials
sold as mulches — pulverised bark, peat, and mushroom
compost — but they all create problems if you use them
at this early stage in the garden's development, because
windborne weed seeds germinate on the surface, and
the little seedlings grow like mad with their roots down
in the mulch.

## DECAYING MATERIALS AND FUNGI

Chopped bark can also form the first instalment of
your introduction of dead wood and decaying material
to your woodland edge. This is a vitally important part
of woodland habitat. So many of the small woodland
creatures spend at least part of their life munching
through dead wood or hiding under damp logs.

I was lucky when I made my wildlife garden for
TV. All along one boundary there had been a row of
majestic old elm trees. Sadly they had succumbed to
the dreaded Dutch elm disease several years before
I arrived on the scene, and had been chopped down.
Anyway, the previous owners had kept a good many of
the big slices of tree trunk, and used them for garden
stools, pergola bases, and anything else they could think
of. I heaved several of these logs into two or three
piles, carefully positioned where they would be safe
from disturbance. I also used another dozen or so of
them to retain a bank of soil in the woodland edge.
The first autumn I was rewarded with a spectacular
display of fungi of all shapes and sizes — neat spherical
pink blobs and big tough brown brackets — at one point
my woodland edge looked like a bit of Walt Disney
fairyland. The toadstools are just the fruiting part of the
fungi, of course, and although most of them appear in
autumn, there are usually one or two in evidence most
of the year. If you can accumulate logs from a variety of
different types of tree, then you will discover that their
fungi vary, too.

The bulk of the fungus (the mycelium) is below the
surface, extending deep down into the dead tissue of the
rotting logs. It helps to break the timber down to a soft
pulp which other organisms are then more easily able
to digest. For the most part, fungi are harmless in the

## WEEDS

If you are planting a woodland edge habitat from scratch,
then I suggest you concentrate on establishing the tree
and shrub layer for the first year or two. Once the shade
begins to develop you can start introducing wildflowers.
In the first couple of seasons there will still be wide
gaps between the trees and shrubs, and of course every
gardener knows this is an invitation for weeds to grow.
It may come as a bit of a surprise to find that you need
to control weeds in a wildlife garden, but I do not want
a tangle of sow thistle and groundsel choking my tree
and shrub planting. Naturally I'm keen to avoid using
chemical weedkillers if possible, though I must admit that
there are a few over-enthusiastic weeds such as ground
elder and couch grass that do get a dab of systemic
contact weedkiller gel, even in my garden. I find the best
way to avoid most of the weed problem, however, is
to spread a mulch over the soil surface. If you can get it,
or afford to buy it, one of the best materials, particularly
in the woodland edge habitat, is 7.5–10cm chunks of
coarsely chopped tree bark. Alternatively, although it
cannot look, feel or smell so woodlandy, a square metre
of roofing felt, or even a sheet of cardboard around the

## INVASIVE FUNGUS

There is one fungus, *Armillaria mellea*, the honey fungus, which can grow on dead wood and attack and kill living trees and shrubs. It sends out long underground threads or hyphae from the infected dead log, and enters the tree through the roots. The victim is killed as the fungus blocks up the tubes inside the plant. The underground threads are black and tough, and give *Armillaria* its other popular name of bootlace fungus.

Most of the time it does no harm at all, but if there are big, old, sickly trees around, then honey fungus does seem to seek out and kill them. Vigorous, healthy specimens are generally not affected, but just occasionally the fungus seems to act more aggressively, and there are certainly some well-known gardens where several trees and shrubs have been killed in a short space of time. The fungus produces its toadstools in September. They are about 4cm across, golden yellow with a slightly darker brown colour in the centre of the 'cap' and they pop up in clusters at the base of infected trees and logs.

It is obviously important to be aware of risks such as this. Frankly, though, wildlife gardening is much less hazardous than intensive chemical gardening. The rich diversity of natural fungi that you find in mature woodland seems to help reduce the impact of honey fungus to a modest, almost insignificant level, and it's reasonable to suppose that the same will be true in your garden. Penicillin is a fungus which is successful at suppressing the effect of other, harmful fungi, and it could well be that one or other of the many different toadstools found in a wood, or in your new woodland edge habitat, may have a similar influence over the deadly bootlace. In any event, however neat and tidy you are in your garden, there is still plenty of scope for this fungus to affect you. So far as infectious dead wood is concerned, a gate post or fence post is just as good a host as your pile of carefully selected logs. On balance I'm happy to take the risk. I keep an eye out for honey fungus toadstools each autumn, and as a precaution I've positioned the pond between my log piles and a lovely old apple tree which I think might be particularly vulnerable. In all honesty, though, I know that if an extra vigorous strain of honey fungus does visit my garden there is little I can do, and all the other fascinating toadstools, insects and organisms of decay my woodland edge attracts are more than enough compensation for the slight risk I'm taking.

garden, just a useful and interesting part of the natural recycling process – the ecological balance I've talked about. One or two species of toadstool are poisonous, and it is as well to have a book or chart somewhere in the house, where you can check suspicious-looking growths for safety. Failing this, simply adopt the policy that all toadstools are likely to be nasty to eat, and are best left to the wildlife. Incidentally, I've been amazed at just how much wildlife the fungi do attract. There are celebrated examples of smelly toadstool species such as the stinkhorn which are irresistible to flies. The insects zoom in from the neighbourhood, crawl around on the evil-smelling green jelly which covers the tip of the toadstool and, of course, in so doing they pick up fungal spores which they then cart off somewhere else. My elm logs have been particularly good for producing big, brown, striped bracket fungi in both spring and autumn, and these in turn have been the focus of attention for slugs and snails, which seem to delight in crawling around all over them, chewing off great lumps. Each morning the fungus looks more and more 'got-at' and all around it on the log there is a telltale network of silvery snail trails revealing the recent activity of visitors.

ABOVE A healthy compost heap will recycle waste and increase the concentration of worms and other small organisms of decay – rich pickings for songbirds, slow worms and other garden predators.

## COMPOST AND MULCHES

The best way of minimising the risk of a damaging infestation is to encourage a healthy level of decay at the surface of the soil. Chopped bark is chosen as weed-suppressing mulch because bark takes a long time to decay. Once your planting is forming a reasonable density of natural cover it is well worth adding much more mulching material as a way of improving habitat and adding to natural structure of the soil. I have an effective composting bin, bought from Sweden years ago, which takes all my kitchen waste and converts it to a sweet-smelling black compost. I usually shovel out the lower layers in early spring and spread the compost on the garden. Alternative composts are available commercially, and another useful mulch material is wood chip. If you have room to store the machine, then a garden shredder will convert twig, prunings and other woody garden waste into a marvellous mulch, although you must beware of shredding fresh material from plants such as brambles and willows, since you can find yourself with scores of freshly rooted cuttings mixed unintentionally with the mulch and spread around the garden. Leave the wood chip to weather in a quiet corner for a few months before you spread it, and if you can mix it with leaf sweepings, so much the better.

## WOODLAND MINI-BEASTS

You can expect masses of animal life to make use of your organic mulches and dead wood. There are a great many insects and other invertebrates which tunnel away inside the logs. Many beetles in particular spend their larval stage there. The elm logs in my garden were full of big, squidgy, white grubs, anything up to 2cm long. I found the first few when I was splitting a spare log for the fire, and that persuaded me that the more rotten, soft-centred lumps of timber should definitely be reserved for the wildlife. I've since discovered that these are the grubs of the lesser stag beetle, and in fact when I turn over a log in my woodland edge there are usually a couple of handsome, dull black adults lying there on their backs, slowly waving their legs in the air and looking disgruntled by my rude disturbance. The logs I used to retain the earth bank are full of insect life too. All through the summer there is a constant coming and going of tiny black flying creatures. Sit and watch carefully for a few minutes and you will see that the logs are peppered with neat little holes. These insects are wood wasps of various types, which lay their eggs in the tunnels that they or some other creatures have dug. Some of the wasps have an amazing ability to fly straight into their tunnel at breakneck speed. Other species seem rather less foolhardy, landing beside the hole first, and then reversing cautiously in, presumably preparing to lay an egg. Their caution is sensible, too, because often the hole they have chosen is already occupied, and they come whizzing out rather more quickly than they went in.

## LARGER WILDLIFE

Much larger creatures use the log piles too. It generally stays damp and cool under the logs, and so a lot of moisture-loving animals hide there during the day, and then creep out after dark to hunt among the dew-covered damp vegetation. Slugs are commonplace, of course, though their variety of texture, colour and pattern deserves far more attention. The most fascinating creatures that shelter under my logs, though, are the young amphibians. Yearling newts in particular seem to love the damp conditions, and while the current season's newtlets are still sporting gills and darting jerkily about in the pond, the yearlings can be found huddled together under the logs. I've discovered anything up to fifteen young smooth newts under one elm log on some days, and the next day just one or two remained. This rather confirms the theory that they shelter there in the daytime, and move out to feed on lesser beasties after nightfall.

With so much life crawling in and around the dead wood of the woodland edge, it is not surprising that larger predators find it a useful place to visit, too. Garden spiders stake their claim almost the minute the logs hit the deck, and string up their beautiful webs in the hope of

**BELOW** Some woodland creatures can be quite spectacular. My closest encounter with a male stag beetle was in a London garden with mature oaks on its boundary.

**BOTTOM** Visit your woodland edge habitat after dark and you may well hear shrews and other secretive creatures rustling in the undergrowth.

**RIGHT** A healthy population of garden spiders is a sure sign that there are plenty of small flying insects in your garden glade.

trapping the unfortunate wood wasps. Hunting spiders will move in too. My bark mulch and dead logs are alive with crowds of little black spiders which dart away as I approach. They are brilliantly camouflaged, and invisible – until they move. They do not build webs, but instead make their living by lying in wait, and then pouncing on poor unsuspecting flies and creepy-crawlies. Fascinating, though. Look closely at these apparently dull little grey spiders and in mid-summer you will find that some of them have what appears at first glance to be a knobbly back end. If the spider stands still long enough you will see that the knobbles are a mass of tiny baby spiders, carted around by their mother for safekeeping.

Where there are spiders, you will often find wrens, and certainly I have a pair of these handsome, noisy little birds in my garden. They are numerous in the UK, although their numbers tend to dip significantly in a harsh winter. A large part of their diet is spiders, and when they have a brood of chicks to feed they spend a great deal of their time hunting among the logs and flying back to the cluster of eager open mouths poking out from the nest hole in the eaves.

Although hedgehogs have become a great rarity over recent years, they do still turn up in my inner city garden from time to time, and if I am lucky enough to see or hear them, they always check out the log pile for slugs and beetles. Blackbirds are forever pecking away at the soft ground beneath the edge of the pile, scattering bark in all directions in their frantic search for food, and even the local fox knows that it is worth turning the logs over from time to time, on the off chance of picking up a wood mouse or one of my beautiful beetles.

## FOOD CHAINS AND NATIVE SPECIES

Woodlands are not just full of dead wood, of course. They are a wonderful collection of living plants, too, and a great many species of animals live on leaves, flowers and fruits. So far as shelter and protection are concerned, any species of tree or shrub is useful, but to make the best wildlife habitat you should try to include some native species. Remember that you are no longer interested simply in the way a plant looks. You're interested in the part it can play in attracting and supporting wildlife. It is a simple fact that the native

animal life of any country depends fundamentally on native plants. In our case we have a complex, mixed community of wild plants and animals which have 'grown up together' since the last Ice Age, eight to ten thousand years ago. Not all our animal life feeds directly on plants, of course, but even the most carnivorous of predators feed on other animals which themselves feed on plants, or on other plant-eating creatures. The leaves and shrubs of native plants provide the basic platform for our animal life, and it is important to understand just how particular many of our lower forms of wildlife are about what they eat. Many of the plant-eating insect larvae, for instance, only eat the leaves of one specific type of plant, and when that is the case, that plant will always be a native one. This is why it is so important to plant native trees, shrubs and wildflowers in your woodland edge, and in every other wildlife habitat you create. The greater the variety of natives you include, the larger the menu you are providing, and the wider range of animals you are likely to attract.

Some species of plants support more different dependent leaf-eaters than others, and each species of plant will have its own special range of animal life. If

you want to make a simple comparison, look at the oak trees you can buy in your garden centre.

The native English oaks, *Quercus petraea* and *Q. robur*, are capable of providing a home for an amazing 284 different species of invertebrates – many of which can eat nothing else but English oak. By contrast, the American red oak, *Q. rubra*, the cut-leaved, hairy acorned Turkey oak, *Q. cerris*, and the evergreen holm oak, *Q. ilex* can be eaten by no more than four or five native British species altogether. Go to North America, Turkey or the Mediterranean where these exotic species grow as natives, and you find that there they support as wide a range of their own native fauna as our oaks do here.

## LEAF-EATING INSECTS

In a good, healthy bit of garden wildlife habitat there will be hardly a leaf that has not had a bite taken out of it. Some of the smaller species live inside the leaves, and you can see thin wiggly lines snaking around beneath the surface. Look for these leaf miner tunnels particularly on bramble, holly and birch leaves, and on the leaves of woodland wildflowers such as red campion and primrose. The patterns are generally made by the

LEFT, FAR LEFT ABOVE AND BELOW Telltale circular holes in the leaves of roses are a sure sign that you have leaf cutter bees. The discs are then transported to the nest – in this case an 'insect hotel' created with lengths of bamboo cane in a pipe.

BELOW This is a colourful male redpoll feeding on English alder seeds. Look out for them in winter flocks of tits and siskins.

caterpillars of tiny moths, and again they are often absolutely specific about which plant's leaves they can live in.

There is one particular leaf-using insect that I am always thrilled to see at work in my garden. Leaf cutter bees do not eat leaves. They use sections of leaf to build their nesting shelters and if they are visiting your garden then the evidence is recognisable. The bee cuts perfect circular discs out of the leaves of roses and one or two other types of plants. Look out for the evidence and then watch carefully. The bee flies in, lands on the chosen leaf and without a moment's hesitation it slices out a perfect circle of leaf a couple of centimetres in diameter. When the circle is complete and the leaf disc is loose the bee flies away with it to add to the nest. I have a big old dog rose just outside my office window, and the first time I watched this wildlife spectacle I could hardly believe my eyes. Now I wait eagerly for the first circular holes to appear in my rose leaves every spring with the same sense of anticipation that I reserve for the first frog spawn or the scream of the first returning swift.

RIGHT (top and below) In a wildlife garden, plants need to multi-task. The dog rose has delightful flowers with a subtle scent and a valuable crop of seed-filled fruits to follow. The thorny stems also provide protection for nesting songbirds.

OPPOSITE Multiple layers of vegetation are the key to a successful woodland edge habitat.

## SEEDS

Other animals rely on your woodland edge plants, too, and not all of them are leaf-eaters either. Many of the birds will be looking for seeds. Jays will gorge themselves on acorns in the autumn, and do a good job of spreading them around too, when they bury them in soon-to-be-forgotten larders. Siskins are lovely little birds that look like slimmed-down greenfinches. They spend winter here and summer further north. They feed in flocks on the seed of English alder, and you can sometimes see twenty or thirty birds feeding together on cold January days. Look out for redpolls too – these pretty little birds often join the siskins in mixed feeding parties. There was a time when these winter visitors were rare in gardens, but with the development of more sophisticated bird food they have become a much more familiar sight.

Even at the creepy-crawly end of the woodland wildlife community, seeds are an important food source. If you find an empty hazelnut with a small neat hole in it, when you crack it open you will find the kernel has been eaten away by a small insect larva, and the hole is the point at which the mature insect left after the food ran out. The reason that wildflowers such as foxglove

and campion produce so many thousands of seeds from each plant is that they need to compensate for the enormous majority that are eaten by something or other. There are complex specialisms too. The seeds of greater celandine and primrose are both covered with a waxy outer coating which ants seem to like eating. When the seeds are ripe the ants cart them away from the parent plant, strip off the coating, and leave them in a bit of your woodland edge where they can germinate and grow, or perhaps be eaten by yet another creature.

## CHOOSING YOUR PLANTS

In the panel on pages 68–69 there is a long list of native plants suitable for your woodland edge habitat. Many of them are beautiful. Being native they are unlikely to suffer in cold winters, and being part of the naturally balanced native community they are unlikely to be eaten to the point of destruction in the way that exotic plants sometimes are. Within the recommended three-layer structure you can pick and choose the plants you like best. For small gardens it is obviously sensible to avoid big trees, or plants which spread like mad. You do not have to stick exclusively to natives either. I hope

I've made it clear how critical it is to include some native plants, but there are masses of woodland shrubs and flowers from other regions of the globe that also enjoy this habitat. Some of the cotoneasters and berberis are good berry producers, and plants like azaleas and mock orange are beautiful shrubs to have in any garden, filling the air with perfume and providing lots of pollen and nectar. Just bear in mind, however, that each time you plant an exotic instead of a native plant you are taking up a bit of space which could be supporting a greater diversity of wildlife.

There are several native plants which I think are particularly useful for garden woodland edge habitat. Among the trees, silver birch (*Betula pendula*) is marvellous because it looks so beautiful in every season, its seeds are popular with tits in particular, its leaves feed interesting creatures like the birch sawfly larva, and it casts a light shade which makes it easy to grow other layers of plants beneath it. English alder (*Alnus glutinosa*), rowan (*Sorbus aucuparia*) and wild gean or cherry (*Prunus avium*) are the other tallish trees I would suggest you have a look at.

Coming down a layer there are lots of attractive woodland edge shrubs. Bird cherry (*Prunus padus*) is particularly handsome with its long plumes of white blossom covered in bees in the spring, and small cherries to feed the blackbirds and thrushes in autumn. Hazel is a must, with its lambs-tail catkins in the early spring and its cobnuts for the mice and squirrels in the autumn. My hazels also support a wonderful species of shield bug about the size of my little fingernail and shiny brown and green. It spends a lot of its time sheltering from predators under those thick green leaf-sheaths that surround the hazelnuts and has an unusual characteristic for an insect – it protects its young. Hawthorn and field maple are always worth growing if you have room. They can also be used to make a hedge. Wild dog rose (*Rosa canina*) is a plant I love to have in the garden. Its thorns are rather vicious but the flowers are so perfect, the rose hips are spectacular to look at and popular with the birds, and if you are lucky you may find a robin's pincushion or two decorating the rose twigs. These are galls which the rose is stimulated to produce by yet another little resident creature. Several eggs of this particular gall wasp are laid in a bud in the spring, and as the bright red 'pincushion' matures it provides a mini-habitat for a whole host of other even smaller creatures

# WILDFLOWERS FOR THE WOODLAND EDGE HABITAT

**Solomon's seal** (*Polygonatum multiflorum*) (above) An unusual wildflower, with arching stems of small white flowers and blue-green leaves.

**Lords and ladies** (*Arum maculatum*) Dramatic at every stage of growth, from black-blotched fresh green leaves in spring, through the flowering stage, with its weird, creamy hood-like flower, to the clusters of bright orange berries.

**Foxglove** (*Digitalis purpurea*) Up to 2m tall. Grows as a biennial, so new seed must be allowed to germinate each year, to provide flowers the year after. May/June is the best time for flowering.

**Bluebell** (*Hyacinthoides non-scripta*) Spreads well once established. You can buy bulbs from specialist nurseries, but beware of pink garden varieties and the much coarser Spanish species. Nothing could be more beautiful than our own, increasingly rare, native bluebell.

**Snowdrop** (*Galanthus nivalis*) Probably not a true native but so easy to grow that it is a must. Transplant plants in leaf if you can get them. Otherwise bulbs are readily available, but they can take a season or two to settle down.

**White deadnettle** (*Lamium album*) A super ground cover for the woodland edge. It flowers in spring and autumn most years, and is a marvellous bee plant.

**Yellow archangel** (*L. galeobdolon*) Much more open habitat than the deadnettles, with a rich golden flower colour. An indicator of ancient woodland in the wild.

**Red deadnettle** (*L. purpureum*) Not so tall as its white relative, but with more colourful leaves and a capacity for carpeting shady ground and flowering for six or seven months of the year.

**Wild daffodil** (*Narcissus pseudo-narcissus*) Still thriving in a few lucky corners of England and Wales. Never dig them up from the countryside. Bulbs are available from specialist nurseries, and that is the way to grow them.

**Primrose** (*Primula vulgaris*) Easily swamped by taller vegetation. Grow without too much difficulty from seed, and they do make the woodland edge complete.

**Red campion** (*Silene dioica*) Seeds happily into rich soils in dappled shade. Tones perfectly with foxgloves, and flowers a second time in late summer.

**Lily-of-the-valley** (*Convallaria majalis*) Grows like mad in some gardens, and proves impossible in others. Drought-tolerant, with a wonderful fragrance from the white flowers in spring. Look out for the red berries in late summer, too. This plant dies down completely in the autumn, but is easily transplanted. Rare in the wild.

**Common violet** (*Viola riviniana*) An important butterfly food plant and a lovely addition to the spring garden.

**Sweet woodruff** (*Galium odoratum*) Whorls of pretty little white flowers on long, thin stems. Can be grown as a tight carpet or allowed to sprawl over other woodland wildflowers.

**Herb robert** (*Geranium robertianum*) (below) A colourful little cranesbill with red stems and small pink flowers.

**Stinking hellebore** (*Helleborus foetidus*) Dark green

leaves all year round. A handsome plant, growing up to 60cm tall, and producing green flowers in early spring.

**Greater celandine** (*Chelidonium majus*) (left) Yellow sap is poisonous and stains fingers (and anything else it touches). The leaves and flowers are pretty.

**Stinking iris** (*Iris foetidissima*) The flowers are a rather insipid browny-yellow, but beautifully marked. The evergreen strap-like leaves are useful through the winter but the star feature is the fruits. Heavy seedpods split in late summer to reveal neat rows of dazzling orange berry-like seeds.

**Hedge woundwort** (*Stachys sylvatica*) This has tall, handsome flower spikes, followed by shiny little black seeds in clusters of four.

**Garlic mustard** (*Alliaria petiolata*) A pretty spring flower with a deep rootstock. It grows as a biennial, and is an important food plant for orange tip butterflies. Can be invasive.

**Lesser celandine** (*Ranunculus ficaria*) Invasive, but beautiful nevertheless. Prefers moist ground.

**Ramsons** (*Allium ursinum*) Introduce this wild garlic at your peril. It is invasive – spreading by both seed and bulb division. The white flowers are striking. The leaves are handsome, and even the oniony smell is rather pleasant in small doses.

**Wild strawberry** (*Fragaria vesca*) (left) A low-growing wiry little plant with white flowers in late spring, and miniature strawberries in midsummer. The fruits are delicious, but you need an awful lot to fill a bowl, and the blackbirds and squirrels usually get there first.

**Nettle-leaved bellflower** (*Campanula trachelium*) Tall, handsome flower with unusual leaves. Pretty blue.

**Green alkanet** (*Pentaglottis sempervirens*) A piercing blue flower this time, but the plant is rather coarse and it can be untidy. Cut back after flowering and you may get a second performance if you're lucky. It seeds prolifically and can become a nuisance.

**Wood anemone** (*Anemone nemorosa*) (left) Pretty white 'wind' flowers.

too. When the gall-fly larvae hatch they feed on the plant tissue that makes up the centre of the gall.

## A CARPET OF WOODLAND WILDFLOWERS

Down at ground level, the choice of native plants is enormous, and these shade-loving wildflowers are some of the most beautiful things you could ever wish to grow. Most of them flower in spring to make use of the sunlight early in the year, before the trees and shrubs close canopy. Almost all are easy to grow from seed if you cannot buy them from a nursery. However tempting it might be you must never dig up wild plants for your garden. Fortunately this selfish practice is now against the law anyway, but if you are interested in helping nature then the last thing you should be doing is raiding the few rich bits of countryside to stock up your garden. In just thirty or forty years, the primrose has become a rare plant in the wild, and one of the main factors leading to its decline has been thoughtless transplanting. Most of them are now readily available to buy as nursery-grown seedlings. You may even see advertisements for native bluebells and wild daffodils, but do check the source carefully. They can only be dug from the wild under the strictest of licences, and since they are slow to grow from seed the more unscrupulous traders may try to sell you the invasive and less pretty Spanish bluebell, or cultivated hybrid daffodils.

Primroses are one of the obvious woodland wildflowers to grow. I have a large patch in my mini-woodland, growing in the sandy soil around the log bank, and they flower their heads off from March through April and on into May. By splitting the clumps every two or three years, and by watching out for volunteer seedlings in the veg patch and the flower borders I am gradually managing to carpet a great deal of the garden with these lovely little wildflowers. Violets are happy in the same habitat, and I have a few oxlip plants among mine because the yellow and purple flowers go so well together. Other low-growing woodland edge flowers you must include are wood anemone, with its dark green, deeply-cut leaves and pure white flowers, and the wild strawberry, which scrambles about, rooting down all over the place. Its pretty white flowers are followed by delicious miniature strawberries in July and August. Sweet woodruff is another favourite with a modest habit. If you have plenty of space, you may be brave enough to plant wild garlic – ramsons. This has a

BELOW My own shady inner-city garden is a carpet of primroses in the early spring. They are always a delight and they are extremely well-behaved.

RIGHT Spring bulbs such as snowdrops and winter aconites blend well with the modest wildflowers of the woodland floor.

beautiful white flower in early spring, and the leaves are delicious in salads, but it seeds like mad and does give off rather an overpowering smell of onions, particularly if it gets crushed. Another native woodland wildflower which is common enough in gardens but rare in the countryside is lily-of-the-valley. This is one of the few flowers that will grow well in the driest of soils, so if you have a big tree casting heavy shade and stealing all the soil moisture, lily-of-the-valley is just the thing to fill that space. The leaves are an attractive green and the perfume from the spring flowers can be overpowering on a still evening in May or June.

Of the taller woodland wildflowers, foxgloves are a must. It is well worth collecting a little seed from wild plants, rather than planting the slightly different garden hybrids. There is nothing to beat the elegant beauty of those large pink bells with the chocolate-brown spots inside, and I sit for hours in early summer watching huge bumblebees visiting each pollen store in turn. Remember that foxgloves are biennials. Once a plant has flowered it dies, and seedlings take two years to reach maturity, so you need to sow seed for two consecutive years if you want to establish a colony which will produce flowers annually. There is another wonderful wildflower which is almost the same shade of deep pink, and begins flowering a little earlier than the foxgloves. Pink campion is one of my favourite woodland edge plants. It grows up to about 60cm tall, flowers off and on from March to October, with its major display early in the spring, and it produces a carpet of seedlings wherever there is a gap it can reach. Its close relation white campion is just as beautiful, but tends to need more light and often grows as an annual in cultivated but weedy cornfields. Greater celandine is about the same height as the campions, but has lime-green leaves and a wonderful little yellow flower. It is much more closely related to the Welsh poppy than the familiar lesser celandine, and if you break off a leaf or an unripe seedpod, you will find that the plant contains a deep yellow sap which will stain your fingers, and was used by our ancestors as a dye for wool.

There are many more woodland wildflowers to choose from, of course – bluebells and Solomon's seal, nettle-leaved bellflower and perhaps the best of all the ground carpeting bumblebee plants, white and red deadnettle – but few if any of these plants will find their way naturally into your new habitat. Woodland plants tend not to produce mobile seed in the way wasteland plants do. That's why they are so easily lost forever when a wood is destroyed. All of the wildflowers I have mentioned so far are available commercially as seed. I suggest you begin by growing and planting easy ones such as pink campion and primrose, and as the woodland edge habitat develops you can add in the plants like wood anemone which are a bit more difficult to get going.

There are a few particularly invasive woodland wildflowers that are probably best resisted. Herb robert

is a pretty wild geranium that will seed everywhere given the chance. Ground elder is a nightmare once it takes root and although lesser celandine is a favourite of mine, with its bright stars of butter-yellow flowers and its marbled green leaves, it is all too capable of taking over entire flower borders.

## WOODLAND CLIMBERS

Finally, there are a few plants which make their living by growing up through several layers of this habitat. These are the woodland climbers. You need to wait until your trees and shrubs are strongly established, otherwise they could be overwhelmed, but once you have a sturdy structure emerging it is well worth planting honeysuckle, and possibly the more vigorous wild clematis or old man's beard if you are lucky enough to have a large, rambling garden. There are herbaceous climbers too, such as white bryony, with its fascinating double-spiral tendrils, its bee-busy white-green flowers and its strings of orange, yellow and red poisonous fruit; woody nightshade, with its bunches of wonderful blue-purple and yellow flowers in summer and its equally colourful but slightly less poisonous berries in autumn;

and large bell bindweed, whose beautiful white flowers draw such compliments from garden visitors, but whose twining stems can swamp the whole garden in no time at all. Each of these plants has its place of course. I love to see the way bryony can grow from nothing to twenty feet in a summer, and I encourage it to crawl across my inherited conifer hedge, but as with so many of our wild plants, they can get out of hand quickly, and they provide a timely reminder that, although wildlife gardening may mean working much more closely with nature, it is still gardening. My artificial woodland edge habitat is artificial, and there is no point pretending that the rich habitat garden doesn't require some regular effort on your part. What I can say is that for the gardening work you put in, you will reap far, far more rewards, and certainly your effort will be appreciated by a huge number of grateful wild plants and animals, many of which are too small for you ever to see.

TOP LEFT Climbing and scrambling plants add an extra dimension to the wildlife garden boundary. Here white bryony decorates a conifer hedge with stems that will turn to strings of orange fruit if kept until late summer.

LEFT Wild clematis or old man's beard is far too vigorous a scrambling plant for any but the wildest of large gardens, but there are several garden cultivars that also produce similarly attractive fluffy seed heads.

ABOVE Our native honeysuckle is more subtly beautiful than the flamboyant cultivars and exotic species. Its perfume will fill the garden on a still summer's evening. Its stems provide support for birds' nests, and strips of its bark are popular as nest-lining material. It even yields a crop of berries in the autumn.

## RHS GARDEN HARLOW CARR

❛ RHS Garden Harlow Carr has a naturalistic feel, with dramatic rock banks and water courses designed to complement the wooded landscape. Wildflower meadows have become an important feature, the more formal flower borders are magnificent and woodland has been successfully enhanced through horticulture. The gardens are managed with wildlife in mind, so even in the icy depths of winter the borders' seedheads put on a bold display.

Harlow Carr is one of the best places to see both native and exotic woodland and meadow flowers successfully combined. The northern branch of the RHS's Lindley reference library is housed in the exemplary environmentally-sound Bramall Learning Centre, and there is a year-round programme of courses and guided walks, many of which make a particular feature of the garden's wildlife. ❜

The flowery hedgerow of
a country lane can be the
inspiration for the boundary
of your wildlife garden.

5

# HEDGEROWS AND CLIMBER-COVERED SCREENS

ONE ASPECT of wildlife habitat destruction that has received a great deal of publicity in recent years has been the loss of farm hedgerows. Although some of the tens of thousands of kilometres which have been grubbed out were old – Saxon boundaries dating back a thousand years for instance – most of the hedges were relatively modern in landscape terms. The enclosure, which carved up the common land and led to so much hedge-planting mainly took place between 150 and 200 years ago. These hedgerows were much more modern than, say, the ancient woodlands, but they were extremely important for wildlife. Because they were planted in the Arcadian days before intensive farming, when there were wildflowers and butterflies everywhere, the 'new' hedgerows were able to inherit an extremely rich woodland overspill. The wildflowers and less mobile invertebrates of the deepest woodland were unable to move out and occupy this new eighteenth-century habitat boom, but many of the more mobile species did take up residence, and as the original woodlands were then destroyed, the field hedgerows became more and more important as a mini-habitat for refuge woodlanders.

The other, perhaps even more significant contribution which hedgerows made to wildlife in the farming countryside, was to provide a green, sheltered, relatively safe corridor system for animals and plants to move along. As the arable fields and pastures were made more hostile to wildlife, the hedgerows became the only relatively pollution-free means of travelling from one sanctuary to another. Now many of the hedgerows have gone. They are simply not compatible with the scale of modern mechanical farming. With heavy machinery and a grant to cover the costs, it has been all too easy to remove even the most critical of ancient landscape features without a second thought.

## WILD HEDGEROWS AT HOME
When I first began to appreciate the role that gardens could play in nature conservation, the garden hedge seemed an obvious asset. The thousands of miles of boundaries that define our mosaic of domestic gardens offered a significant scale of compensation for the loss of rural field hedgerows. Unfortunately, as modern gardens have become more compact, and the taste for maintenance-free designs has become fashionable,

LEFT Hedge woundwort is one of those modest wildflowers that deserve closer examination. It is a great plant for pollinators and its shiny black seeds are a delightful detail.

RIGHT Don't waste the autumn leaves. Rake them together as habitat heaps beneath the boundary hedgerows.

BELOW Edges are important. They form the connecting wildlife corridors that link gardens together, and they offer secluded routes around the landscape for secretive creatures such as weasels, toads and hedgehogs.

the timber deck has replaced the lawn, and fencing has become much more popular than hedging. Even with the use of a mechanical hedge trimmer, a hedge presents a serious maintenance challenge. This is unfortunate. In the wildlife garden, a good mixed country hedgerow can provide a marvellous scaled-down version of the woodland edge, in much the same way as it did 200 years ago in the countryside. You get a lot of habitat in little space, and if enough of your neighbours plant or conserve hedges, then you will set up a good ecological corridor system which will shelter hedgehogs, weasels, mice and small birds as they roam around from garden to garden. Modern garden hedges can be good nesting habitat. The mere act of clipping produces a dense, twiggy cover, and no matter how alien the plant species, birds such as the song thrushes, blackbirds and hedge sparrows will happily build there. As you will have gathered from all my talk of 'native species' in the previous chapter, though, there is more to habitat creation than just providing physical support for birds' nests. The same principles apply here. There is a whole range of vigorous native shrubs which have been used for generations as hedgerow plants in the countryside.

In fact, a hedge is perhaps the best way of all at garden scale, to provide a comprehensive range of native leaves and soft, juicy shoots for the caterpillars and grubs of all those native invertebrates. Even forest tree species can be kept at a manageable size by clipping as a hedge, and although some dependent insects seem to need their oak or beech leaves to be blowing in the wind 30m above ground, many are just as happy munching away in a hedge as they would be in a forest-size tree.

## WILDFLOWERS FOR THE HEDGE BOTTOM

It is possible to grow a range of woodland edge wildflowers along a hedge bottom, too. Some of them do need shade, and will do best on the side away from the sun, and many of them have problems if the ground becomes dry, but given a reasonable soil, and perhaps a bit of extra water in dry weather, you should be able to grow a smashing, colourful ribbon of wildflowers along the strip immediately in front of the hedge. Woodland edge species such as foxglove, campion, primrose, greater celandine and violet will all thrive, and several other species seem to grow better here. Where there is shelter but lots of light, hedge woundwort (*Stachys sylvatica*) is a marvellous plant, with tall spikes of brownish-purple flowers. This is truly a bee plant, but the lipped flowers are not big, and so the relatively small species of bee find that they have an advantage. I grow it through a carpet of more prostrate white and red deadnettle, and in early spring the whole hedge bottom does buzz with activity. The detail of many of these wildflowers is exquisite, and a feature of hedge woundwort which I love is the way the seeds are packaged. Look deep into the old flower socket when the blossom has fallen, and you will see a neat cluster of three or four tiny shiny black seeds peeping out at you.

Cuckoo-pint is another dramatic hedge-bottom wildflower, exciting at every stage of its development. The blotched leaves are a remarkable rich, deep green when they burst through and unfold in early spring. The flower structure is spectacular – a subtle, soft green colour for the delicate-looking hood-like spathe or sheath, and in the centre, the rather phallic spadix. This gives off a faint smell of unpleasant decay which seems irresistible to flies. Once pollinated, the sheath withers and a column of fresh green berries develops. These berries turn brilliant vermilion in the late summer, and brighten up the hedgerow, though the berries are poisonous. Another common name for cuckoo-pint is lords and ladies, and there are any number of theories about the erotic origins of that name.

One more hedge-bottom wildflower that it is worth finding a place for is garlic mustard. This common white flower, with its fresh green leaves, tinged with purple, has nothing whatever to do with garlic, but if you crush the leaves there is a faint oniony smell. The other common name you sometimes hear is Jack-by-the-hedge. This plant flowers early in the year, and is an important food source for overwintering butterflies as they emerge from hibernation. It is also one of the three or four types of plant which orange tip butterflies lay their eggs on, and for that reason alone there should always be a place for it in our wildlife gardens.

The hedge bottom is the traditional place to throw rubbish. Pull into any rural lay-by and I'm afraid you will see all too clearly what I mean. I'm certainly not advocating a wildlife habitat made up of old mattresses and bicycle frames, however good that may be for certain species, but I do think it is a good idea to let more natural garden rubbish build up along the hedge bottom. When you sweep the autumn leaves from the lawn, or chop down the spent raspberry canes at the end of the summer, do not burn them. Put them under the hedge as organic mulch. There they will provide food for a whole mass of mini-beasts, and could even be the spot your local hedgehog chooses for hibernating.

## PLANTING YOUR HEDGE

I do hope you will find somewhere to plant a hedge. In the *Bluetits and Bumblebees* TV garden, I replaced about 50m of rickety wooden fence with new hedgerow planting, and used another hedge to screen off the vegetable patch. It was cheap and easy to do, and within a couple of years lots of wildlife had moved in and colonised the new slimline habitat.

There is a big choice of species you can use but if you want my specific suggestion, then why not plant a mixture of 75 per cent hawthorn, to give you a thorny, dense hedge which blackbirds and finches will nest in, 15 per cent field maple, a shrub with a similar shaped leaf to hawthorn but with lovely soft brown shades in the spring regrowth and no thorns, and then 2 per cent each of holly and native wild privet, for a splash of evergreen winter leaf colour, dogwood for the red colour of its stems, guelder rose and dog rose. Plant two-year-old seedlings, which are readily available from any good nursery, and I suggest you use about five plants for each metre of hedge. I find it helps establishment if I plant the seedlings so that they all slope along the line of the hedge in the same direction at about 45 degrees.

If I cut off the side shoots and about one third off the top of each plant, then by the end of the first summer the hedge is already pretty dense at the base. My mixed field hedge is also helped by mulching with two parallel strips of a material much like roofing felt, which is manufactured specially for the job.

BELOW Clipped hedgerows provide tighter protection for nesting birds, and looser, more natural hedgerows are generally better for blossom and fruit. If you have room, try to accommodate both.

RIGHT When a hawthorn hedge is loose enough to flower and fruit, the benefit to wildlife can be most rewarding. Here a redwing from the frozen north is gorging on hawthorn berries ahead of harsher winter weather.

I do love the way all the different leaf shapes blend together into a kind of living tapestry. But of course, if you do not want this kind of mixed hedge, then you can always plant a single-species hedge. Any of the species in the mixture will do, or there are colourful alternatives like beech, or more sombre native shrubs such as yew or box. The one native shrub to avoid is blackthorn. I love it for the early display of bright white blossoms that clothe the bare twigs, and the deep purple sloes in autumn, but it suckers aggressively, its spines are vicious and it will take over the garden in no time.

Whatever you choose to plant, do try to experiment a little, particularly when it comes to clipping. If you get it right, with just one cut a year in early summer, you can get a neat hawthorn hedge to cover itself with May blossom. A cut at the end of winter will provide you with plenty of regrowth in the dogwood to give you red stem colour right through to the following spring. Do not forget, though, that for maximum wildlife value the hedge does need to produce some soft, chewable leaves and shoots, and please remember never to cut the hedge during the nesting season. You may not physically damage the nest, but the disturbance and the

dramatic change to the look of the surroundings almost always leads to the parent birds deserting, and that is the last thing you want to happen.

## CLIMBERS FOR ALL SPACES

I promised at the beginning of this book that you could attract wildlife into even the tiniest of town gardens. So far I've talked about nothing but mini-woodlands and country hedgerows, and obviously if you look out on little more than a light well then I cannot have helped much. Your salvation comes with climbers. In the wild there are several plants that scramble and twine their way up bushes and tree trunks, or cascade down cliff faces. None of them are particularly choosy about what they use for support, and if you have any kind of reasonably solid, vertical surface you should be trying to cover it with plants.

Of all the climbing plants you could possibly grow, there is no doubt in my mind about which is the best for wildlife – ivy. No wonder the ancient Brits thought it had magical properties. First of all, it is easy to grow. It likes shade best, and a reasonably rich soil, but in fact it will grow pretty well anywhere. It grows up vertical

surfaces without any need for wires or bits of string, though it sometimes needs some encouragement at first. If you buy a plant in a pot, it will probably be tied to a cane and looking rather forlorn. Plant it at least 30cm away from the bottom of the wall or fence, so that its roots are outside the hostile drought zone. (That is good policy whichever climbers you choose.) Then summon up all your courage, forget about how much you've just shelled out for the cane, and chop the plant down to 10cm or so above the ground. What that apparently brutal act of vandalism does is give a boost to the roots and stimulate the production of vigorous young side shoots with instant sticking power. If the ivy is planted on the sunny side of the wall, then it seems to help in the first few months of growth if you shade the plant. Just lean a piece of wood or a sheet of corrugated iron against the wall so that it leaves the young plant in a shadow. It is important that you water climbers in the early stages, too. It can get dry at the bottom of a wall. The foundations tend to absorb soil moisture and make the problem particularly bad.

The great thing about ivy as a wildlife climber is the variety of ways in which it supports wild creatures. Being evergreen it provides good cover throughout the year, of course, and an ivy-covered wall is a favourite nesting site for wrens and robins. Blackbirds often build in older ivy, too. Ivy is particularly important as wildlife cover in the winter, with several species of butterfly hibernating among its leaves. The brimstone, for instance, often the last butterfly to be seen around in the autumn, and a real harbinger of the following spring, seems perfectly camouflaged for overwintering among the ivy. When it flies, its wings are a wonderful soft lemon-yellow, but when it settles, and its wings close, the colour and pattern are exactly like those of a dead ivy leaf. When it hangs itself up for the winter it simply seems to disappear.

In my garden there is ivy growing tightly over a low brick wall by the back door. In the daytime it looks innocent enough, but if I take a torch out, particularly on a damp, warm night, there are dozens and dozens of snails gliding around the wall and the surrounding paths. Obviously the deep, cool shade of the ivy foliage is just what snails like to keep them safe during the heat of the day. Ivy provides much more than simple physical protection: its flowers last longer into the winter than almost any other British plant, often carrying golden blobs of sweet life-giving nectar right through into December. It only flowers once it reaches maturity, and it seems to need to climb up to at least a metre or so too, but once it starts, an arborescent flowering ivy will pull in late autumn insects from the whole neighbourhood. I watched a bank of good ivy flowers in a park one October and counted an average of seven fabulous small tortoiseshell butterflies to the square metre, all gently sipping away at the nectar to the point of intoxication. The flowers on my own ivy attract a marvellous variety of hoverflies in October and November, and do provide a focus for insect-watching at that time of year.

After the flower comes the fruit, and again the ivy is terrific. Most years the clusters of berry-like fruits are only ripening to their mature purple-black stage at the end of the winter, when most other natural foods such as hips and haws have been eaten up. Redwings and fieldfares often gorge themselves on ivy fruits before leaving for the long journey back north to their breeding sites, and each spring comical, portly wood pigeons entertain us for hours, trying to balance on the thin

OPPOSITE Cover walls, fences and other vertical surfaces with vegetation. There is no better way of increasing the natural nesting opportunities for songbirds such as wrens, blackbirds and robins.

BELOW Non-native garden climbers such as this *Clematis alpina* can provide excellent shelter and nest support.

twigs at the top of the elm hedge, while they reached out desperately to grab at the ivy crop.

People worry terribly about the effect on their buildings of climbers such as ivy. All sorts of stories circulate about demolished masonry. The fact is that climbers are much more likely to protect your brickwork, insulating it from the effects of frost and direct sunshine. Problems only seem to arise if the wall is already on its last legs, and even then, ivy is only likely to speed up the problem if the wall is old enough to have been built with relatively soft lime mortar instead of the less hospitable modern cement.

## NON-CLINGING CLIMBER CURTAINS

If you decide to stick to more traditional climbing vines, but want to avoid those with self-clinging aerial roots that attach to the house, there are plenty of climbers that will cling to other structures. Apart from the climbing hydrangea, ivy and Virginia creeper, most garden climbers need a wire or a pole to cling to. Wildlife will make most use of the gap between the outer leaves and the wall or fence, and for this reason it is worth manipulating this habitat a little. Normally

## LIVING WALLS

There is growing concern about the way that climate change is threatening to make our towns and cities much hotter and less healthy in the summer months. Living plants have the ability to cool and moisten the air while also filtering pollution. Consequently there is increasing enthusiasm for living green walls as a contribution to more healthy and comfortable urban living. Sometimes the green walls are simply clad with climbers rooted into the soil at the base, but there are more sophisticated alternatives. Suspending a special planting structure against a blank wall is enabling horticulturists to establish vertical communities of a whole range of non-climbing plants.

In the UK, New Street railway station in Birmingham now has a living wall several hundred metres long, growing a wonderful display of flowering garden plants, wildflowers and culinary herbs. In London, there is a living wall on Buckingham Palace Road, close to Victoria station, covering the entire gable end of a four-storey hotel. As our cities heat up and our desire increases to see more nature on the doorstep, we can expect green walls to become much more commonplace.

ABOVE Living walls were almost unheard of thirty years ago. Now they are increasingly popular. They help to insulate buildings, cool the air, make use of rainwater from the roof, and of course they can provide more habitat for pollinating insects, bats and birds.

OPPOSITE Don't forget night-flying insects. Pale flowers and strong perfume generally mean that climbers such as this evergreen honeysuckle will attract nocturnal pollinators such as hawkmoths.

you would expect to fix your climbing wires a few centimetres from the wall. Traditionally, gardeners have used flat nails with a hole in, known as vine-eyes, to hold the wires a little away from the surface. What I suggest is that you strain your climber support at least 10cm away from the wall. You can do this easily, either by making use of any brick piers or projecting fence posts that already exist; fixing 10cm square blocks to the wall and stretching wires between their outer faces, or driving in special new posts a little way out from the wall and effectively erecting a wire fence along them. Fit in a few simple wooden ledges and platforms between the wall or fence and your climber framework, and then train your climber up to form an outer screen. You will be delighted by the amount of wildlife activity that takes place on the other side of the green curtain. Birds will nest there, butterflies will hibernate and you may even accommodate a bat roost if you are lucky.

## A VARIETY OF BENEFITS
Of the non-clinging native climbers you can choose from, honeysuckle probably gives the best value. It climbs by twining its stems around the support, and may

need a bit of tying in at first, until it gets the idea. There is no more dreamy perfume on a June evening, and by growing it against a wall you can bury your nose right in among the blossoms. Honeysuckle is one of the classic moth flowers, and it can be particularly successful if you train it up a wall with an outside light on it. You can look forward to the sight of large hawkmoths bobbing meticulously from flower to flower, hovering at the entrance and then probing deep inside and sucking up the nectar. If the perfume does not captivate them, then the lamplight will do so. Insist on the native honeysuckle, rather than some garden hybrid, and then you will be sure of a good crop of scarlet berries to follow the flowers. The young shoots are often attacked by blackfly too, and from now on you can view this as an asset, since the aphids will quickly be followed by ladybirds and lacewings, and the larvae of such insects as the spectacular, but harmless, scorpion fly. Where would the wildlife gardener be without aphids?

Even the bark of honeysuckle has its uses, believe it or not. On an old plant, the bark tends to strip off in long, tough, stringy lumps, a bit like short lengths of raffia. This makes marvellous nest-building material, and in early spring you will see everything from house sparrows to blackbirds tugging strips off. In ancient oak woodland, where honeysuckle grows naturally, one species of rare bird, the pied flycatcher, depends almost entirely on honeysuckle bark for nest-building, while dormice eat the flowers and use the bark to build their nests. As coppice woodlands have become neglected, honeysuckle has tended to die out, and the visiting pied flycatchers and dormice are sadly becoming rarer and rarer.

BELOW Edges are very important. Hedges, climbers and tall shrubs all help to create shelter and enclosure, they provide both cover and corridors for wildlife movement, and tall plants such as these foxgloves are shown off to better effect.

RIGHT A dense curtain of honeysuckle is terrific value, especially where space is limited.

## EXOTIC CLIMBERS AND SHRUBS

Several exotic climbers and wall shrubs are also recommended. Some of the honeysuckles have as rich a perfume and nectar supply as our own native species. Several species of clematis produce even fluffier seedheads than our own wild old man's beard. Shrubs like *Ceanothus* and *Cotoneaster* are first-class pollen plants, and *Pyracantha* is famous for its autumn berries. All of them will give you the wildlife shelter you need, and they are popular in cultivation because they are beautiful to grow.

One more native climber deserves special mention. In fact this time it is normally more of a scrambler. How about growing a bramble up your wall? It will mean a lot of work if you are to keep it under control, but there are few plants more beautiful, and for wildlife the blackberry bush is a winner. It's easy to grow from a cutting or a layering, and since brambles vary enormously in the wild I suggest you choose a parent plant which has proved to be a heavy, sweet fruiter, and propagate your garden plant from that. Train it on wires, and prune it the way you would a cultivated loganberry, on a two-year rotation, cutting out the old canes after their second season, once they have fruited. In the formal fruit garden you would probably remove the old stems from the base in early autumn, but in the wildlife garden I suggest you leave these on until the spring. That way you will provide maximum shelter each winter. The bramble is a native plant which supports a great many dependent insects. A quick glance at the old leaves will show you how many little creatures have given them a bite or at least a nasty suck. The beautiful blossoms are a particularly good source of pollen, and popular with bees, and they also attract the late spring butterflies. Gatekeeper, speckled wood, peacock, small tortoiseshell and comma butterflies all feed on the bramble flowers in my garden. From mid-August onwards there will be colourful bunches of blackberries for you and the wildlife to enjoy. Masses of them hang over the garden wall outside my window, and each year the crown fruits at the tip of each bunch seem to ripen just in time for the mother blackbird to pluck each one, and feed it to one or other of her enormous, impatient offspring. There is lots of colour in the leaves and stems of the bramble, too, and in a sheltered spot, particularly when it is trained as a wall plant, you can expect the handsome five-part leaves to turn shades of crimson, copper and gold, and to cling on right until the last frost of spring. Often the new side shoots are several centimetres long before the old leaves fall, so it is virtually evergreen.

## ANNUALS FROM SEED

There is one final category of climbers that is well worth mentioning, and that is the annuals. When you think about it, there are a lot of climbing, twining plants you

**BELOW** Large dragonflies such as this southern hawker will often be found resting in the sun at the woodland edge between feeding flights.

**RIGHT** I always grow runner beans in my small garden. They quickly reach 2m in height, they provide food for me and the pollinating insects, and they are extremely cheap.

**BELOW RIGHT** Nasturtiums have been a favourite all my life. They thrive in the poorest of soils, they help to draw cabbage white butterflies away from food crops, their flowers are great for bees (and salads) and the climbing varieties will cover several square metres of wall by early summer.

can grow from seed, and they are useful, particularly in the early years when you are waiting for the more permanent perennials to become established. You may have to change your ideas a bit, but how about growing a curtain of runner beans up your wildlife garden wall? You will be able to watch bees squeezing their way into the bright red flowers all summer long, and have the added bonus of a crop at the end of it.

If you watch carefully, you will probably observe some of the insect pollinators 'beating the system'. Instead of struggling to open the jaws of the bean flowers, a few of the bees have developed the trick of biting a small hole in the base of the flower, and pinching the nectar without ever fulfilling their part of the bargain by pollinating the plant. If you do not see the cheats in action, you will be able to find plenty of the little holes they leave behind.

Old varieties of runner beans usually had scarlet flowers and tended to produce rather stringy beans unless they were harvested very young. For this reason I have always tended to grow climbing French beans as stringless alternatives with a wider range of cream, red or purple flowers, but modern varieties of runner bean

LEFT The cup-and-saucer vine, *Cobaea scandens*, is another climbing annual with flowers that suit bumblebees perfectly.

RIGHT As a child I was fascinated by ornamental gourds. Then it was their weird shapes that held the appeal. Now I grow them for their ability to cover the ground rapidly and for their flowers' appeal to pollinators including tiny beetles.

have been bred to provide very similar characteristics, and they do tend to grow taller and more vigorously.

Nasturtiums are well worth their place in the wildlife garden, too. Choose a vigorous climbing strain, preferably with a perfume, plant in poor soil for maximum flower colour, and stand well back. Once they get going, these annual climbers grow at an amazing pace. The flowers are popular with bees, and a range of small pollinating beetles, too. The seeds are presumably eaten by small mammals in the winter, and the leaves are an alternative food source for caterpillars of the cabbage white butterfly. It would be nice to think that, if you grew nasturtiums, the caterpillars would leave your cabbages alone, but I'm afraid the more probable outcome is simply an extra supply of egg-laying females the following year. Cabbage white caterpillars are not alone in eating nasturtium leaves, aphids enjoy them too. Several other kinds of caterpillar seem to like them, and I'm rather partial to them myself. They add a lovely sharp, peppery zing to summer salads. One of the great flavours of childhood, too, comes with that moment when you bite the pointed tip off the back end of your first nasturtium 'hat' and suck out the sugary nectar. The bean-flower robber bees don't have all the tricks!

Next spring, when you are stocking up with seed packets, and pretending to yourself that this year they will get planted, look out for annual climbers. There are ornamental gourds with huge yellow flowers, the cup-and-saucer vine (*Cobaea scandens*), with wonderful purple bell flowers; canary creeper (*Tropaeolum peregrinum*); love-in-a-puff (*Cardiospermum halicacabum*) and a few more. Start them off in a pot on the kitchen windowsill, train them up your climber support and you could have an irresistibly picturesque setting for your spotted flycatcher nest by the end of May.

## 6

Liberate your lawn. Even the smallest patch of flowering grasses and meadow wildflowers will trigger nostalgic images of the lost countryside, and the garden wildlife will love it.

# LIVE-IN LAWNS AND WILDFLOWER MEADOWS

IF YOU close your eyes and drift off into your ideal imaginary landscape, I guarantee that within minutes you will be climbing over a stile or squeezing through a kissing gate – into a sunny, wildflower meadow. All those Monet and Renoir reproductions on birthday cards, and the pictures in our earliest school reading books have helped build up this romantic image of the countryside. Things are rather different when you set off in search of your dream landscape, and meet up with the harsh reality of wall-to-wall sugar beet, zero grazing and green deserts of ryegrass. In Britain, wildflower meadows are almost entirely a thing of the past. You may still see the odd field of buttercups or dandelions, and the National Lottery has helped the Wildlife Trusts to buy up one or two of the best examples of truly ancient meadow, but the statistics show clearly that we are now left with less than 2 per cent of all the unimproved pasture that still existed as recently as 1949. We must have quarter of a million hectares of regularly mown lawns in our suburban gardens, and at least as much again in our urban parks. It seems such a shame to adopt the high technology of chemical agriculture here, when we could

be providing a valuable habitat for all those refugee cowslips that have nowhere else to go.

Certainly it is possible to conserve a great many of our meadow wildflowers in wildlife gardens. It is also possible, if enough people take the plunge, to reverse the falling trend in the population of many of our grassland insect species too. In the first year of managing my old lawn as a meadow I had meadow brown and common blue butterflies breeding – and the whole thing was less than 10m across. I know there must be small mammals in there too, because the local kestrel drops in from time to time, and, rather less pleasingly, next-door's cat has a field day. I suspect we are unlikely to see skylarks nesting in gardens. The cats would certainly make their life difficult, and probably they need a minimum size of meadow, but I am convinced that if we could persuade the local authorities to bring back wildflower meadows to our parks and public open spaces, we could have lots of skylarks in the heart of town, and even corncrakes would return. Their near extinction is particularly sad because they fly from Africa to Britain each summer to breed. We are self-satisfied

about our conservation conscience compared with that of some countries in the developing world, yet we have destroyed the corncrakes' breeding habitat to such an extent that within less than fifty years they have been driven to the furthest corners of their territory. The few that still survive fly all the way over the barren lands of Britain's productive farmland, and if they are lucky they find a pocket of flowery, unimproved meadow in the Outer Hebrides, the Orkneys or the west of Ireland. They won't be safe there for long either, as vast sums of public money are used to drain land and pour on chemicals in a desperate effort to bring crofters into the agricultural surpluses jamboree. Wouldn't it be marvellous if migrant corncrakes were able to drop with a croak of relief into one of your dream meadows in Birmingham, or Manchester or Glasgow? Start the ball rolling with your pocket handkerchief and I'm sure it will happen in the parks.

## ROOFTOP LANDSCAPES

One exciting recent development is already making a positive contribution. Brown and green roofs on some of the larger factories and warehouses in our towns and cities are providing successful nesting sites for skylarks and other ground nesting birds. These high level habitats are not generally actively managed since mower access is often impossible, but the best of them have poor infertile soils, relatively sparse vegetation and plenty of scope for wild flowers to thrive. The bare earth between the plants plays an important role as habitat for some of our rarest burrowing insects and sheltered spots for birds to nest. Perhaps most significantly of all, the roof is usually one place which is out of bounds to predators such as cats, foxes and weasels, although there is still every chance of a kestrel attack from above. Some of the best of these rooftop landscapes are deep in the heart of our industrial landscapes, where ground level open space can be in short supply, and in East London the impact has been particularly striking. Skylarks, lapwings and several other ground-nesting birds are now known to breed successfully two or three storeys above street level.

## MOWING PATTERNS

All our rich grassland wildlife succeeded as a happy spin-off from traditional farming of one sort or another. It

LEFT This rooftop meadow benefits from very thin, stony soil and the less polluted air above street level. It is also safe from predatory cats and foxes.

BELOW Skylarks are not thought of as urban birds, but there are signs that even these iconic ground-nesting creatures may be adopting rooftop wildlife habitats.

was the regular, methodical, annual cycle of mowing and grazing which provided the ideal conditions for all those wildflowers, butterflies and birds we miss so much. It is a change in this pattern which has led to their decline. The success of the wildflower meadow in your garden will depend basically on your willingness to adopt a particular pattern of mowing, and sticking to it. You can see how true this is if you look at any normal garden lawn. Presumably it will have been mown on the same steady cycle of a cut every Sunday for summer after summer. That particular pattern favours some of the lawn grasses, which is why we do it, but it also provides a suitable habitat for several species of wildflower. These are generally the species that can live for years without the need to flower, and which hold their leaves close to the ground. We call them lawn weeds, and everyone is familiar with them. The most common ones are daisies, plantains and cat's ears, all with the same growth pattern of a flat rosette of leaves. There are creeping plants too, that sneak about below the mower blades, and the commonest of these are self-heal and speedwell. These are the wildflowers best suited to a 'formal lawn' pattern of mowing regime, and if you want

# WILDFLOWERS FOR THE SPRING MEADOW

Should be mown from July onwards and the clippings left uncollected.

**Yellow rattle** (*Rhinanthus minor*) (right) A modest little plant, semi-parasitic on grasses, and producing large (10cm diameter) seed pods in which the seeds rattle. Helps to improve the success of other meadow flowers by reducing competition from suppressed grasses.
**Cowslip** (*Primula veris*) Clusters of yellow flowers. Prefers slightly limy soil but can cope with clay.
**Snake's-head fritillary** (*Fritillaria meleagris*) Plant as corms. Beautiful purple-chequered or white flowers. Prefers moist, non-acidic soils.
**Self-heal** (*Prunella vulgaris*) A tough little creeping

plant with blue-purple flowers. Can quickly spread into surrounding borders.
**Lesser stitchwort** (*Stellaria graminea*) (left) Present in many old lawns. Sprinkles the grasses with tiny white flowers.
**Bugle** (*Ajuga reptans*) Similar to self-heal, but with taller spikes of blue flowers and a preference for damp conditions.
**Daisy** (*Bellis perennis*) What can I say?
**Cat's ears** (*Hypochaeris radicata*) A common rosette weed of poor lawns. Lovely bright yellow flowers on 30cm stems.
**Rough hawkbit** (*Leontodon hispidus*) Similar to cat's ear, but less wiry and much taller.
**Dandelion** (*Taraxacum officinale*) A sign of deep, rich soil. A useful butterfly nectar plant, and bullfinches love pulling the clocks to pieces and eating the seeds. No better way of telling the time.
**Salad burnet** (*Sanguisorba minor*) Purple flowers over attractive foliage. Prefers moist soil, and the leaves taste like walnut oil (if you have a vivid imagination). Nice addition to cheese sandwiches.
**Milkmaids or lady's smock** (*Cardamine pratensis*) (left) Pink flower; 30cm tall. Food plant of the orange tip butterfly.

# WILDFLOWERS FOR THE SUMMER MEADOW

Mow until June and again in late September.

**Sheep's sorrel** (*Rumex acetosella*) (above) Lends a lovely orange haze to the summer meadow. The seed is an important food for finches, and the leaves are used for egg-laying by the small copper butterfly. An indicator of slightly acid soils.

**Knapweed** (*Centaurea scabiosa*) A tough plant with dark, hairy stems and a thistle-like purple flower. An important nectar plant in late summer.

**Lady's bedstraw** (*Galium verum*) Masses of tiny little bright-yellow flowers, sprawling around in clusters among the grass stems. A food plant for some of the more spectacular moth caterpillars, and once widely used as a dried 'strewing herb' to cover the floor and disguise the smells of mediaeval living.

**Field scabious** (*Knautia arvensis*) One of the prettiest of our meadow wildflowers. Pincushions of mauve-blue flowers. Popular with beetles and moths as a source of nectar and pollen.

**Ox-eye daisy** (*Leucanthemum vulgare*) One of the easiest meadow flowers to grow, though it will tend to die out after four or five years unless the 'meadow' is disturbed a little – perhaps by trampling.

**Hardhead** (*Centaurea nigra*) Similar to knapweed.

**Meadow buttercup** (*Ranunculus acris*) So much more handsome than the creeping buttercup. The divided leaves are up to 5cm across and the beautiful single flowers stand up to 1m tall on elegant, slender, green stems.

**Perforate St John's wort** (*Hypericum perforatum*) (above) A rapid coloniser, and a useful insect plant, growing up to 30–45cm tall in solid stands. The flowers are yellow and orange.

**Yarrow** (*Achillea millefolium*) A lawn weed that spreads like mad. Its fern-like leaves are pretty, and the plates of white flowers are an important source of mid-summer nectar.

**Devil's-bit scabious** (*Succisa pratensis*) Much smaller, darker blue flowers than field scabious, and with no outer 'frill' of ray-flowers. Leaves are the food plant of marsh fritillary butterflies, and this plant will bloom from July until November. Prefers damp conditions.

**Musk mallow** (*Malva moschata*) A big meadow plant, growing up to 1.5m even in mown conditions. Well worth growing for its lovely pale pink flowers up to 5cm across.

**Harebell** (*Campanula rotundifolia*) Can get overwhelmed in all but the poorest of soils, but if you can grow it successfully it gives a real reminder of the countryside.

**Goat's beard** (*Tragopogon pratensis*) Much more than just 'another dandelion'. The seedheads are huge – real 'grandfather clocks' and they seem to stay in one piece rather longer than ordinary dandelions. They look spectacular in the shallow light of evening.

to keep them you must stick to the usual timetable, and keep dragging the mower out each week. You can give yourself a treat each year, though. Some time around the middle to the end of May, take a couple of Sundays off. After just a few days of neglect, flower stems will rise up from the centre of each of your rosette lawn weeds. Cat's ears (*Hypochaeris radicata*) will give you sheets of yellow, daisies will mingle with the bright blue carpet of speedwell, and plantain will surprise you with the beauty of its pollen-covered stamens. You can repeat this lawn-weed wildflower exhibition year after year, but you must return to close mowing again within a month or so, otherwise the lawn grasses will grow up, overshadow the leaves of the rosette plants, and your daisies and plantain will wither away.

You may decide you would like to change your style of management completely for part of your lawn. I wanted a meadow at the far end of my garden, beyond the pond, and was keen to leave the lawn uncut until high summer so that the grasses would get a chance to flower. It was easy enough to do. I simply avoided mowing the new meadow area until the grasses had flowered. Within a couple of seasons, as I expected,

Conservation charities such as Plantlife manage inspiring wildflower meadows all over the UK. Here one of their Coronation Meadows contains meadow buttercup, dyers wintergreen, knapweed, red clover and common spotted orchids as well as numerous wild grasses.

all the daisies had gone, but I had a pleasant surprise, too. Some of the plants which had been growing in a suppressed form among the closely mown grasses grew up, flowered and survived the competition of the taller vegetation. The most successful of these was yarrow, which is present in many people's lawns as a tight, fern-like, emerald-green carpet. It now graces my meadow with its plates of nectar-rich white flowers from mid-July to September, and its leaves have grown up among the grasses. The flowers seem particularly attractive to small copper and skipper butterflies, which is a bonus in sunny summers. There were a few other meadow flowers

lying incognito in my lawn too. One of the prettiest was lesser stitchwort, and its clouds of bright white flowers are sprinkled everywhere throughout the spring meadow. I had sheets of milkmaids, or lady's smock – the cuckoo flower – growing there. They cannot have had a chance to flower for years, and yet as soon as I stopped mowing, up came all these beautiful pink flowers, and down came the orange tip butterflies to feed on the nectar and lay eggs on the leaves.

## SOIL FERTILITY

I was particularly fortunate with my lawn. It was old, and weedy, and the soil beneath it was poor – almost pure sand in fact. This low fertility is important. If you have rich, deep soil then the grasses do well, particularly tall, coarse species like cock's foot, and the only wildflower that is likely to survive the competition is cow parsley. You can use your lawnmower to lower the soil fertility, and that may be the best policy for the first couple of years. Keep mowing closely, but make sure you take off the clippings each time, and resist all temptation to add any fertiliser. Each time you cart away a bag of clippings you are taking out a little more of the fertility, the coarse

plants will do less and less well, and you will improve your wildflowers' chances. Mix in the clippings with the compost heap, or add them as a mulch to the vegetable garden where the fertility will be a positive advantage.

Low fertility is a real advantage when establishing a colourful wildflower meadow. It helps the broad leaved plants to outcompete the vigorous grasses. If you are brave enough, then stripping off the topsoil and establishing wildflowers on the infertile subsoil certainly works. The meadow at Sticky Wicket in Dorset is a brilliant demonstration of the effectiveness of this technique. In a small garden, stripping a modest patch of the lawn is relatively simple, and I strongly recommend that you try it. On a much bigger scale there are a few schemes in parks and school grounds where heavy machinery and a deep plough has been used to turn over the top half metre of soil. This buries the fertile topsoil and brings the poor subsoil to the surface, and some of the resulting wildflower meadows are spectacular.

## ACHIEVING VARIED MEADOW STYLES

If your garden is big enough, you might like to develop two or three slightly different meadow communities.

Perhaps the area nearest the house will remain closely mown, with that flowery hiccup in June to surprise the neighbours. Obviously, closely mown lawns are useful in a garden. It would be silly to leave yourself with nowhere to sit on sunny days. A second area might be managed specifically for spring wildflowers. If you mow it regularly after the end of June, this will allow flowers like lady's smock, fritillary, self-heal, bugle, ox-eye daisy, cowslip, and dandelion the time to flower and set ripe seed, but will give you a usable lawn for the summer holidays. Mow as the seed ripens and this will help the spring flowers spread and germinate.

Some of our most spectacular wildflower meadows are managed more or less along these lines. North Meadow, in Wiltshire, for example, has been mown for hay in early July for generations. The cropped field is rested for a couple of months, and then cattle are put out to graze the late summer growth of grass, known as the aftermath, through the late autumn and winter. This pattern of management has produced a wonderful community of spring meadow flowers. Almost the entire surviving British population of wild snake's-head fritillaries grows here, setting seed in June before the

hay is cut. The cattle's grazing prevents the swamping of spring flowers by coarse grasses, and also plays an important role in lightly trampling or 'poaching' the ground. Without the cattle churning the surface with their hooves, the wildflower seed would be much less likely to get down through the mat of grasses and germinate. If you want to simulate the trampling of North Meadow accurately in your garden then you need to organise a garden party in late August, where you can ply your livestock with gin and tonic, and then wheel out your mechanical grazing machine, the lawn mower, for an extra couple of cuts at the end of the growing season.

Some meadow flowers do not bloom until August or September, and if you adopt the spring meadow cycle then obviously they will not survive. I'm thinking of the taller species such as field scabious, knapweed, hardhead, meadow clary and musk mallow. To encourage these particular plants you need a third mowing regime, which leaves the meadow uncut until the end of the summer – say mid to late September. You must cut then, of course, and you must take away the hay. If you leave all the cut stems through the winter

LEFT Some meadows are particularly special. North Meadow, in the Thames' flood plain at Cricklade, Wiltshire is home to half a million snake's-head fritillaries. Well worth a visit in early May.

BELOW Cowslips used to be commonplace. Now they are rare, but easy to grow in our gardens. They are pretty enough to hold their own in a flower border, but with seasonal mowing they will quickly colonise a mini-meadow. Sow fresh green seed if you can.

you will have a tangled mess by spring, and the only wildflowers that are likely to survive that treatment are nettles and hogweed.

Late-summer meadows are lovely. All the flower colours seem to be pastel shades of mauve and lilac, and the shallower sunlight at the end of the year produces some beautiful effects. A few of these taller, late-flowering species do not begin to grow until midsummer, so if you are short of space you can mow this section of the meadow in the early part of the year, and use

it as a rough lawn while the cowslips and fritillaries of the spring meadow are out of bounds elsewhere. Do not cut the grass too close, though, or you will damage the wildflowers and they will gradually disappear. Five centimetres should be the minimum.

Adopting a different mowing regime will provide the right habitat for meadow wildlife, but apart from a few odd plants like yarrow, you are unlikely to have the meadow species already in place and ready to take up residence. The more mobile animal life will find your new habitat surprisingly quickly, but most of the wildflowers will have to be introduced artificially – just like the primroses and foxgloves of the woodland edge. In the wild, the flower seed is scattered around in the wind, and then pressed into the soil by the cattle, and you can try sprinkling packets of cowslip seed among your garden-party guests if you like. However, even in the cow pasture the success rate is extremely low, and with wildflower seed the price it is, I suggest you adopt a more efficient technique. Plan to introduce a selection of species which will flower to suit the particular mowing regime you have adopted. It is worth checking the type of soil you have, too. You may just happen to have one which is particularly acid or chalky, extra wet or well drained. If it is extreme in some way, then that will restrict the range of wildflowers you can grow, though it may offer you possibilities that are unavailable to wildlife gardeners with more normal, middle-of-the-road kinds of soil.

## CHOOSING AND SOWING YOUR SEED

Once you have made your selection, buy the seed in individual packets, preferably from one of the seed houses that deal only in native stock. There is a difference between subspecies of some of our wildflowers when you compare native flora with their counterparts in France or Holland, for example, and certainly it is better for wildlife generally if we try to avoid introducing foreign seed stock, even into our gardens.

When your seeds arrive, rather than sow them straight on to the meadow, where few of them are likely to germinate successfully, sow them instead in pots or seed trays filled with a normal, sterilised seed compost – John Innes No. 1, for instance. The best time to sow most species is in late summer. If you think about it, this is the natural time of year for seed to reach the soil anyway. Put the pots outside in a cold corner of the

# WILDFLOWERS FOR THE CULTIVATED CORNFIELD WEED PATCH

Rake over a patch of your poorest soil and sow these cornfield annuals for a colourful display throughout the summer.

**Cornflowers** (*Centaurea cyanus*) (above) Another of those penetrating blues. Cornflowers must have made our countryside look magical when they were common weeds in cornfields. Avoid all those new fancy pinks, mauves and whites if you possibly can. Cornflowers last surprisingly well as cut flowers.

**Corncockle** (*Agrostemma githago*) Tall and elegant – and now extremely rare in the wild. The big, black seeds are easy to sow but they are poisonous, so need handling with care. The mauve flowers stand up to 1m tall, and are extremely beautiful.

**Scarlet pimpernel** (*Anagallis arvensis*) A tiny creeping plant with poppy-red flowers which open in the sun and close at the first sign of rain. A common garden weed.

**Corn marigold** (*Glebionis segetum*) One of our prettiest wildflowers, and an easy annual to grow. The yellow daisy-like flowers lend splashes of colour.

**Red deadnettle** (*Lamium purpureum*) Often crops up in the first year after cultivation. The leaves have a purple tinge to them too, and the plant seems able to tolerate the shade of the taller annuals, and creeps around beneath the more colourful weeds.

**Pineapple weed** (*Matricaria discoidea*) One of those evocative smells of childhood. Squeeze the plump green flower between finger and thumb and smell the pineapple perfume that gives this common weed its name.

**Common poppy** (*Papaver rhoeas*) (below) A great favourite, and rightly so. The colour is spectacular, and poppy seedlings will reappear year after year if you simply rake over the surface at the end of each summer. It is no use trying to grow poppies in the meadow, though. They are annuals and must have a disturbed habitat.

garden and forget about them. Avoid leaving the pots inside through winter. If you do this, then some of the species will germinate in December or January, and you will be landed with a mass of seedlings and nowhere to put them. They will be too tender to plant outside. Most of the seed, though, will probably not germinate at all if you keep it inside. A great many of our native wildflowers need a period of cold weather, with many degrees of frost, before they are in a suitable condition to germinate. It is a strategy which helps them survive in the wild, by preventing early germination in mild mid-winter weather, and then premature death in the frost that follows. By putting your autumn-sown seeds out in the cold you are helping to prepare them for effective germination the following spring. Once April comes, make sure the compost is kept moist, and all being well you will have germinating seedlings by the end of the month.

A few species may not germinate the first year, even after frost treatment. Cowslips are one example of a species the seeds of which germinate only if they are extremely fresh (and that can never be the case with packeted seeds) or when they have had two or

ABOVE It's hard to create a colour clash with wild flowers. Here the yellow of welsh poppies seems to blend perfectly well with pink campion and bright blue speedwell.

OVERLEAF A meadow setting is perfect for long summer lunches or a cool drink at the end of a hot day.

even three winters of cold weather treatment. It may be frustrating but just be patient. Keep an eye on the pots each spring, and just when you have abandoned all hope, up will come the cowslip seedlings. This is one of the reasons why it is so important to use sterilised compost for seed-growing. It may take cowslips several winters before they germinate, but if you sow them in ordinary soil, dozens of other 'weed' species will germinate at the first sign of spring, and you will never find your cowslips, even if they do manage to come to life. I know a great many people who have bought wildflower seed in the past. If they have chosen an easy

species then they have been delighted, and perfectly satisfied. But many of them have gone for difficult seed, like cowslips, and all too often they have thrown the apparently barren compost away, not realising that their precious seeds are just taking their time.

## PLANTING ON

Once your seedlings are big enough to handle, usually at the three or four leaf stage, tease them gently out of the moist compost, and plant them on into individual pots, this time using slightly richer potting compost such as John Innes No. 2. Put them in a sheltered spot where you can keep them watered and watch them grow. I would choose 6 or 7.5cm plant pots, and leave the seedlings in these for a whole summer. They should grow into good healthy plants, filling the pots with roots and producing lots of leaves. If they start to produce flower shoots, cut these off, and concentrate the plant's energy on growing roots. At the end of the summer, when the 'hay crop' has been cleared and the last tidy-up mowing has been done, usually at the beginning of October, you can plant out your pot-grown seedlings. Back in 1985, when I planted my wildlife garden at Chelsea, it was almost impossible to buy commercially

grown wildflowers. Now you can order them by mail, or pick them up at most good garden centres. Those in large pots are expensive, but many wildflowers are also available as substantial seedlings, grown in trays of 'plugs', and although these take an extra season to establish, this is an efficient and economical way to acquire a wildflower meadow.

## PLOTTING OUT YOUR MEADOW

Remember to allocate plants to the appropriate bit of meadow. Place out the pots first, so that they form bold groups of a single species rather than a spotty mixture of different things. Space the plants 20–40cm apart, depending on the eventual scale of the particular species, and when you are sure the layout is right, plant them. Ideally you should try and remove a plug of soil just the right size to make room for the pot of roots. If the pot is small enough you might get away with using a bulb planter to cut out the holes; if not, then a sharp trowel does the job perfectly well. Remove the pots put the plant roots in the hole, and firm the whole thing with your heel. Do not worry too much about squashing your precious seedlings, they should be tough enough to withstand a bit of trampling. Try to avoid leaving any

loose soil on the surface of the meadow, or bare earth around the new plants. This is an open invitation for weed seed to float in and germinate, and it's the classic way that thistles and dandelions in particular get into meadows. In the countryside it is molehills that often create the opportunity for incomers, and while you may have moles in your lawn, you may as well take the trouble to minimise the risk of weeds by being as tidy as possible when planting.

If the meadow conditions are right, then your wildflowers should multiply year by year. Those which do best will give you a useful clue as to which other species might be worth introducing, and certainly I would suggest that you build up the list gradually by growing a couple of new species each year.

## EXOTIC BULBS

There are one or two meadow wildflowers that are available for planting in a rather more convenient form. These are the meadow bulbs, and you may choose to include a few exotic bulbous species in your meadow too, to increase the range of flowers. Wild daffodils, snowflakes, snake's-head fritillaries and meadow saffron are all wildflowers which you can buy as bulbs or corms,

though you may have to order from a specialist nursery. It is likely that the stock you buy will be of foreign origin, since these plants are all so rare in the wild now, but none of them are likely to leap off and interfere with the surviving fragments of the native population, so unless you live next door to a wild colony, where there is a risk that cross-pollination with imported stock could weaken the natives, I think you are safe to plant your bulbous wildflowers from whichever nursery source you choose. Do make sure, however, that they are certified as nursery-grown, and not plundered from the wild.

## FROM THE SOIL UP

If yours is a new garden, then you will need to start your meadow from scratch. In fact, even in an established garden it is not a bad idea to start from bare earth if the existing lawn is fertile and vigorous.

The essential requirement for a new wildflower meadow is low fertility. Poverty tends to favour a wide range of wildflowers, and gives them a bit of an advantage over the more greedy, coarse species. If you're buying a brand-new house, try to persuade the builder to leave you with a well-drained poor sandy subsoil for the meadow if you possibly can. What you

normally get is the opposite of this, of course: the worst compaction that twelve months of building site traffic can produce, covered with 15cm of 'topsoil' which has been stockpiled just long enough to build up a massive bank of dock and thistle seed. If you can get poor soil, all well and good, but if you are landed with highly fertile material then it is worth taking a couple of summers to lower the fertility before you attempt sowing your meadow.

Grow greedy crops like potatoes, maize or marrows and avoid leguminous vegetables like peas and beans because they will build up the nitrogen levels in the soil. When you've harvested your corn on the cob, or dug up your spuds, cart away all the nutrient-rich waste plant material and compost it for use on the permanent vegetable garden. You can speed up the de-fertilising process by stripping off a layer of the topsoil, too, though the practicality of this remedy rather depends on how big the area is. Certainly it is a good way of preparing an existing over-fertile lawn. Strip the turf, perhaps 7.5cm or even 10cm thick, and stack it, grass-to-grass until it rots down to form a wonderful crumbly compost for use elsewhere.

Once you have your low-fertility soil, make the drainage as good as you can get it. Of course there are some lovely wildflowers that grow in wet meadows, but unless you can guarantee that your poor drainage is going to be permanent, and is not a temporary legacy of the building contractor, it is well worth sorting the drainage out right at the start. Dig a soakaway or two if need be. Just make a deep hole, perhaps a metre or so deep and about the same distance across. Fill this with coarse material – all those half-bricks the builder so thoughtfully left behind for you – and cover the top with a few upside-down turfs and a layer of soil. If you put your soakaways at low points in the garden the 'floodwaters' will run down among the bricks and should disappear.

PREPARING THE SEEDBED

The soil preparation of the seedbed for your well-drained, low-fertility meadow is perfectly orthodox – just like any normal lawn. The seed will only germinate evenly if the seedbed is fine and crumbly and firm, so you need to rake away until you have broken up all the big lumps, and pulled out all the stones. Shuffle over the

LEFT A mown path makes the longer meadow grass look more intentional and improves access without trampling the wildlife habitat.

BELOW, TOP Salad burnet is one of the more uncommon meadow flowers. Its leaves have a mild walnut flavour.

BELOW, BOTTOM One surprise for many first-time meadow gardeners is just how beautiful wild grasses can be when they're allowed to flower.

whole area to firm the surface, or roll it with a light roller if the area is big enough, and then wait. The best time to sow your meadow seed is late August, with mid-April as a reasonable second choice. You need to allow a gap of at least three weeks between soil preparation and sowing, so that means you should finish your raking at the end of July or in late March. The reason for the three week wait is simple. The newly prepared soil will be full of seed already. Within a couple of days, provided it's not too hot and dry, you will see a green sheen develop over your handiwork. The cultivation and sudden exposure to sunlight will have triggered off the germination of thousands and thousands of 'weed' seeds. You may also have bits of root in the soil from such aggressive die hards as couch grass, creeping thistle and ground elder. Few, if any, of these weed species can survive in an established meadow, but they are all much more efficient than your meadow species at establishing in newly cultivated soil, so it is well worth getting rid of as many as possible before you sow. The most efficient way of wiping them out is to wait until the flush of seedlings is about 5cm tall, and then, before any of them have a chance to flower and seed, kill the lot with a non-selective, non-residual systemic weed killer. Look for something in your garden centre that answers to this description, mix it according to the instructions, and apply it from a watering can, taking great care not to let it get on any of the surrounding plants.

If, like me, you are suspicious of the so-called 'safe' garden chemicals, and would rather not use them, then you can burn the weed seedlings off with a flame-thrower. These are generally fairly easy to hire these days, and although they look rather terrifying, they will certainly do the trick. The only problem with the non-chemical approach is that it will not deal completely with the weeds that grow from bits of perennial root. They will just keep coming back for more.

Another possibility is simply to hoe or rake the seedling crop to uproot and kill it, but more often than not that aggravates the perennating root problem, and it also stirs up another lot of weed seed. In a normal lawn, the regular mowing will quickly get rid of pernicious weeds such as ground elder and couch grass, but in a meadow, with only a couple of cuts a year, you may be left with a permanent problem. If you have permanent weeds, and your conscience stops you spraying them even once, then I suggest you adopt a fairly orthodox mowing regime for a couple of seasons, mowing say once every ten days. This will establish a weed-free lawn of fine grasses, and then, when you've mown out the ground elder and couch grass, you can introduce wildflowers as you would in old, established lawns.

## STARTING WITH GRASSES

The species you choose to sow obviously have a major bearing on the quality of meadow you produce. Essentially, what you are hoping for is a mixture of attractive low-growing, non-aggressive grasses, and a selection of wildflowers that suit your chosen mowing regime. There are a great many pre-selected seed mixes available, but there is only one golden rule. Whatever else you do, never sow a mixture which contains ryegrass. This is the tough, wiry grass used to produce hardwearing sports pitches and play lawns. It must be kept out of your meadow. The grasses you do want all have relatively small seeds, and since you want to leave plenty of gaps for the wildflowers to germinate, the second important rule is to sow small quantities.

You can produce a good-looking meadow simply by selecting a 'no-ryegrass' mixture straight off the shelf at your local garden centre, and sowing it at about one fifth the recommended rate. That is difficult, since you are talking about little more than a pinch or two to the square metre. You can simplify even sowing at these low rates by mixing the seeds thoroughly with sawdust or silver sand. This has the double advantage of giving the different sized seeds an extra mix, to counter any separating out that might have taken place in the packet, and it also gives you a much clearer picture of where you have sown. Your grass mix should contain at least three or four non-rye species. Red fescue (*Festuca rubra*), common bent (*Agrostis tenuis*) and smooth meadow grass (*Poa pratense*) are all fairly standard, and then you might like to add one or two specifically hay-meadow species such as meadow foxtail (*Alopecuris pratensis*), Timothy (*Phleum pratense*) and Yorkshire fog (*Holcus lanatus*). To give your meadow that special 'new-mown hay' smell you need to include a little sweet vernal grass (*Anthoxanthum odoratum*) too. If you are sowing in the late summer, as I suggested, then you can use a simple, standard fine grasses mix and spice it up a bit by visiting the nearest attractive stretch of unmown roadside verge and collecting a handful or two of the seed of those grasses you like the look of. The total weight of fine

grass seed you need to sow is no more than 2g per square metre, and that is why it is so helpful to bulk it up with a carrier. In fact, to get a even coverage I find it is worth dividing the quantity of seed into two halves, and sowing one half in one direction, and then broadcasting the other portion at right angles to it.

## ADDING YOUR WILDFLOWERS

After the grass seed has been sown, you can then oversow with the seeds of various wildflowers. With these I think it is better to deal with individual species, and sow them either in drifts on their, own, or mixed in simple combinations of two or three species. This means that you can sow cheap, predictably successful species such as moonpenny or ox-eye daisy (*Leucanthemum vulgare*) and yellow rattle (*Rhianthus minor*) over the whole area, and restrict the more precious seeds to pockets where they will be particularly valuable, or particularly well-suited to some peculiarity of the site, such as a wet patch or a shaded area. I definitely favour a fairly simple range of wildflowers for starters, with more species added as pot-grown seedlings when the meadow has settled down. For the spring meadow I

LEFT Meadow cranesbill, seen growing here with lady's bedstraw, is one of the easiest and most persistent meadow wildflowers, especially where the soil is limey.

BELOW Sheep's sorrel does well in acid soil. Its flowers give the grassland a rusty-red sheen, and the leaves provide food for the caterpillars of small copper butterflies.

would start with cowslip (*Primula veris*), speedwell (*Veronica chamaedrys*), self-heal (*Prunella vulgaris*), hoary plantain (*Plantago media*), common sorrel (*Rumex acetosa*), and a generous proportion of ox-eye daisy. For the late summer meadow I would still include ox-eye daisy, because it looks so marvellous in early summer, and should survive. Other basic species include meadow buttercup (*Ranunculus acris*), lady's bedstraw (*Galium verum*), wild carrot (*Daucus carota*), common knapweed (*Centaurea nigra*), field scabious (*Knautia arvensis*) and meadow cranesbill (*Geranium pratense*).

## AIDING GROWTH

When all the seed has been sown, run gently over the surface of the seedbed with the back of a rake, to cover the seed lightly. Then re-firm the whole thing either by treading or by light rolling. Finally, stretch some lengths of cotton across from side to side, with twists of aluminium foil or newspaper tied in to scare away the sparrows. Ideal conditions for germination are provided by dull, drizzly weather, so you might like to make certain of that by booking your holidays for the week following sowing. If the weather is dry, then it is worth

watering, but do be careful to avoid washing the surface and disturbing the seed. If you get it right, the soil should be thoroughly soaked by a continuous fine spray. If you get it wrong, then seed will germinate in pretty, wave-shaped narrow bands. All being well, an August sowing will give you a good covering of grass before the winter, though most of the wildflowers will stay dormant until the spring. If the growth gets any taller than 7.5cm, then it is advisable to go over it with a mower, and chop off the tops. Do not cut any lower than 5cm, and do, please, make sure you use a sharp mower or shears, as the seedlings are still weak. The roots will not be well established and a blunt lawnmower can pull the plants out of the soil. Go over the area with a light roller, or firm feet, immediately after cutting, to push back any loosened plants. In the first year after sowing you should expect little in the way of flowers. The seeds will germinate, but the plants will mainly be producing root and leaf. For this reason there is nothing to be lost by mowing through the summer. In fact, this is a good idea in the first year. Set the blade as high as it will go, and keep taking the clippings off. This will encourage the grasses to spread, and will concentrate all the plants' energy into root establishment. In the second spring after sowing you can adopt your permanent mowing cycle, and you should be rewarded with a colourful display of flowers. In the first year of my sown meadow one or two ox-eye daisies managed to bloom, but in the second summer the wildflowers completely dominated the meadow for week after week.

## HAYMAKING

You may be wondering what to cut your meadow with. Certainly it is not easy fighting your way through two-foot tall grass with a little manual cylinder mower. The best tool of all is probably a scythe, and if you are feeling energetic it will give you a tremendous sense of satisfaction to see the swathes of hay falling away beneath your blades. Scything is marvellous for the waistline, too – which probably tells you that I use a mowing machine myself. In fact, the best machine of all is a motor-scythe with what is called a reciprocating blade. This works like a vicious-looking row of scissors, and cuts through the stems. Alternatively you can use a strimmer. The length of nylon thread at the business end whizzes round at a terrifying rate and slices through everything but the patio windows. The fourth option is

a rotary mower, but you need one with wheels so that you can set the blades high, and it has to be pretty hefty to cope. Remember that you are only going to have the problem once, or possibly twice, a year. One solution might be to keep the existing mower for cutting the lawn, and if it is not powerful enough for the meadow, and you are not strong enough to use a scythe, you can hire an appropriate machine for the two days of annual harvest. When you have cut the hay, leave it on the surface for a day or two before taking it off – this allows it to dry, the wildflowers can shed their ripe seeds, and any caterpillars and other meadow mini-beasts that have survived the mowing can migrate down into the stubble and out of harm's way. You must remove the hay eventually, though. Put it on the compost heap, or offer it as bedding for the local hamster population.

## KEEPING YOUR MEADOW ECO-FRIENDLY

There is one final, and obvious thing to say about meadow management. Having established your low-fertility, high-species-diversity grassland community, do not spray it with chemicals. No matter what the experts tell you about autumn lawn dressings and the horror of the leatherjackets, remember that your meadow is there to provide a habitat for wildlife. If you are ever in the slightest doubt, just take five minutes to watch the swallows swooping backwards and forwards over the grass and flowers and look down into the tangle of stems at the mass of different creatures living there, or sit quietly in the magic half-hour just after nightfall and listen to the squeaks and scuffles in your new habitat. That's the way you will know your meadow is successful. The fact that it looks more and more beautiful each summer is just a welcome bonus.

## RHS GARDEN WISLEY

‛     The essence of RHS Garden Wisley has always been to provide visitors with a combination of pleasure and learning. Now that gardening for wildlife has become an important theme of the research work at Wisley, there is a spectacular 'pictorial meadow' combining native wildflowers, grasses and more exotic meadow plants, to create a glorious summer display (shown here).

Wisley is a large and mature garden, created in 1904 for the Society's centenary. It has more than 500 mature oaks, each contributing to its natural richness, as well as a great many features to provide valuable practical inspiration for domestic gardens. The borders around the centenary glasshouses are good for attracting bees and other pollinators over a long season and a small area with a bird hide overlooks a natural wetland and attracts local bird life.

The traditional flower borders provide living proof of the species and cultivars most visited by insects, and these observations have led to important garden wildlife research. *The Plants for Pollinators* project has applied scientific rigour to the study of plant preferences: over four years, the RHS has compared the effectiveness of native and non-native garden plants for attracting butterflies, bees, hoverflies and other pollinating creatures, and the findings are invaluable when selecting the best plants for small gardens. ’

With water in the garden
you will never be short of
wildlife entertainment. Birds
need to bathe in order to
keep their plumage clean,
especially when they need
the insulation in cold weather.

7

# GARDEN PONDS AND OTHER 'WETLANDS'

A WILDLIFE garden without a pond is like a theatre without a stage. The woodland edge habitat and the mini-meadow create the countryside atmosphere, certainly, and the wildlife they support is fascinating, but the real thrills, the real dramas of the rich habitat garden take place in and around the pond. I sit for hours every summer, captivated by the aerobatics of the dragonflies that hunt, mate and lay their eggs there. In the depths of winter, when snow covers the whole neighbourhood, I am entertained day after day by the squabbling, splashing crowds of starlings and other birds which bathe in the icy shallows. Winter bathing is essential, apparently, to give the plumage maximum fluffability on killingly cold nights. Mini-wetlands in towns have proved more than anything else that urban nature conservation can provide some positive compensation for habitat destruction in the countryside. The common frog, in particular, would be virtually extinct by now were it not for the gnome-fringed ponds of suburbia, and the same will soon be true of diving beetles, damselflies, pond skaters and many more of the fascinating creatures whose survival depends on small stretches of unpolluted, shallow water. The ponds of the countryside have mostly been filled in now. The ditches have been piped to make way for bigger, combinable fields, and those wetlands that do survive have suffered terribly in the past from fertiliser run-off and chemical over-spray. A garden pond provides you with a guaranteed means of helping wildlife to survive, and the life it brings to your doorstep will enrich every aspect of the enjoyment your garden gives you.

## WETLAND HAVENS

The wetland habitats of the British Isles are especially important for international conservation. Bird migration is particularly dependent on our estuaries, lakes and marshes, with visiting wildfowl travelling here in vast numbers each autumn to escape the frozen winters of northern Russia, Greenland and Scandinavia. In the summer our wet woodlands provide nesting habitat for willow warblers from Africa, the soft mud around our lakes and ponds is used for nest-building by migrant house martins, eroded river cliffs are the natural nesting sites for sand martins, and of course the constant supply of newly-hatched mayflies, midges and other aquatic insects provide the thousands of swallows and swifts that visit us with a large proportion of their high-protein diet.

One of the most spectacular urban wildlife sights I know is the latter-day Battle of Britain that takes place every day throughout the summer, where the sewers meet the Thames at Kingston. Hundreds of swifts, swallows and martins swoop and dive with breath-taking agility as they snap up the clouds of insects among the buses and lorries on the A307.

Massive post-war building programmes have created some new wetlands, to compensate for the loss of lakes and ponds elsewhere. All that tarmac and concrete takes a great deal of gravel, and all those extra people drink a lot of water. Along many floodplains you will find wet gravel pits, and there have been a good many new reservoirs built this century, too. With care the new wetlands can become immensely rich wildlife sanctuaries, and in fact the gravel pits in particular have provided us with most of our new wetland habitat creation techniques. For an inspiring demonstration of successful wetland habitat creation on a grand scale, visit the Wildfowl and Wetland Trust's London centre, beside the Thames at Barn Elms.

The open, deep water of reservoirs and glacial lakes are of relatively little wildlife value, though they do provide a safe roost for the large flocks of urban seagulls. In fact, in London, by failing to consider seagull ecology the planners have created a traffic hazard, as thousands of big, engine-clogging birds commute twice daily across airport flight paths from their reservoir roosts to their feeding grounds on the rubbish tips.

LEFT Muddy margins are invaluable. Here a house martin is gathering nest building material.

OPPOSITE Even in very large lakes, like this one at the London Wetlands Trust, most of the action is at the edges. Remember that when you're making your much more modest garden pond.

BELOW The stickier the mud, the easier it is for house martins to build their nests under the eaves.

## FLOODS

It is the shallow waters that are the great wildlife resource. Most of the wild plants and animals live in the relative warmth among the reeds and rushes of the reservoir margin, and even the deep-water fish tend to move into the safety of the shallows to breed. Wetlands do not stop at the water's edge either. Flood meadows, marshes, wet pasture and waterlogged willow and alder woodland are all vitally important to their own particular dependent community of wild plants and animals. Sadly, these habitats have probably suffered even more than the ponds and ditches in recent years. Land drainage has been made all too easy with the powerful machinery we have available. Well-drained land is agriculturally more productive than marshy ground. Farmers can grow potatoes and wheat where previously they could perhaps only graze cattle for part of the year. Hundreds of millions of pounds of public funds have been poured into agricultural land drainage – lowering water tables, straightening rivers and destroying wetland habitat. One consequence of all this increased efficiency in land drainage has been an escalation in the rate of rainwater runoff. Water that would once have been retained

in ponds and marshes now flows off the land with dramatic, and often disastrous results. The increasing incidence of urban flooding is due in part to the more extreme weather that climate change seems to be triggering, but the lack of absorbency in the upstream landscapes makes the situation much worse.

## A NEW APPROACH

Even without all the deliberate destruction of the post-war years, wetland habitats are particularly vulnerable. Ponds and lakes gradually silt up as the rainwater washes particles of soil from high ground down to the lowlands. Leaf litter accumulates, trees and shrubs colonise and sooner or later the wetland turns into dry land. I spent my childhood playing in an old industrial river valley on the edge of Sheffield. In its heyday, at the end of the nineteenth century, the river Rivelin had been harnessed for water power by building a whole chain of millponds, but by the time I came on the scene half a century later, almost every one of them had silted up completely and was supporting a dense tangle of tall willow and alder trees. Of course, the old mill managers would never have let that happen. They would have employed men

BELOW Most of my own front garden is a wildlife pond, with a mix of gently shelving planted margins and hard edges for safe accessibility.

RIGHT For garden birds, clean water is as important for bathing as it is for drinking, and shallow margins are essential.

to keep the mill races clear, dredge out the silt and cut back the overhanging trees, but when steam and then electric power overtook the waterwheel, the wetlands were abandoned, and nature reclaimed the land.

Now, at last, the single-mindedness of agricultural land drainage seems to be tempered by a growing public demand for common sense. A number of high profile conservation campaigns in the 1980 – in Lancashire's Ribble Valley, the Somerset Levels, Halvergate in the Norfolk Broads, and elsewhere – persuaded policy-makers that flooded wetlands were a desirable alternative to artificial drainage. The growing frequency of urban flooding has also helped to strengthen the case for holding back stormwater upstream, and now there are signs that a more holistic view of land and water management is beginning to emerge. Money is being spent on blocking drains, rewetting upland peat bogs and creating many more opportunities to make landscapes more water-retentive. The planners' term for this new approach is *sustainable drainage*, and in a few parks, housing landscapes and other urban open spaces there are good examples of working with nature to deal with increasingly heavy rainfall. When the principles of wildlife gardening are used to shape these sustainable urban wetlands, then the impact on frogs and dragonflies and a whole host of other water-loving plants and animals can be dramatic. They can also provide the next generation of children with the kind of watery playground that I enjoyed so much.

All of this may seem rather remote from the issue of garden ponds, gnomes with fishing rods, and jamjars full of frogspawn, but it seems to me that the two ends of the wetland story are undeniably linked. The more people there are in towns who have had the first-hand thrill of seeing an ugly brown creature crawl laboriously up the stem of a flag iris and heave itself clumsily into new life as a dazzling blue damselfly, or have gasped as the early morning sun picked out the beautiful, tattered pink flowers of the ragged robin, the more chance we have of winning the battle for conservation and re-creation of our rare, precious and fast disappearing wetlands in the countryside.

## SITING YOUR POND OR WETLAND
Creating a garden wetland is probably easier now than it has ever been. In the past, the only choices

for waterproofing were either concrete or clay, but the great revolution in garden pond-making has come with the development of flexible waterproof sheet liners. With a bit of manipulation these can be used to create bogs and marshes as well as pools. Choose a part of your garden which is reasonably sheltered and, preferably, easily visible from inside the house. If you have your wetland fairly close to the building, then you may be able to tap into the rainwater guttering, and there is no doubt that the best artificial wetlands are those kept wet by rainwater instead of tap water.

Generally speaking, it is best to choose a position which is light and sunny. There *are* some wild creatures that inhabit the gloomy, leaf-filled pools of deepest woodland, but you will certainly have more colourful action on your doorstep if you go for a well-lit pond. If your garden slopes, try to choose a spot for the wetland at the lower end. It is not absolutely crucial, but artificial ponds and marshes always look more convincing if they lie in a natural hollow or at the bottom of a slope. Having said that, in my experience it is advisable to avoid wet hollows for artificial

LEFT In a family garden, make sure the pond has very gently sloping edges.

OVERLEAF Wildlife gardening is all about comfort and close observation. Make sure you have a comfortable seat where you can blend into the background.

Avoid overhanging trees if you can. For one thing, the autumn leaves are a nuisance. You will inevitably get some in your pond, even in a treeless garden, but overhanging branches guarantee difficulties ahead. The other reason for avoiding trees is that your excavations will damage the roots. It can be rather embarrassing if you site your pond to reflect the wonderful sculptural form of the mature beech tree, and then the mature beech tree promptly keels over and dies.

The ideal setting from the wildlife point of view would be a south west-facing corner of the garden, where part of the shoreline can be tucked into the dense undergrowth of the woodland edge, and the remainder can sit naturally in the meadow grassland. Paved or mown access to one or two parts of the pond edge will give you the chance to watch the wildlife at close quarters, and the adjacent shrubbery will provide a sheltered, safe approach for the more timid of your garden creatures.

When you've chosen the ideal spot for your mini-wetland, I'm afraid you have no alternative but to face up to the next rather strenuous stage. You will have to dig a big hole. Do make absolutely sure you are happy with the siting before you start. Digging is hard work, but filling in again is disheartening. I like to mark out the shape of my ponds with some canes first, and leave them for a week or two. This helps me to visualise the new pond and marsh, and I often adjust the shape and the position a lot before I finally dig the hole.

I cannot recommend sufficiently the benefits of a garden pond. When you are deciding how large yours should be, go for the biggest you can afford. However, in my first garden I had a tiny pond which I made by sinking a 60cm-square water tank into the ground. Even that was full of life in no time. To get the best habitat

ponds. Although that may seem like the most perfect place, you will regret the decision when you have to dig underwater. The airless ground conditions underneath the pond liner can sometimes promote the production of methane, which may cause the liner to bubble up embarrassingly. You will have nowhere to drain any surplus water to, either, which could well give you a flood problem in wet weather. If you have a naturally wet hollow, plant that with marsh plants and position the pond slightly higher up the slope; then it can overflow into the natural wetland.

PUDDLED CLAY
## PUDDLED CLAY

Traditionally the technique of choice would have been puddled clay. This is the sticky material that keeps the water in most of our canals, and it works well unless it dries out. Then it cracks and leaks. Ideally, the clay should be laid in blocks a bit like brick paving. Pack the blocks tightly together, water them and then 'puddle' for all you are worth. You need to trample the wet sticky clay thoroughly until it smears together and forms a watertight lining. Traditional clay-lined farm ponds were successful because their margins

would have been continually re-trampled and re-sealed by drinking livestock. The old navigators used to drive herds of cows and flocks of sheep along the bed of their new clay-lined canals to puddle them in. You might prefer to invite all the kids in the neighbourhood round, and tell them on no account to set foot in the new pond. You may be fortunate in having a local supply of suitable clay, in which case it's worth a try, but if you have to start paying for transport, then I strongly recommend that you choose one of the cheaper, easier and more reliable alternatives.

possible, you should allow for at least one area where the pond is shallow. If you cover the liner to bring the soil back up to top water level, then you will be able to grow marsh plants in the waterlogged conditions. The other absolutely critical characteristic of a first class wildlife pond is a depth of at least 60cm somewhere in the centre. The ideal shape of hole you should dig is a gently sided saucer, and if you are going to get down to the depth I suggest, then you will need a fairly big area. The deep water is necessary to allow pond life to survive below a sheet of the thickest ice in the coldest of winters, and the shallow edges are crucial as a habitat for many of the wetland water plants, and also as a safe access route for the wildlife that climbs in and out of the pond. It also makes the whole thing much safer for people at the water's edge.

## MAKE USE OF A GARDEN STREAM

If you are lucky enough to have a stream in your garden, then you can create a pond and marsh relatively simply by building a dam. Before you do, though, you should discuss this with the local office of the Environment Agency. You may need to take professional advice on the dam structure, too, if you are attempting anything more ambitious than a railway sleeper or a pile of four or five sandbags. Even a small pool contains a surprising volume of water, and if your inadequate dam bursts, you will be liable for any damage the floodwater causes downstream. One of the most inspiring garden schemes I have seen in recent years is in the Dutch city of Arnhem. Here, a whole group of neighbours investigated their shared problem of flooded cellars

and discovered that their houses had been built over a stream in a cracked culvert. They worked collectively to bring the lost stream back to the surface, and to direct it through all their front gardens. The result is a whole street of delightful watery wildlife gardens and the cellar flooding has become a thing of the past.

## WATERPROOFING

Most of us have gardens without streams. In this case you can choose from a number of different methods for waterproofing your wetland. For years, most people lined their garden ponds with concrete. If you have inherited a concrete pond, the odds are it now leaks, because although concrete is strong under pressure it cracks easily under tension, and you only need a bit of uneven settlement, or an exceptional frost, to fracture the concrete. The other thing that puts me off concrete pool construction is the speed at which you have to work. One of my earliest childhood memories is of dad racing to make use of a load of pond-lining ready-mix concrete before it turned to stone and cut off access to the car in the garage. That pond is still there, more than half a century later, but I must confess that it has leaked for years.

I think by far the best waterproofing method is the flexible sheet liner. Indeed if you have inherited a leaking concrete pond from a bygone age, then adding a modern sheet liner is the quickest and most reliable way of restoring it. There are now several different grades and types of waterproof sheeting available. The cheapest option that works is 1000 gauge black polythene. There are plastic sheets which have a tough

nylon mesh incorporated into them for extra protection against ripping, but the tough rubberised fabric liner known as butyl sheeting is the pond liner of choice. Butyl can be expected to last for at least twenty or thirty years. The other two materials can work well too, but you must adopt a technique of using them which protects them adequately from sunlight. The ultra-violet rays can make exposed polythene brittle enough to crack and leak within a summer, even beneath a metre of murky pond water, and any exposure at the edges of the pond almost inevitably leads to early failure.

## GET DIGGING

I recommend the same technique for all the different flexible liners, and so far it has proved pretty successful. You need to excavate your hole 15cm deeper than the depth you want your pond to be. If you want a shallow margin with 10cm of water in it, dig down 25cm. If the deepest point in the centre is to be 60cm deep, dig down 75cm and so on. Remember to shape the excavation so that it has gently sloping contours only. Do not leave any sharp changes of direction that would be difficult for the liner to follow. Excavate the ground

15cm deep for an extra half a metre or so all around the edge of the pool, too. You will need the overlap to anchor the liner, and do check and double check that the edge is the same level all the way round. You can do this with most garden ponds by using a long board and a spirit level.

Once the shape is right, go over the whole surface, carefully removing any sharp stones, bits of broken glass or china or anything else that might work its way up and puncture the liner from beneath. The next task is to spread a cushioning layer of some material or another over the whole of the excavated surface, as an extra precaution against puncturing. Five centimetres of the 15cm extra digging is there to allow you to spread a layer of sand in the hole. That is one of the cheapest materials you can use. There are various alternatives. Old carpets are good. Lots of tough old polythene sacks, sheets of dampened cardboard or thick pads of folded newspaper will all help. The best material of all is polypropylene matting specially made for the job. It is tough – virtually impenetrable – but it does cost a lot. It is used by engineers beneath roads that have to be constructed across badly drained land, and you can buy

# NATIVE WILDFLOWERS FOR THE POND: FLOATING-LEAVED AND BOTTOM-ROOTED

Many pond creatures need protective cover. Floating leaves are a good place to find the eggs of pond snails, dragonflies and newts.

**Water crowfoot** (*Ranunculus aquatilis*) (above) Pretty, simple white flowers and green, indented leaves about 3cm across. Flowers in early spring and disappears by midsummer. The leaves below the surface are much more fern-like.

**White waterlily** (*Nymphaea alba*) This is a vigorous native plant, capable of growing up in 3m of water, and producing large lily pads. It is too big for small garden ponds, though its flowers are beautiful.

**Fringed waterlily** (*Nymphoides peltata*) (right) Available from garden centres, and much less aggressive. Delightful little single yellow flowers stand a few millimetres above the water surface and the circular leaves are about 7.5cm across.

**Broad-leaved pondweed** (*Potamogeton natans*) Lovely dark brown-green oval leaves lying flat on the surface. Insignificant flowers.

**Amphibious bistort** (*Polygonum amphibium*) (right) One of the best pond plants, with oval floating leaves and pretty little pink flowers standing proud of the water. Snails lay their blobs of sticky eggs on the underside of the leaves and the seed is a popular food with several species. It also straddles the boundary between water and damp soil effectively.

## MINIATURE WETLANDS

If you only have a small space to play with, I still think it is worth trying find room for one or two of the prettiest wetland wildflowers. Even a bucket or sealed plant pot filled with soil can provide a habitat for a stunning display of purple loosestrife, flowering rush, marsh marigold and water forget-me-not if you keep it waterlogged by topping up with water during dry periods.

it at a builders' merchants or from pond liner suppliers.

Run your protective layer up and over the lip of the hole. The edges are obviously the most likely parts to get punctured, because there is the added pressure of careless feet to contend with. Once you are satisfied that the bed of the wetland is puncture-proof, spread your sheet liner out on the lawn, carry it across and stretch it over the hole. Make sure you've allowed plenty of overlap, and then weigh down the edges with smooth-bottomed heavy objects. (Bricks are ideal.)

Now here my recommendations differ from those of most people. Other books and guidelines say you should put a hosepipe into the middle of the sheet, turn on the tap, and let the weight of the water stretch the liner down to hug the walls of the pond. That does work well, but it leaves you with the liner shining up at you through the water, and it is difficult to cover it effectively with a sunshine-filtering, protective layer of anything. I prefer to ease the liner into the hole gradually, under its own weight. I then spread a further protective layer of matting, folded newspaper or the equivalent on top of my liner, making sure that if I need to step into the hole I always tread on a protected bit, and as the liner is covered over, I complete the protection by shovelling in an over-layer of subsoil or fine gravel. The waterproof liner is securely anchored under 15cm of soil all around the edge, and I am then left with an empty waterproof hole, lined with an impervious sheet sandwiched between soft protective layers of padding and soil.

The last stage in the operation is obviously the filling. With soil at the bottom, you do not want simply to splash the hosepipe in – you will end up with a mud bath. What I do is rest the hosepipe on top of a square of polythene or a piece of the protective matting, and let the water trickle in over that. It is a trick I learned from watching Arab nurserymen in the Middle East watering their young tree seedlings with a 5cm hose, and it should be possible for you to fill the pond completely without stirring up the soil in the bottom. The water itself can be an issue. Tap water is certainly bound to be pretty sterile, since it is treated for drinking, but in some areas it can be quite rich in nitrates which tend to encourage the growth of slimy green algae. If you can manage to tap into a source of rainwater this will generally be preferable, but even when you are able to divert your rainwater pipes from the roof into the pond, the filling process is likely to take much longer.

Personally I have always resorted to tap water, and then taken the trouble to pull out any strands of algae that appear in the first few months.

## PRE-FORMED PONDS

A practical alternative method for creating a small garden pond is to install a pre-formed rigid fibreglass or plastic pond. You will find these stacked against the wall at your local garden centre or aquatic specialists, and they come in all shapes and sizes. As a relatively foolproof method of containing the water they are excellent. You still have to dig the hole, of course, but you do not have to worry so much about settlement, and the job is certainly a lot quicker and less strenuous than either concrete or clay. Pre-formed ponds have two disadvantages as wildlife habitat. The first problem is the edge. All these ponds seem to have vertical sides which stand up at least 10cm and often higher. This is an obstacle for many of the smaller amphibians and for any mammals that tumble in, though you can overcome the problem to some extent by piling rocks on the ledge inside the pond, providing an access route that way. The other difficulty is caused by the steep slope and the shiny finish. These combine to make it almost impossible to cover the bottom with soil or gravel, and that makes the pond pretty hostile to wildlife. You are left with no alternative but to grow your water plants in pots or baskets standing on the bottom, and while this makes them easier to keep under control, it never produces the tangle of underwater vegetation and the layer of mud that creates vital shelter for the smaller pond creatures.

## INTRODUCING PLANTS

The best time to plant up your wetland is April or early May, though with pot-grown garden centre plants you can do it at any time. There is little point bothering in winter, though, as almost all the plants die down to nothing in the autumn. You have to get into the water to plant properly, and this can be pretty chilly. If you have a layer of soil in your pond, plant straight into it. This may mean your water plants run a bit wild, but they are easy enough to control if they get out of hand, and you are aiming to establish a healthy habitat as rapidly as possible. If you have chosen a concrete or pre-formed pond, then plant into those perforated plastic containers which are sold in water plant centres.

### SLIME MANAGEMENT

When nutrients accumulate in a garden pond, the plants respond by growing more strongly, and the quickest to respond are the fast growing algae. Some are useful and attractive pondweeds, and they provide cover and egg-laying habitat for a range of pond creatures. However the most successful plant in many ponds is blanket weed. This sometimes goes by the romantic name of angels' tresses, but to most of us it is known as 'that dreadful green slime'.

This is a particular problem in the first season of a new pond, when there is no established alternative vegetation, and when the nutrients from tap water and fresh soil are over-abundant. As the pond settles down the more desirable plants will take the place of some of the slime, so patience is often rewarded, but to reduce the slime effect, four techniques can be combined:

- Top up with rainwater rather than tap water. This avoids the addition of even more dissolved nitrates and other feeding chemicals.
- Harvest the surplus pond vegetation in late summer before the leaves have time to collapse and decompose.
- Try to stop autumn leaves falling into the pond.
- Gently pull out strands of green slime regularly through the first few summer seasons.

# NATIVE PLANTS FOR THE POND: SUBMERGED AQUATIC PLANTS

These plants provide oxygen and cover for the more secretive pondlife.

**Spiked water milfoil** (*Myriophyllum spicatum*) (right) Prefers 'hard water' and produces a mass of feathery green underwater stems. Flowers above the surface.

**Curly pondweed** (*Potamogeton crispus*) Crinkly leaves all the way along the stem and modest little flowers held just above the water surface.

**Hornwort** (*Ceratophyllum demersum*) A solid-looking plant with much-branched stem. Brittle but easy to anchor again.

**Water starwort** (*Callitriche* spp) Delicate in appearance, these pale-green plants can cope with seasonal drought.

**Water crowfoot** (*Ranunculus aquatilis*) A pretty plant with white flowers above the surface and oxygenating leaves below.

## NATIVE BEAUTY

The plants you need to introduce fall into several categories, and again you will produce the richest habitat if you stick to native species. That is no hardship with wetlands. Our indigenous marshland and pond plants are beautiful. The first and most essential category of plants is the submerged large green algae. These are generally sold in bundles, often tied with a strip of lead to weight them down and you will find them under the label 'oxygenators'. These are the plants that spread across the bottom of the pool and provide a hiding place and food source for most of the smallest pond creatures. Although you can just lob them into the water and trust in the lead to carry them down to the bottom, I prefer to anchor them more firmly. Try and stick some of the cut ends into the soil, and then make sure they stay put with a half brick. These filamentous green plants are highly buoyant, and if you do not take this precaution you are likely to find them all floating on the surface again half an hour later. It is infinitely preferable to get your submerged oxygenators from some other established pond, rather than in bundles from a nursery if you can. Most pond owners will be happy to rake you out a bucketful, particularly later in the spring or summer, when the plants are growing well, and you have the possibility of gaining a bonus in the form of pond snail eggs or even more exciting mini-beasts. Beware, though. Some passengers are not so welcome. Check the donor pond is free from blanket weed. You will probably get it sooner or later anyway, but there is no point in encouraging its introduction. Watch out for the more vicious predators, too. Diving beetle larvae hide in pondweed, and it is unfortunate to introduce such aggressive residents at this early stage. One exotic aquatic that you should avoid is Canadian pondweed (*Elodea canadensis*). This is much more vigorous than native oxygenators such as millfoil and water starwort. It isn't the end of the world if you do introduce it. You just have to spend a lot more time pulling out piles of it with a wire rake.

## FLOATING GRACEFULLY

There are one or two rather nice water plants that grow with their roots in the bottom, and their leaves floating on the surface half a metre or more above. For large pools you can't beat the native water lilies, yellow and white, and for smaller pools there are few more valuable and attractive plants than amphibious bistort, with its pretty pink flowers, and common pondweed. Both have similar oval, olive-green leaves, and look lovely growing together. The fringed water lily is a useful plant for a small pond, too. Its leaves are more or less circular and only 5cm or so across, and it has beautiful, simple yellow flowers emerging one after another throughout the summer. One floater to avoid is *Azolla* – the fairy fern. It may look lovely, but it's a menace.

## IN THE SHALLOWS

When you reach the shallows there is a terrific choice of the plants we call 'emergents'. They all seem to have a preference for a particular depth of water, but in garden ponds they will tend to find their own level pretty quickly. At the deep end, bog bean (*Menyanthes trifoliata*) is perhaps the plant whose flower I love the most. It makes up for its rather slapstick name by producing a spike of the most exquisite, feathery white flowers in June. Its three-lobed blue-green leaves look rather like those of broad bean and it seems to grow happily in water as deep as 60cm. There are a couple of

other emergents that will grow up through deep water, but you should avoid them in a garden pond. One is the plant most people call bulrush. Technically it should be called greater reedmace or *Typha latifolia*. The other is *Phragmites communis*, the common reed, and that is even more of a nuisance. Once established they just spread like mad, and overwhelm everything else. If you cannot live without bulrushes, then try the more slender, elegant and less aggressive lesser reedmace, *Typha angustifolia*.

BELOW This mini-monster of the deep is the larva of a great diving beetle. Your tadpoles better watch out.

## NATIVE WILDFLOWERS FOR THE POND: EMERGENT PLANTS

These wildflowers will grow in deeper water and send their leaves and flower stems up above the water's surface.

**Bog bean** (*Menyanthes trifoliata*) (above) The most delicate of white flowers, standing above strong, blue-green leaves that look like those of broad beans.

**Burr reed** (*Sparganium erectum*) (right) Tough, sword-like leaves and spiky, globe-shaped fruits. The seed is particularly popular with birds.

**Greater spearwort** (*Ranunculus lingua*) Rare in the wild, but extremely invasive in 'captivity'. Tall stems up to 1.5m tall, with large leaves and topped by enormous buttercup flowers.

**Lesser reedmace** (*Typha angustifolia*) This is a rather more elegant and less aggressive relative of the popular plant we generally call bulrush, *T. latifolia*, which is too invasive for garden ponds. Leave the seedheads to ripen and you will eventually see them ripped to bits by the sparrows.

**Flowering rush** (*Butomus umbellatus*) (right) Extremely beautiful. Clusters of pretty pinkish-mauve flowers on a single 1m-tall stem, and tufts of slender, bright green leaves.

# NATIVE WILDFLOWERS FOR THE POND: MARGINAL PLANTS

The marsh plants will all grow happily around the edge of the pond. The following will cope with water as much as 15cm deep.

**Water forget-me-not** (*Myosotis scorpioides*) (above) Pale blue and beautiful.

**Yellow iris** (*Iris pseudacorus*) (right) A beautiful wildflower with wonderful bright green sword-like leaves, and yellow flowers which bloom through June, and are followed by pods of brown seeds. Can be invasive, but there are always people eager to adopt a clump or two.

**Water plantain** (*Alisma plantago-aquatica*) Pretty little pale lilac flowers on wiry tiered stems. Seeds and colonises the shallows rapidly.

**Brooklime** (*Veronica beccabunga*) Bright blue flowers on fleshy-leaved prostrate stems.

**Lesser spearwort** (*Ranunculus flammula*) A delicate little yellow 'buttercup' which creeps around in the shallows. Looks particularly beautiful when the electric blue damselflies settle on them.

**Water mint** (*Mentha aquatica*) (right) Aromatic leaves, and lovely pink flowers which attract butterflies in August and September.

## INVASIVE WATER PLANTS TO AVOID

There is no doubt that domestic garden ponds are beneficial for wildlife, however, there is great concern that some popular pond plants are prone to invading the wider landscape. This is a problem in many parts of the world. Purple loosestrife has become a nightmare coloniser in the wild watercourses of Canada, while water hyacinth is such a problem in the paddy fields of the Far East, that it is seriously threatening people's livelihood in many rural communities. The following water plants are particularly problematic. However delightful they appear to be in the confines of the garden centre, please do not be tempted to introduce them to your garden pond.

1. *Azolla filiculoides* (water fern)
2. *Myriophyllum aquaticum* (parrot's feather)
3. *Hydrocotyle ranunculoides* (water pennywort)
4. *Ludwigia* (water primrose)
5. *Crassula helmsii* (New Zealand pigmyweed)
6. *Elodea canadensis* (Canadian pondweed)
7. *Glyceria maxima* (reed sweet-grass)
8. *Phragmites communis* (common reed)
9. *Typha latifolia* (reedmace)
10. *Lemna* (duckweeds)
11. *Nuphar lutea* (yellow water lily)
12. *Stratiotes aloides* (water soldier)
13. *Hydrocharis morsus-ranae* (frogbit)
14. *Cabomba caroliniana* (fanwort)
15. *Eichhornia crassipes* (water hyacinth)
16. *Lagarosiphon major* (curly waterweed)
17. *Pistia stratiotes* (water lettuce)
18. *Sagittaria latifolia* (duck potato)

Around the shallow margins of the pond you can grow several plants which are both beautiful and valuable for wildlife. Yellow flag iris (*Iris pseudacorus*) is one which I am particularly fond of, though it does need controlling firmly. Flowering rush (*Butomus umbellatus*) is much less invasive, and it must be one of our most beautiful wildflowers. When its cluster of coral-pink flowers is blooming, visitors to the garden will never believe that it is a native water weed. Water plantain, water mint (*Mentha aquatica*) and the bur reeds (*Sparganium spp*) all grow happily with their 'feet' in a few centimetres of water, and all of them are fast disappearing in the wild. One shallow water emergent which needs treating with caution is the greater spearwort (*Ranunculus lingua*). This is one of the most spectacular of all the buttercup family, growing a metre tall and carrying a pure yellow flower at the top of a handsome stem. It has become rare in the wild, but in garden ponds

it seems to go berserk, sending out long horizontal underwater shoots and springing up all over the place. I put three small pieces in the shallows the first spring, and by the following summer there was a spearwort forest decorating half the pond. The flower is beautiful, though, particularly when it is chosen as the perch for a turquoise-blue darter dragonfly, and it is easy to keep under control by weeding out any unwanted stems every now and again.

### VIBRANT MARSHLAND

The marshy, waterlogged ground around the edges of ponds is an important habitat for another range of equally attractive wildflowers, and I am delighted with the colour my artificial marshland brings to the summer garden. In the band of meadow which is underlaid with a pond liner, and therefore kept permanently moist, I can grow the more delicate marsh-grassland flowers, and the shallow arm of the pond which I filled in with soil again up to water level provides an ideal habitat for the taller ones.

Along the damp grass margin I now have ribbons of brilliant blue and yellow all summer long. The blue is a mixture of water veronica or brooklime (*Veronica beccabunga*) and water forget-me-not (*Myosotis scorpioides*) and the yellow is a close relative of the invasive giant buttercup, this one growing only 15cm or so tall and going by the name of lesser spearwort (*Ranunculus flammula*). Creeping along at damp ground level there is also the bugle flower (*Ajuga reptans*) with its purple spikes so popular with insects, and the delicate little yellow creeping Jenny (*Lysimachia nummularia*). That most beautiful of wildflowers, grass of Parnassus (*Parnassia palustris*), and lady's smock (*Cardamine pratense*) do well there.

In the deeper, soggier soil of the marsh proper there is room to grow the vigorous, wetland wildflowers that you see now mainly in overgrown ditches in the more remote parts of Britain. Most of them flower in August, though there is a bit of colour earlier on. One of the prettiest of plants is ragged robin (*Lychnis flos-cuculi*)

**BOTTOM** Damselflies like these are relatively common, but their mating performance is fascinating nevertheless.

**BELOW** The banded agrion is mainly a damselfly of flowing water, but if you have a stream nearby then a visit is always possible.

# NATIVE WILDFLOWERS FOR THE MARSH

These colourful plants will flourish around the margin of a pond or in a permanently damp corner of the garden

**Purple loosestrife** (*Lythrum salicaria*) (right) A dramatic plant producing tall, slender spikes of mauve flowers up to 2m tall. Popular with bees and large white butterflies.

**Meadowsweet** (*Filipendula ulmaria*) Lovely summery perfume from clouds of fluffy cream flowerheads. Grows about 1.5m tall and attracts lots of bees.

**Salad burnet** (*Sanguisorba minor*) An unusual wildflower with edible leaves that taste of walnuts. Purple flowers and fresh green cut-leaves.

**Ragged robin** (*Lychnis flos-cuculi*) One of the most beautiful of our wildflowers – growing best in wet meadows. A lovely 'tattered' pink flower which blooms all summer long.

**Marsh marigold** (*Caltha palustris*) (below) Big yellow flowers on solid foliage about 30cm tall. Avoid the double-flowered form, which is sterile and does not set seed.

**Bugle** (*Ajuga reptans*) A prostrate, creeping evergreen plant which is shade-tolerant and produces 15cm tall spikes of blue flowers. Good for bees and butterflies.

**Creeping Jenny** (*Lysimachia nummularia*) Pale green leaves on long creeping stems, punctuated with bright yellow little flowers.

**Marsh woundwort** (*Stachys palustris*) (below) Similar flower to hedge woundwort – deep purple-brown and good for bees.

**Meadow buttercup** (*Ranunculus acris*) Much more handsome than the creeping buttercup. Tall, branched flower stems 1m tall, and delicate palmate leaves.

**Hemp agrimony** (*Eupatorium cannabinum*) One of the best butterfly plants. Grows 1–2m tall. Produces flat heads of pink flowers, which develop into fluffy seedheads.

**Codlins-and-cream or hairy willowherb** (*Epilobium hirsutum*) A lovely loose habit, and masses of pink flowers with cream centres. Popular with bees, but producing clouds of fluffy seeds and colonizing rapidly.

BELOW The more pond snails you can encourage in your pond, the better. They slowly scrape up the green slime and help to keep the water clear.

RIGHT I never tire of seeing great diving beetles. They are magnificent creatures, spectacular hunters under water, and able to fly from pond to pond.

with its bunches of delicate pink flowers. It flowers in June and deserves a place in every garden. It is now one of our officially 'threatened' wildflowers. By midsummer my marsh is over 1.5m tall, and a riot of frothy pinks and whites. Meadowsweet (*Filipendula ulmaria*) has a lovely summery perfume, and pretty little cream flowers, a bit like elder. Purple loosestrife (*Lythrum salicaria*) sends up spectacular spikes of magenta blossoms which look particularly dramatic when they attract the odd white butterfly. Hemp agrimony (*Eupatorium cannabinum*) is another marvellous butterfly plant, particularly popular with bees as well, and Hairy willowherb, which I prefer

to call by its much more romantic alternative name of codlings-and-cream (*Epilobium hirsutum*), completes the picture. If you have room for a waterside shrub then you could do worse than to plant bog myrtle. It prefers slightly acid, peaty soil, but the aroma from its leaves is delicious.

## NEW LIFE

One of the most fascinating things about creating a new pond is the way in which aquatic animal life manages to colonise it unaided. You will be amazed by the variety of pond insects that arrive from nowhere, almost as soon as the water goes into the pond. Pond skaters and whirligig beetles are normally the first to arrive, but in no time at all you can expect to have diving beetles, water boatmen and masses of wriggly little larvae, too. Dragonflies are mobile, and may well have been visiting your garden in search of insect prey for years, but damselflies and one or two of the other desirable water creatures do not travel so much, and you may need to introduce them. Resist this temptation for a year at least, though, and enjoy the pleasure of seeing what turns up on its own.

## INTRODUCING SPECIES

As suggested earlier, the introduced water plants will provide the vehicle for a lot of the smaller creatures, and certainly a good many eggs will arrive that way. The round-ended oblong blocks of jelly are made up of masses of water snail eggs, and they are an absolute must if you hope to have a pond with clear water. If you do not inherit snails with your pondweed beg a few from a friend's pond, or buy a dozen from the pet shop. They soon multiply. Another way of introducing the more sedentary species of pond life is by transplanting a bucket or two of mud from some species-rich wetland. I scooped up half a bucket of black oozy slime from among the plants on the edge of a derelict canal I know, and poured it into my pond. As the black cloud mushroomed across the bottom of the pond, little wriggly creatures shot out in all directions. Some of them were almost certainly the damselfly larvae that emerged later that summer, climbed a few centimetres up the base of the nearest flag iris, and emerged as iridescent blue fairy-tale insects, darting around the pool margin just above the water surface before coupling with a mate and performing amazing egg-laying gymnastics on the water lily leaves.

## FEEDING YOUR NEW FRIENDS

The water in a well-balanced pond is a rich soup of tiny aquatic animals, all feeding either on rotting vegetation, even tinier green plants or on one another. In a new pond, there is bound to be a shortage of dead plant material, and that can slow down development of the wildlife community. Researchers at the Game Conservancy devised a clever way of solving this problem way back in the early 1980s, and it is a technique which you might like to try in your new pond. Take an armful or two of clean straw, chop it into short lengths, and float them out across the pond surface. This looks ridiculous, but after a day or two the straw will all have sunk to the bottom, and you will see a dramatic increase in invertebrate activity. This approach has the added advantage of tackling the build-up of green algae, and the technique works so well that pads of barley straw are now available in garden centres.

## ENCOURAGING COLONIES

Frogs, toads and newts all depend on ponds for breeding. They spend the winter hibernating under logs, stones or other damp, safe places, and most of the summer wandering around in the long grass hunting for slugs and small insects. In the spring, though, they return to their home pond, where they mate and the females lay their spawn. Most people are familiar with frogspawn, which comes in big blobs of spotty jelly. Toad spawn is laid as long double strands of eggs which sink to the bottom and wrap around the pondweed, while female newts stick their eggs to individual underwater leaves. Because of the strong homing instinct, there is little point trying to establish a breeding colony of amphibians by transplanting adults. That is cruel and in the case of some species it is a serious offence. It is worth transferring the spawn, though. Collect it when it is fresh, and try only to remove it from a pond which is overpopulated, or where the misguided owners are 'anti-frog'. In small ponds people often supplement the tadpoles' diet with a little cat food, but if the pond is well established, with plenty of resident plant and animal life, there should not be any need to feed them.

## FISH IN YOUR WILDLIFE POND

It is not a good idea to have goldfish in a wildlife pond. Certainly you should never introduce frogspawn or tadpoles along with goldfish. The fish will eat them. Mind you, the frogs, or at least the toads, do sometimes get their own back. I have had several upset goldfish fanciers complain to me that a passionate lovesick male toad, desperate to wrap its arms and legs around anything resembling a fertile female, has seized one of the prize koi carp and hugged it to death. I must say I find the newts that live in my pond infinitely more fascinating than fish, and certainly more needful of habitat help. However, if you are keen to introduce a fish or two, I suggest you go for sticklebacks if the pond is reasonably big, and perhaps a small tench or two to help vacuum clean the debris in the murky depths, if you have an angler friend who can come up with the goods.

## MAINTAINING YOUR POND

One problem with artificial garden wetlands is that they have a nasty habit of losing water by evaporation in hot dry weather. The problem is worse in a wildlife wetland because all the plants that you have growing with their roots in the water act as a collection of efficient wicks, and pump out the water even faster than normal. If you can collect the rainwater from the house roof, all well

BELOW Common frogs are not so common these days, but garden ponds have been their salvation. Listen out for the quiet purring of amorous males as early as February, and remember that the frogspawn and the tadpoles help to feed a host of other creatures. Only a few need to survive each year.

RIGHT Great crested newts are the stars of my own garden pond – best enjoyed by torchlight after dark.

and good, though you will obviously need to store a lot. The drought problem cannot be solved otherwise, since of course there will not be any rain coming gushing down the drainpipe in the periods when you need it.

For one reason or another, you are likely to finish up putting in the hose pipe and turning on the tap. This can lead to problems. Tap water can be high in nutrients. In the big cities it may have been through at least one other pair of kidneys before it reaches you (via another purification plant of course) and some of the surplus artificial fertilisers we pour on the land inevitably

find their way into the waterways. When you add nutrient-rich water to the pond, you can find that you stimulate the growth of green slime. This 'algal bloom' is a perfectly natural response to extra fertility, but it is not attractive, it can lock up the oxygen which the pond creatures need, and if it gets bad it can even cut out the light. Chemical controls are no longer available for killing blanket weed, but they never tackled the cause of the problem anyway, they just obscure the effect for a while. There are biological controls available commercially, and some of these may fast-track the establishment of a natural balance in the pond, but with a little patience and appropriate planting the algal problem should be relatively easy to control.

Rake out the green slime if it gets bad, and put it on the compost heap. Take out some of the other vegetation towards the end of the summer too. That will help to reduce the nutrient surplus in the pond. The best advice, though, seems to be to leave well alone, and let nature take a hand. I had thick green blanket weed in my new pond the first year. I raked a lot of it out, but the second year there was a boom in the snail population. These amazing creatures sucked and

munched their way casually around the pond, sweeping up any spare bit of algae that floated by, and the water remained crystal clear, despite top-ups from the tap and an exceptionally sunny summer. The golden rule with wildlife gardening and habitat management seems to be 'if in doubt, leave it alone'. It is remarkable how often nature finds a way of sorting out the problem and restoring a healthy balance.

# RHS GARDEN ROSEMOOR

‘ A well-established Devon garden in the deep south west of England, RHS Garden Rosemoor is particularly good for learning about water gardens, with a stream, waterfalls, fountains, ponds and bog gardens fringed with a rich diversity of garden and wild flowers. Attracting wildlife is a high priority, and otters and herons are among the regular visitors, but this is also a garden where more modest garden wetland creatures such as dragonflies and amphibians flourish.

Anyone who gardens on heavy clay will find Rosemoor particularly instructive. This is a wet part of the country, and that combination can create a sticky mess, but the gardeners at Rosemoor have achieved remarkable results. It has wonderful flower borders, but there are also meadows and woodland glades for inspiration. For a real treat, it is even possible to stay the night in rented cottages at Rosemoor, and this is a place where the wildlife is particularly magical at the crack of dawn, or just as the sun goes down. ’

# PART III

# SUPPLEMENTING THE HABITATS

Many of our most familiar cottage garden flowers (left) are brilliant for bees and other pollinators, and borage (below) is one of the very best. The bright blue flowers also add a dash of glamour to summer drinks and salads.

8 |

# COTTAGE GARDEN SERVICE STATION

THE GARDEN can be a richer habitat than anything you might find in nature. Although the size eventually puts a limit on the number and variety of species you can have *living* with you, it is possible to boost the habitat, and develop your garden as an attractive service station for extra, passing wildlife. Your pond will tend to serve as a magnet anyway, with flocks of birds and a stream of small mammals visiting it to drink, but moving on elsewhere to breed. One of the joys of calm summer evenings in my wildlife garden is the bats. Two or three individuals arrive every night at dusk, and fly silently round and round the pond, a few metres above the surface. They are presumably sweeping up the last few unsuspecting midges that have hatched during the day, but they generally swoop down and snatch a drink from the pool while they are there, too. I had always assumed that my bats were pipistrelles. They are the most common town bats, although like all their relatives they are declining in numbers at a worrying rate. I recently had a 'bat expert' visiting the garden, who felt my bats might be a rather less common species called Natterer's bat. I do not much mind whether the wildlife in my garden is rare or common. The sight of these visitors flitting across the moon is thrilling, and since even the tiny pipistrelle is capable of gobbling up 3,500 insects in a

night, they are helping to reduce the chances of any of those midges and mosquitoes biting me. The point is that, so far as I know, my bats do not live here. They simply visit on a regular basis because they like the menu at my service station. Without the pond and its midges they would probably still fly over from time to time, but they would not come right down low, where I can watch them perform.

## STOCKING THE LARDER
The most important feature of any service station, wildlife or otherwise, is the food and drink, and this is where you can score if you know what you are doing.

Native plants are critical for a balanced, ecologically sound wildlife community, but many of the more mobile and spectacular creatures, particularly insects such as butterflies and moths, and the songbirds, feed mainly on nectar, pollen or seed. You can give a tremendous boost to their larder by planting colourful flowery 'cottage garden' style borders, and I strongly recommend that you concentrate them near the house. This will bring the butterflies and birds close to your windows, and provides an orthodox landscape around the buildings, emphasising the more relaxed countryside atmosphere in the rest of the wildlife garden and keeping any unconverted neighbours happy. The RHS has a helpful app, available through its website, with scope for searching specific habitat types, so the following lists are just a start. The list on p146–147 suggests garden plants which are especially good for providing food for passing insects. When I began teaching horticulture to landscape designers, way back in the 1970s, one of my mature students, Mary Mountain, was an extremely experienced bee keeper. She was a fountain of knowledge so far as pollen and nectar plants were concerned, and I

BELOW Be brave and leave some of your seed heads standing. Your reward may well be a charm of goldfinches.

RIGHT  Great Dixter in Sussex is a garden that inspired me as a student. There can be very few more magnificent mixed borders, and there is always wildlife in abundance.

remember her enthusing about the miraculous pulling power of borage. That early source of knowledge and experience has been refined and enhanced in recent years by the excellent scientific studies carried out by the RHS at their gardens at Wisley, under the *Perfect for Pollinators* research project.

The ideal 'larder border' is a mixture of flowering and fruiting shrubs, herbaceous perennials and colourful seasonal bedding. Your aim should be to provide a source of 'natural' food for as long a period of each year as possible, and that means starting in early spring with some of the garden bulbs, and leaving herbaceous plants to run to seed as an attraction to finches in the late autumn. There are lots of books around which discuss mixed borders. The idea began at the end of the nineteenth century when they were championed by the great garden writers William Robinson and Gertrude Jekyll. My personal hero of post-war planting design was Christopher Lloyd. His long border at Great Dixter in Sussex must be a dream come true for the local bees and butterflies, and my own little flower borders have owed a great deal to his ideas over the years. Although Christopher died in 2006, the gardens at Great Dixter continue to be a living inspiration, and they now provide a unique training facility for future generations of plant lovers. When *How to Make a Wildlife Garden* was first published in 1985, I think it was the enthusiastic welcome from Christo that helped to persuade the gardening establishment to begin taking the idea much more seriously.

## NATIVE CHOICES
There are a lot of native plants which are more than a match for the flamboyant herbaceous hybrids.

# GARDEN BORDER FLOWERS FOR NECTAR AND SEED

Listed in approximate order of flowering – January to December.

**Christmas rose** (*Helleborus niger*) (below)

**Lenten rose** (*H. orientalis*)
**Winter aconite** (*Eranthis hyemalis*)
**Elephant's ears** (*Bergenia cordifolia*)
**Spring crocus** (*Crocus chrysanthus* and hybrids)
**Grape hyacinth** (*Muscari armeniacum*)
**Polyanthus, primrose and cowslip** (*Primula* spp)
**Soldiers and sailors** (*Pulmonaria saccharata*)
**White arabis** (single) (*Arabis alpina subsp caucasica*)
**Honesty** (*Lunaria annua*)
**Aubrieta** (*Aubrieta deltoidea*)
**Wallflowers** (*Erysimum cheiri*)
**Forget-me-not** (*Myosotis* spp)
**Bugle** (*Ajuga reptans*)
**Thrift, sea pink** (*Armeria maritima*)
**Leopard's-bane** (*Doronicum* × *excelsum*)
**Sweet rocket** (*Hesperis matronalis*)
**Golden alyssum** (*Aurinia saxatilis*) (below)

**Sweet William** (*Dianthus barbatus*) (below)

**Cornflower** (*Centaurea cyanus*)
**Ragged robin** (*Lychnis flos-cuculi*)
**Water avens** (*Geum rivale*)
**Poached-egg plant** (*Limnanthes douglasii*)
**Shasta daisy** (*Leucanthemum* × *superbum*)
**Fleabane** (*Erigeron* spp)
**Cranesbills** (*Geranium* spp)
**Sweet bergamot** (*Monarda didyma*) (below)

**Evening primrose** (Oenothera biennis)
**Oriental poppy** (Papaver orientale)
**Red valerian** (Centranthus ruber)
**Musk mallow** (Malva moschata)
**Clustered bellflower** (Campanula glomerata)
**Foxglove** (Digitalis purpurea)
**Jacob's ladder** (Polemonium caeruleum)
**Sweet alyssum** (Lobularia maritima)
**Angelica** (Angelica archangelica)
**Viper's bugloss** (Echium vulgare)
**Common bistort** (Persicaria bistorta)
**Tobacco plant** (Nicotiana langsdorfii)
**Mignonette** (Reseda odorata)
**Corncockle** (Agrostemma githago)
**Common poppy** (Papaver rhoeas)
**Yarrow** (Achillea flipendulina)
**Alkanet** (Anchusa capensis)
**Chicory** (Cichorium intybus)
**Yellow loosestrife** (Lysimachia vulgaris)
**Small scabious** (Scabiosa columbaria)
**Hollyhock** (Alcea rosea)
**Snapdragon** (Antirrhinum majus) (below)

**Nasturtium** (Tropaeolum majus)
**Hemp agrimony** (Eupatorium cannabinum)
**Wild candytuft** (Iberis amara)

**Californian poppy** (Eschscholtzia californica)
**Sunflower** (Helianthus annuus)
**Purple loosestrife** (Lythrum salicaria)
**Tree lavatera** (Lavatera olbia)
**Spider flower** (Cleome hassleriana)
**Blue lace flower** (Trachymene coerulea)
**Golden rod** (Solidago canadensis)
**Phlox** (Phlox paniculata)
**Common fennel** (Foeniculum vulgare)
**Teasel** (Dipsacus fullonum)
**Garden speedwell** (Veronica longifolia) (below)

**Spearmint** (Mentha spicata)
**Globe thistle** (Echinops ritro)
**Wild marjoram** (Origanum vulgare)
**Purple top** (Verbena bonariensis)
**Cosmos** (Cosmea bipinnatus)
**Cherry pie** (Heliotropium arborescens)
**Michaelmas daisy** (Aster/Symphyotrichum spp)
**Orpine** (Sedum telephium)
**Meadow saffron** (Colchicum autumnale)

**NOTE** many of these plants will flower in autumn if you cut off some of their dead summer flowers. Do not forget to leave some to seed.

Some of them are fantastic wildlife attractors, and I strongly recommend them. There are a few plants too, which began life as garden flowers, escaped into the countryside years ago, and are now classified as 'wildflowers', so the situation is rather confused anyway. I will leave you to consult the panels in this chapter for a full choice of service station species, but there are one or two particular 'stars' which I think are worth a special mention

Top of the charts for me is the teasel. This is a biennial, which means you have to sow seed for two consecutive springs if you want flowers every year. (I mentioned this earlier in connection with foxgloves.) Once you have teasels established, though, you will never be short of them provided you allow a few seedlings to survive each year. They are good at colonising. The plant itself is exceptionally handsome. It grows as a flat rosette in the first year, and the cartwheel of leaves is covered in short, knobbly spines. In the second spring your teasels will rumble into life in April, and shoot up to more than 2m in height to produce perfectly symmetrical flower stems of paired side shoots as elegant as any candelabra.

I love to watch bumblebees drenching themselves in the pink pollen of teasel flowers.

# NATIVE WILDFLOWERS FOR THE FLOWER BORDER

I have grouped these suggestions according to colour, to make them easier to design your borders with.

## BLUE

**Viper's bugloss** (*Echium vulgare*) (right) One of the best wildflowers for hot, dry gravel soils. Friends of mine have it naturalised all over their gravel drive. Flower spikes up to 1m tall, all summer long.

**Meadow cranesbill** (*Geranium pratense*) A low, spreading herbaceous perennial, 45cm tall, preferring limy soils. Popular with bees.

**Bluebell** (*Hyacinthoides non-scripta*) Plant as bulbs. Seedlings take several years to reach flowering size. Wonderful perfume on still, damp days. Grows best in the shade of deciduous shrubs and trees. (Note: the Spanish bluebell is more readily available to buy, but has now become a seriously invasive weed that threatens our native bluebell woods, so please help to eradicate it where you can.)

**Chicory** (*Cichorium intybus*) Startling blue flowers for four months through the summer. Flower stems well over 2m tall, and a constant source of bee activity.

**Cornflower** (*Centaurea cyanus*) An annual, now available in a whole range of colours. Grow the native cornflower-blue type mixed in with poppies and corn marigold for a spectacular summer display.

**Great bellflower** (*Campanula latifolia*) Sturdy flower stem up to 1m tall, covered in large flowers. Best in moist soil and half-shade.

**Nettle-leaved bellflower** (*C. trachelium*) Similar to above and a well behaved coloniser I wouldn't want to be without.

**Harebell** (*C. rotundifolia*) A favourite wildflower. Tough, wiry stems and the most delicate of bell-like flowers. It grows wild among dwarf grasses in acid soils, but thrives in the kinder conditions of a flower border, so long as the soil is not limy.

**Clustered bellflower** (*C. glomerata*) Similar to *C. latifolia* but with a bunch of bellflowers at the tip of each stem.

**Devil's bit scabious** (*Succisa pratensis*) Week after week of pretty blue flowers, nodding about 60cm above the leaves. Food plant for the caterpillars of marsh fritillary butterflies.

**Germander speedwell** (*Veronica chamaedrys*) Invasive, but not overwhelming and relatively easy to pull up when necessary. Pretty ground cover with sheets of flowers in May. Important for early foraging bees.

**Self-heal** (*Prunella vulgaris*) A lawn weed that is transformed by cultivation. Deep purple-blue flowers up to 10cm tall, above a carpet of deep-green leaves. Good ground cover and a useful bee plant.

**Bugle** (*Ajuga reptans*) Lots of garden varieties, some with variegated leaves. Prefers shade and moisture. Spikes of flowers up to 15cm tall in May and June.

**Green alkanet** (*Pentaglottis sempervirens*) Another dazzling blue flower. Grow it among the nettles in a damp, shady corner, but beware. It can quickly spread, has deep roots, and when it starts to become a problem you may curse it. Grows over 1m tall by midsummer.

**Wood forget-me-not** (*Myosotis sylvatica*) More delicate than the highly refined garden varieties. Beautiful, shade-tolerant and flowers for months on end.

Continues on p154

LEFT Teasel seeds are irresistible to goldfinches. Their toughened facial feathers protect them from the sharp spines as they tease out the seeds.

BELOW Hollyhocks beside the path bring pollinators right up to eye level, but make sure you plant the single flowered varieties.

In the angle of each side shoot there is a large, watertight pocket, formed by fused bracts wrapped around the stem, and this is the first wildlife feature. Rainwater collects in these little reservoirs, and you will almost certainly see sparrows drinking there by late spring. The water also seems to trap a surprising number of small insects, and there is some discussion as to whether teasels might be slightly carnivorous. The teasel flowers generally bloom in mid-July. The flower head is the size and shape of an upturned egg cup, covered in soft green bristles at this stage, and the flowers open just like a mauve belt around the middle. This first band of miniature blossoms lasts a day or two, and as it fades, a pair of replacement rings opens, one above and one below. As the week goes by, the two bands of flowers move wider and wider apart, until all the flowers have been pollinated and the performance is over. The colour of the teasel pollen is deep lavender-pink, and there is a great deal of it. Big bumblebees seem to be the main pollinators, and they look like rather overweight punk-rocker 'wall of death' riders as they crawl horizontally around each belt of flowers, covering themselves with pink

pollen. The flowers are also popular with summer butterflies, and the ones in my garden often seem to attract the small species such as common skipper, common blue and small copper. Blue butterflies on pink flowers are particularly pretty.

Once the teasel flowers have been pollinated and the seeds begin to form, the whole of the flower head hardens and turns to a rich brown colour. The bristles stiffen, and even nowadays there are teasels grown commercially, particularly in Somerset, for use in the weaving mills of Yorkshire. Long rows of dried teasel heads are used to fluff up or 'tease' the surface of the best worsted. If you look closely at the brown seed heads you will see a densely packed honeycomb of little chambers, each one containing a large brown seed. Some of these will be shaken out by the wind, and a few will germinate to produce next year's seedlings. However, the vast majority never stand a chance. Teasels are particularly popular with goldfinches. They seem to know instinctively when to begin visiting the seed heads, and there is no more colourful sight on a frosty winter morning, than a 'charm' of these cheerful little birds with their black

and yellow wings and their brilliant crimson faces, fluttering around the tips of the teasels, chattering musically to one another as they tease out seed after seed. Goldfinches have specially toughened face feathers to protect them as they dig down for the teasel seeds among the wiry spikes, and although they have now become one of the most dramatic success stories of the commercial bird food revolution, they still seem to find wild teasel seed heads irresistible.

There are several other tall biennials that are worth including at the back of your borders. The giant mullein (*Verbascum bombyciferum*) has huge hairy grey leaves at ground level, and a spike of yellow and brown flowers more than 2m tall in its second season. It produces tens of thousands of tiny seeds, and its leaves are the food plant for a particularly spectacular caterpillar – the mullein moth. Ladybirds often overwinter among the ripe seed heads.

Angelica is another big biennial which I love to grow. There is a native species, but the herb-garden variety is bigger and even more dramatic. The fresh, green leaves are wonderful as a foliage display, and the huge bunches of tiny green flowers buzz above

your head, attracting dozens of hoverflies and bees. In autumn the dry, brown flower stems are topped by a mass of big golden seeds, visited by greenfinches and bluetits.

One more biennial is worth a special mention. This is the evening primrose (*Oenothera biennis*). Again it can be a little over-enthusiastic in its colonising, but there is no better flower for attracting night-flying moths, and the pure primrose yellow of its 1.5m blooms is lovely. Flowers open each evening, just before sunset, and each one lasts until noon the following day. The perfume at night is wonderful, and if you care to venture out after dark you will find the evening primroses lighting up your garden, and playing larder to a jostling cloud of moths. The oil contained in evening primrose seed is proving to be special – one of the few natural oils that do not aggravate heart disease in humans. I read somewhere that the crushed seed might be a healthy addition to my morning muesli, and that evening primrose could be a future boom crop of British agriculture. That should certainly please the moths, just so long as the farmers also leave them the odd wild corner filled

LEFT *Verbascum bombyciferum*! Even the Latin name of the giant silver mullein sounds magnificent. Its two metre tall flower spikes are spectacular, it colonises open ground and its woolly grey leaves support the very striking mullein moth caterpillar.

BELOW Angelica can grow above head height from nowhere by midsummer. If you have room, then the flowers and the seed heads are really good for garden wildlife and you will soon have seedlings to give away.

RIGHT This biennial evening primrose thrives in poor soil, grows 1.5m tall by midsummer and really glows at dusk. The perfume is lovely, it attracts nightflying moths and produces huge quantities of seeds.

with native plants on which they can lay their eggs. Evening primrose originates in North America, but you can find it growing wild on poor, gravelly soils all over Europe and volunteer seedlings crop up every year in my veg patch.

## PROVIDING SERVICE ALL YEAR ROUND

Try to choose flowers which will turn into useful seed heads wherever possible, and remember you will be particularly popular with the wildlife if you can provide nectar early and late in the season. As you begin to look more critically at the huge range of plants we have to choose from, you may notice that there is a shift of emphasis between native and non-native flowers as the year progresses. In the early summer months of May, June and July we have a great range of delightful native wildflowers to choose from. Just think of primroses and cowslips, pink campion and foxglove, meadow buttercup and marsh marigold. By high summer the choice of native flowers dwindles and in order to keep up the nectar supply, it helps to grow suitable garden cultivars, or wild species from elsewhere in the world that have a different flowering

# NATIVE WILDFLOWERS FOR THE FLOWER BORDER

## MAUVE, PURPLE AND PINK

**Soapwort** (*Saponaria officinalis*) (right) Masses of pink, phlox-like flowers, 7.5cm tall; flowers in August and September. It has a delicate scent which attracts hawkmoths, and the fresh green leaves can be boiled to produce a soap substitute.

**Greater knapweed** (*Centaurea scabiosa*). Thistle-like flowerheads the size of a shaving brush. Flowers in July. Popular with butterflies. Height 60cm.

**Hardhead** (*C. nigra*) Similar to greater knapweed but with smaller flowers.

**Spear thistle** (*Cirsium vulgare*) Elegant thistle 1.5m tall. Purple flower heads all summer. Popular with butterflies. Clouds of fluffy seed heads attract finches in early autumn.

**Lesser burdock** (*Arctium minus*) A coarse biennial up to 2m high that seeds readily. Flowers attract butterflies, goldfinches feed on seeds, and the 'burrs' fix to clothes for ease of transport.

**Hemp agrimony** (*Eupatorium cannabinum*) Beautiful wetland perennial with plates of flowers in July, up to 1.5m tall. Excellent butterfly plant.

**Teasel** (*Dipascus fullonum*) One of the best 'service station' wildflowers. Up to 2m tall and statuesque in form. Birds drink from the rainwater trapped in leaf-forks, bees and butterflies queue up for the pink pollen in August and goldfinches find the seeds irresistible.

**Field scabious** (*Knautia arvensis*) Pretty perennial that flowers all summer. Particularly popular with crimson burnet moths and soldier beetles.

**Foxglove** (*Digitalis purpurea*) Biennial, so it must be allowed to colonise. Seedlings need thinning for the best display. Tall, beautiful spikes of richly marked thimble-like flowers constantly visited by bumblebees in June.

**Woody nightshade** (*Solanum dulcamara*) Poisonous but well worth a safe place in the hedgerow or among shrubs. Scrambling growth, clusters of striking mauve and yellow flowers, followed by bunches of orange and scarlet berries.

**Wild thyme** (*Thymus serpyllum*) Low-growing, aromatic herb. Covered in mauve flowers through June and July, and crawling with bees and butterflies. Needs a sunny, well-drained, slightly limy position to do well.

**Marjoram** (*Origanum vulgare*) Another aromatic culinary herb, this time growing 30–50cm tall. Tolerates poor soil and full sun.

**Hedge woundwort** (*Stachys sylvatica*) Shade-tolerant, with 60cm spikes of snapdragon-like little flowers arranged in tiers. Popular with the smaller species of bees.

**Red deadnettle** (*Lamium purpureum*) A carpeting plant with beautifully marked green and white leaves. Flowers throughout the year. A good shade-tolerant bee plant up to 20cm tall.

**Thrift** (*Armeria maritima*) A grass-like plant of cliff tops, often grown in rockeries. An excellent late-summer source of nectar. The evergreen tussocks provide good shelter for wildlife.

**Rosebay willowherb** (*Epilobium angustifolium*) (above) Treat with caution. This is a most spectacular plant with beautiful tall spikes of cerise flowers in July and August. Bees love it, and the leaves feed the caterpillar of the elephant hawkmoth, but it is invasive, and produces clouds of fluffy seeds each year. Grow a clump in a tub (where it cannot spread) and cut off the flower stems at the first sign of seeding.

**Purple loosestrife** (*Lythrum salicaria*) A tall marsh plant with spectacular spikes of flowers up to 2m tall. Popular with butterflies and bees.

**Musk mallow** (*Malva sylvestris*) One of the prettiest of the taller wildflowers. A loose, branching habit up to 2m tall, with large, open flowers.

**Sainfoin** (*Onobrychis viciifolia*) (above) One of the pea family; tolerates poor soil but prefers slightly limy conditions.

**Betony** (*Stachys officinalis*) (left) A classic bee plant, flowering in mid-summer.

**Herb robert** (*Geranium robertianum*) One of my favourite wildflowers. The whole plant is tinged with red, and the little 'cranesbill' flowers put on a pretty display throughout the summer. Grows happily in cracks in paving and walls, and along the hedge bottom.

**Wood cranesbill** (*G. sylvaticum*) Shade-tolerant as the name suggests, with deep mauve flowers in mid-summer, and lush herbaceous growth to 60cm.

**Night-flowering catchfly** (*Silene noctiflora*) An interesting plant. Pretty little flowers in July and August, and the stems and leaves are sticky. It flowers at night, with a super perfume. Excellent moth plant.

**Corncockle** (*Agrostemma githago*) Perhaps the most elegant of all our cornfield 'weeds'. An annual with open habit, and flowers held on stems up to 1m tall. Provides colour all summer, and produces large black seeds which fall to the ground and germinate the following spring. The seeds are poisonous.

**Red campion** (*Silene dioica*) An easy and beautiful wildflower to grow. The woodland edge and hedge bottom are its preferred habitat. 60cm tall. Flowers in May and again in September or October.

Continues on p159

season. I tend to make heavy use of tender perennials and half-hardy annuals to maintain the nectar and pollen supply through July, August and September, with ornamental tobacco plants (*Nicotiana*), cosmos, snapdragon and even single flowered dahlias and the tall spikes of red-hot pokers all helping to boost the summer service station.

My pollen and nectar garden opens for business in late January, when a couple of days of unexpected sunshine bring out the little yellow flowers of winter aconite. Any insect that happens to have been caught in a warming sunbeam and stirred into activity must be glad to find my garden. After the aconites come the snowdrops, but to be honest not many insects seem to be able to manage the gymnastics involved in tapping their pendulous little flowers.

Grape hyacinth is much more convenient. It seeds itself in ever-increasing numbers under my apple tree, and on one warm day early last spring I watched a small tortoiseshell, a brimstone and two peacock butterflies working their way from flower to flower, dipping into the nectar and no doubt helping with

TOP Some border flowers are especially good for pollinators. *Verbena bonariensis* has the kind of flowering platform that butterflies love, while the spider flower, *Cleome hassleriana*, is shaped to suit the bees.

ABOVE Snapdragons need the bulk of a bumblebee to force open the flower and reveal the pollen.

**LEFT AND BELOW** Leave some seed heads standing through the winter. They will provide a natural food supply for the birds but they also offer shelter to a host of smaller garden creatures such a ladybirds – and of course they look beautiful.

pollination at the same time. The early crocuses are valuable, too. Their flowers are generally too deep for the butterflies to take advantage of, except on those occasional bright, sunny days when the petals fold right back, but the first bees to emerge after the winter certainly make good use of the crocus pollen. Plant the ordinary yellow crocus and you will probably be entertained (or annoyed) by the local sparrow gang too. It is remarkable how they seem to love ripping these innocent little flowers to bits. It looks like hooliganism, but presumably they're after the high protein pollen.

Another early spring flower which I think symbolizes the cottage garden is honesty (*Lunaria annua*). Coincidentally, this is yet another biennial, and again it happily colonises the cracks in paving slabs, or any other soil pockets it can find. Its flowers are a shade of purple which would be vulgar at any other time of year, but in early spring, when there is little else in flower, a patch of honesty is a real source of delight. In recent years a white strain of honesty has established itself in my garden and this might

LEFT Grape hyacinths are among the very best of the early spring bulbs for a wildlife garden. They grow easily and their pulling power with emerging butterflies at the very beginning of spring is unbeatable.

BELOW I have encouraged good old fashioned honesty to spread throughout my garden. The flowers attract pollinators, orange tip butterflies lay their eggs on the leaves, and the translucent silver penny seed heads really catch the low autumn sunlight.

be seen as more tasteful in some circumstances. Butterflies love honesty flowers. The early orange tips are particularly attracted to them, and this plant has become an alternative to the native lady's smock and garlic mustard as the food plant for their caterpillars. As the honesty finishes, its place is taken by sweet rocket, also known as dame's violet. This is yet another biennial and this one provides hundreds of sweetly scented, white or pale pink flowers. Again, orange tip caterpillars can eat the leaves. Honesty is one of those bonus plants which also produce useful seeds. The translucent silver pennies are much loved by flower arrangers, but mine stay firmly on the plants until the last one has been eaten. Bullfinches seem to be remarkably good at tackling these big, papery fruits. They crouch on the ground and then leap up, fluttering their wings frantically, and grab a silver penny in their beak. Their reward is two or three big brown seeds, and the birds have no difficulty at all ripping off the packaging once they are back on the ground.

At the other end of the year, Michaelmas daisies are probably the border flowers that provide the latest heavy crop of nectar. This is most important for overwintering insects. They need to build up their energy store before retiring for the duration, and that is why Michaelmas daisies are so popular with the small tortoiseshell and brimstone butterflies Some of the Michaelmas daisies produce a good seed crop after they have flowered. The species tend to be rather more fruitful than the larger flowered hybrids, so it is worth bearing this in mind when choosing.

Michaelmas daisies are just the last in a long line of good nectar and pollen plants you might like to grow. Some of them seem to prompt amusing antics

# NATIVE WILDFLOWERS FOR THE FLOWER BORDER

## WHITE

**Wood anemone** (*Anemone nemorosa*) (above right) a wildflower of the woodland flower. Difficult to establish but well worth the effort.

**White deadnettle** (*Lamium album*) A marvellous bee plant and a good ground-cover plant. Spreads by seed and runner.

**White campion** (*Silene alba*) Crops up as an annual in weedy cornfields, but you can grow it for several years in the flower border. Purest white flowers, up to 75cm tall.

**Scentless mayweed** (*Matricaria maritima*) A cornfield

wildflower. Grow it mixed with poppies and cornflowers.

**Sneezewort** (*Achillea ptarmica*) (above) A rich source of nectar in late summer. Fern-like, feathery leaves but it can become over-invasive. Height 30–40cm.

**Sanicle** (*Sanicula europaea*) Tiny white flowers, but shade-tolerant and delicate-looking.

**Masterwort** (*Astrantia major*) This is a lovely plant, with delicate, jewel-like flower heads from May onwards. Shade-tolerant and 60cm tall.

**Seakale** (*Crambe maritima*) A dramatic perennial, producing clouds of flowers smelling sweetly of honey. The cabbage-like leaves are handsome too, and the whole plant is spectacular in June.

**Garlic mustard** (*Alliaria petiolata*) (left) An early spring flower, growing as a biennial with a tough rootstock. It seeds readily, is shade-tolerant and its leaves are used as a food plant by the caterpillars of orange tip butterflies.

**Bladder campion** (*Silene vulgaris*) Similar to white campion but not so tall (30cm).

**Greater stitchwort** (*Stellaria holostea*) Pretty star-like flowers throughout the summer – but the plant can be invasive.

Continues on p170

from their pollinators. I grow the large-flowered border poppies, for instance, because I love to watch the bees crawling on their sides, and wallowing in the black pollen. They adopt the same position with several other open flowers. Pink mallow is a favourite, growing 3m tall, and filling the border with colour from late July onwards, and our own native cranesbill (*Geranium pratense*) is a lovely bee plant for the front of the border. There are dozens of garden cranesbills, too. All of them are attractive to bees, and a lot of them produce a good seed crop. Ripe cranesbill fruits are especially beautiful. The panels of the 'beak' peel off from the 'wrong end' to form a five-pointed crown, with the tip of each curved arm decorated by a loosely dangling seed at the outer tip. Again the bullfinches in particular seem to go for them. The garden writer Geoffrey Smith once told me that he believed the cranesbill seeds may be mildly narcotic, and that the bullfinches become addicted – returning each day for a further fix.

Several herbaceous perennials are worth growing especially for their seed. *Achillea*, for instance, is showy in midsummer, with its flat plates of tiny yellow

BELOW This lemon-yellow yarrow is one of a whole range of different coloured cultivars, all of them excellent pollen plants.

RIGHT The globe thistle, *Echinops ritro*, is not for the faint hearted, but its 2m tall flower display is among the very best for bees in high summer.

RIGHT, BELOW Late flowering Michaelmas daisies provide an important nectar boost for red admirals and other overwintering butterflies. Performance varies. Let the bees and butterflies in the garden centre or mature flower border guide you to the most effective varieties.

flowers, and the hoverflies seem to enjoy the nectar, but if you leave the flower stems to ripen they will produce tough seedheads, capable of supporting crowds of sparrows, greenfinches and tits. Golden rod (*Solidago canadensis*) is another border plant that is good for seed. It is invasive, and you will need to keep controlling the size of the clumps, but the great plumes of yellow flowers in August and September are constantly alive with insects, and there must be ten thousand or more fluffy seeds on every stem by the autumn. Globe thistle (*Echinops ritro*), chicory (*Cichorium intybus*), globe artichoke (*Cynara scolymus*), rose campion (*Lychnis coronaria*) and many more produce good seed crops if you let them, so do not chop off all the dead heads the minute the flowers have faded. You are missing a treat if you do. Goldfinches and bullfinches are far and away the most colourful display you could ever wish for in a winter flower border.

## HELPFUL HERBS
The herb garden is a rich source of inspiration for the wildlife gardener. A great many of our culinary herbs

produce pollen-rich flowers, and some of them have good seed heads, too. I mentioned angelica earlier, and two of the best of all herbs for insects are close relatives. One is lovage, which looks similar, but has flatter, smaller flower heads, and the other is fennel, a beautiful plant with feathery, green or bronze leaves and a yellow umbel of flowers like those of lovage. Incidentally, the leaves of both lovage and fennel are delicious for flavouring chicken and fish respectively. Both these umbellifers (the posh name for the cow parsley family) are perennials, and both are well-behaved, so I suggest you plant them as a feature of some sunny border close to the kitchen door. They grow tall – at least 2m by midsummer, but they are both slender plants and do not take up a great deal of room otherwise. When the flowers are open, you can see the droplets of nectar, temptingly displayed to lure passing pollinators, and generally there is a whole collection of different hoverflies, wasps and bees staggering around in the sweet stickiness.

At a slightly lower level, chicory deserves to be grown more often. Its value in the kitchen lies in the roots, which can be dried and ground as a rather

LEFT If your garden is big enough to cope with globe artichokes, then you probably want to eat most of the globes yourself. Leave one or two to flower and run to seed. The late summer pollinators and winter finches will be grateful.

BELOW LEFT Chicory sometimes appears unprompted in wildflower seed mixes and it can spread rapidly. If you have room, a few stems of the sky-blue flowers are well worth fostering for a season or two.

BELOW Fennel is a culinary herb that brings real elegance to the garden. The aniseed qualities of its leaf fronds make it a great garnish, and the flat plates of green flowers are always alive with pollinating bees, hoverflies and beetles. The blue flowers of borage are irresistible to honey bees.

unconvincing substitute for coffee, but it produces a wonderful display of sky-blue flowers all through the summer, stands 1.5m high, and follows its flowers with a useful crop of early accessible bird seed. No one seems sure whether or not chicory is a native, but it can be found growing on wasteland and by the roadside, particularly in southern England. If you stumble across it in combination with evening primroses, the effect can be stunning. Their flowers only coincide for about four hours each day, because chicory opens in the early morning, and both plants have lost their colour by midday

At the ground-hugging level in the herb garden, there are lots of useful insect plants. Chives, for instance, produce their pretty purple balls of flower in June, and are visited by bees from morning till night. I like to grow them alongside cranesbills, some of which have a flower of exactly the same colour. Tansy is a native herb which I grow for the flavour of its deep green leaves, and for the butterflies attracted to its little yellow button flowers. Every summer, throughout the month of August, my tansy clump seems to be adopted by one particularly loyal small

BELOW Rosemary is excellent in the kitchen and the wildlife garden.

RIGHT My first flowering carrots were an oversight. I've grown them ever since. They grow chest high in a matter of weeks, the masses of small white flowers are always full of insect life, and soldier beetles such as these are fascinating to watch.

FAR RIGHT *Buddleja globosa* is much less likely to spread unwanted seedlings than the more familiar mauve flowered *B. davidii*, and it still attracts red admirals and other insects.

copper butterfly, which just spends every hour of every day working its way backwards and forwards over the flowers. Rosemary flowers are good for bees, and lavender is popular with butterflies. Marjoram is now considered to be one of the best insect-attracting garden herbs, and I can confirm that from my own observations but the best bee plant of all seems to be borage. This is a handsome plant which grows easily from seed. It has piercing blue flowers which hang down in bunches, and the bees queue up for a delicious, upside-down drink of the

nectar. Borage flowers are the traditional decoration for gin and tonic, so there is a chance for you to join the intoxicated bees, too.

So attractive are borage flowers to bees, that they were used in a major experiment to improve our understanding of bee communication. Honey bees famously perform a figure-of-eight dance at the mouth of the hive and it has long been assumed that this communicated the location of good nectar and pollen supplies to fellow workers. To try and interpret the secret codes in the bee dance, scientists

planted blocks of borage at measured distances across the landscape, and through careful observation they were able translate the bee dance language and show that the dance contained information about the distance and direction of the borage blocks. Plant borage in your garden and bees will seek it out over considerable distances

Parsley is a herb that we grow for its tasty leaves, and normally it is not encouraged to flower. If you do give it its head, though – and this sometimes happens if the weather is dry and you neglect to cut it for a couple of weeks – then you will find another of those umbelliferous green flowers decorating your herb border. If you want to guarantee a flower crop, then protect the parsley over winter and it will flower like mad in its second year. A lot of insects seem to enjoy parsley flowers, but one in particular, the soldier beetle, seems to turn up as if by magic, and all through the early summer you will see the handsome chestnut-coloured creatures wandering over the flowers. More often than not they seem to be locked together in mating tandem. Mint, sage and lemon balm are three more leaf herbs that you should

encourage to flower. Mint in particular is one of the best butterfly plants there is – almost as compelling as buddleia, and it could not be easier to grow.

SHRUB LAYER

Talking of buddleia, there are one or two shrubs which give an especially useful boost to your wildlife service station. The famous butterfly bush is obvious. It is incredible to see how many butterflies and bees manage to cling on to each spike of perfumed flowers. The common mauve seedlings that have colonised so many of our inner-city demolition sites seem at least as popular as the more sophisticated white, deep purple or red named hybrids although there is now some concern that *Buddleja davidii* has become an invasive shrub, and the RHS is no longer allowing it to be exhibited at their shows. As a child of the post-war bomb sites I have grown up in the company of volunteer buddleia forests and I see no prospect of them disappearing from our urban wild spaces. There are less common species of *Buddleja*, too: *B. sellowiana* and *B. globosa*. They are less prone to widespread seed dispersal, which makes them less

# EXOTIC SHRUBS FOR NECTAR, POLLEN OR FRUITS

**Mahonia spp** (above) The Oregon grape and others are useful evergreens, because they flower so early in the spring. Bees visit them for pollen, and M. *aquifolium* produces a good crop of purple berries in the autumn.

**Pyracantha coccinea** White flowers in spring and orange or red berries. Blackbirds enjoy the fruit. Train it against a wall.

**Cotoneaster frigidus** A semi-evergreen erect shrub, growing 2m tall, and useful as an informal hedge. Lots of berries in the autumn.

**Cotoneaster horizontalis** Deciduous and prostrate habit. Fantastic for bees, which cover the shrub when it flowers in early spring. This plant is now frowned upon in neighbourhoods where there is a risk that it could invade nearby downland.

**Viburnum bodnantense** Flowers with a delicious perfume in January and February. Useful for the time of year.

**Chaenomeles japonica** Japanese quince. Red flowers before the leaves come out, and large apple-like fruit which the thrushes, starlings and blackbirds enjoy once they fall in autumn.

**Amelanchier canadensis** Lovely autumn colour and masses of white blossom in March and April.

**Viburnum tinus** (right) Evergreen, grows 2–3m tall and flowers through the winter. Useful as a nectar source for hibernating insects that wake up unseasonably early.

**Lonicera fragrantissima** Honeysuckle is one of the best shrubs for winter perfume and unseasonal foraging insects. It flowers from Christmas onwards in my Midlands garden.

**Osmanthus x burkwoodii** is one of the great successes of my own front garden. It is a large evergreen shrub, but allows enough light through the open canopy to support carpets of spring wildflowers such as primroses, wood anemones and sweet woodruff, and the perfume from its clusters of white bell flowers fills the garden with delicious perfume throughout the month of May.

LEFT The native broom, *Cytisus scoparius* is a great bee plant. There are garden cultivars with less vigour and more subtle flower colour, but this short-lived native shrub takes some beating.

LEFT, BELOW A quince is a good choice if you want to create dappled shade, a nectar supply for bees in spring, and the most aromatic of fruit crops in the autumn. Any fruits that you fail to harvest will linger on to feed the birds.

invasive and although they have yellow flowers they still appeal to the butterflies.

Flowering currant is another plant that is worth growing. I inherited a couple of big specimens in one of my gardens and was delighted to find that they were good for bees. The tassels of pink flowers come out early – usually well before the end of May, and at that time of year these are probably the richest source of pollen and nectar in the garden. I've noticed that the bluetits spend a lot of time in the bushes, too, but I cannot work out whether they are after the nectar in the flowers, or the aphids and insect eggs around the base of the leaves. Lilac and mock orange are both rich in nectar, but they only flower for a short time. A number of the garden viburnums are useful since they flower as early as January in some years, and the native viburnums, lantana and opulus, are showy enough for the border. Even the common hedging privet is a good insect shrub if it is allowed to flower, though you do need a lot of space for that to happen. I used to love the sweet smell of white privet flowers when I played on the local derelict allotments as a child, and the great columns of black

privet berries are valuable as winter food for birds.

Brooms are extremely good bee plants, and the native, *Cytisus scoparius,* is one of the best flowerers if you have room for it. Broom tends to be short-lived, and usually dies after six or seven years, but at its peak, in years four or five, it is a spectacular blaze of yellow in June. If you have not room to accommodate a plant the size of a mature wild broom, then there are several more compact species. *Cytisus praecox* is particularly good and it flowers a little earlier too.

Shrub roses are perhaps some of the most useful of wildlife ornamental shrubs. There is a whole range of elegant species and modern varieties, some of them growing well over 3m tall, and the various single forms give an extra benefit by producing plenty of pollen and following on with big juicy hips in the autumn. Rose leaves are also the favourite building material used by leaf cutter bees, which cut neat circles to cart away to their nest. The young rose shoots are popular with aphids, of course, and they in turn provide food for a range of insect predators.

A number of other garden shrubs are useful for their fruit crop. There is a whole range of berberis, cotoneasters and mahonias to choose from, and a number flower early in the spring, when pollen and nectar are in short supply. Pyracantha I mentioned as a possible wall shrub, but it can be grown more freely if you prefer, and japonica, or *Chaenomeles,* the Japanese quince, produces fruits which become useful for wildlife once they have dropped off and started to rot a little.

## COLOURFUL ANNUALS

The last and perhaps the most useful range of garden flowers for the wildlife service station garden are the annuals. There is a massive selection of colourful plants which grow from seed-sowing to flowering in just a few weeks. Some of them should be started off in early spring and need the protection of a heated greenhouse or a warm windowsill at the seedling stage, but a number are perfectly hardy, and will fill your borders with colour for next to nothing. There are one or two biennials which are used as seasonal bedding, too.

The spring begins with wallflowers, and certainly they get the pollen season off to a generous start. They are readily available to buy in bunches late in the autumn, and they are easy to grow from seed so long as you remember to sow a year in advance. Their heady perfume in April is one of the real features of the spring garden. In milder gardens, wallflowers will live on for several years, but I've always found I need to plant fresh ones each autumn if I want a predictable display and they respond well to a little lime in the soil. Try to avoid planting wallflowers in the same spot year after year; they belong to the cabbage family and can suffer from clubroot.

Forget-me-nots are a great springtime favourite of

BELOW In a small garden you can ring the changes with seasonal bedding. Single-formed flowers are the key to pollinator appeal. I plant ornamental tobacco plants (Nicotiana affinis) every spring to fill my summer evenings with perfume and night-flying moths.

RIGHT Hardy annuals are unbeatable value for money. There are lots to choose from. A packet of seeds should give you at least a couple of square metres of summer colour, and the Californian poppy is among the very best for attracting hoverflies.

mine. I love their powder-blue colour, and if you give them a good shake as you pull up the spent plants you will produce a sheet of seedlings by late summer, ready for next year's display. Sweet Williams come next, providing a useful late spring nectar supply, and again surviving from year to year in milder districts. There are polyanthus too, though you may be well advised to avoid these colourful garden hybrids if you are trying to maintain a colony of native cowslips. The two are rather promiscuous, and you can end up with some strangely coloured cowslips in your meadow if they are close enough to interbreed.

### HALF-HARDY ANNUALS

Of the half-hardy summer garden flowers, I think *Nicotiana*, the tobacco plant, is probably the most useful. There is a lime green variety, but most are mauve, pink or white, and many of them have wonderful evening perfume. They can be planted out in late May, after the last frost, and will flower through until the autumn. I always grow tobacco flowers in pots by the front door, as well as in the main flower borders, and they reward me by bringing a whole variety of night-flying moths close to the house.

I said earlier that single flowers tend to be better than doubles. This is true of the petunia, another half-hardy summer bedding plant worth growing for its pollen and nectar. The heliotrope, cherry pie, is a good butterfly plant, and snapdragons are worth including, too. They have a limited clientele, but make up for this by giving you lots of fun watching bumblebees struggling to force their way into each flower and then struggling to get out again.

The low, honey-perfumed bedding plant, white alyssum, is on the borderline between hardy and

half-hardy. In the south it seeds on from year to year, in the same way as forget-me-nots, but further north you need to replant each spring. Plant a good big block of plants, at about 20cm centres, and by midsummer you should have a continuous white carpet, and lots of nectar-sipping insects. The sweet perfume tells you everything you need to know about the quality of the nectar supply.

HARDY ANNUALS

Half-hardy bedding tends to be rather expensive if you have to buy it. With all that winter heat it costs a lot to produce. If you are looking for cheaper alternatives, then there are plenty of colourful non-native hardy annuals available, and a packet of seed in April will give you masses of summer flowers for next to nothing. There are lots of low-growing front-of-border species to choose from. Candytuft has flowers in the purple to white range, and seems popular with butterflies. Clarkia, Virginia stock and larkspur are all in the same colour range and are better for bees, while *Convolvulus tricolor* attracts hoverflies. In the yellow and orange range you can

produce spectacular results with a combination of hardy marigolds (*Calendula*) and Californian poppies. On sunny days, these flowers are alive with hoverflies of all shapes and sizes. All these low, annual flowering plants will flower on and on if you remove the dead heads as they fade. It is a natural survival strategy for plants to keep producing more and more flowers until they successfully set seed. Deadheading can be a pretty tedious job, particularly with flowers like the Californian poppies, where each bloom only lasts for a day, but it is well worth the effort. A couple of hardy annuals which produce seedlings year after year, and spread around the garden, are Welsh poppy (*Meconopsis cambrica*) and the poached-egg plant (*Limnanthes douglasii*). The latter is particularly good for bees, hence its alternative name of bees' butter, and it is entirely covered with celandine-yellow flowers for the whole of June.

GAINING HEIGHT

It is possible to achieve a lot of height with hardy annuals grown from seed. Cosmos has pink, purple or white flowers sprinkled over a thin structure

# NATIVE WILDFLOWERS FOR THE FLOWER BORDER

## YELLOW

**Tansy** (*Tanacetum vulgare*) (above) Aromatic leaves (used for flavouring sponge cakes) and button-like flowers oozing with nectar in July. Hoverflies and small butterflies are constant visitors. The plant spreads by underground stems, and can be invasive.

**Rough hawkbit** (*Leontodon hispidus*) One of the tallest of the 'dandelion' types. Extremely handsome, and a long summer flowering season, but you must control the seedlings.

**Ragwort** (*Senecio jacobaea*) Pretty, daisy-like flowers and the leaves are food for the caterpillars of cinnabar moths. It is important not to let ragwort seed onto neighbouring farmland as it is poisonous to livestock.

**Corn marigold** (*Chrysanthemum segetum*) A pretty annual. Grow it just like Californian poppies or calendulas.

**Ox-eye daisy** (*Leucanthemum vulgare*) Meadow flowers which can be cultivated to produce lovely cut flowers, just like giant daisies.

**Yellow archangel** (*Lamiastrum galeobdolon*) A woodland plant with spikes of beautiful bee flowers from early spring onwards.

**Cowslip** (*Primula veris*) Prefers lime, but once your clumps are established they will flower for years, and can be split from time to time – just like polyanthus. Cowslips cross-fertilise easily with garden primulas, and you may have seedlings with bronze flowers appearing after a year or two of promiscuous suburban life.

**Oxlip** (*P. elatior*) Like a bunch of primroses on a stem. A woodland plant with a lovely pale cream colour. Looks wonderful flowering among violets in early spring.

**Primrose** (*P. vulgaris*) Grows best in half-shade, particularly on sandy soil with a covering of fallen leaves. If you have the patience to deadhead, primroses will flower almost the whole year round. The leaves are often patterned by the tunnels of leaf miners and ants feed on the waxy coating of primrose seed.

**Rockrose** (*Helianthemum nummularium*) A tiny native shrub of limestone grasslands. Evergreen, with lots of single and double garden varieties in all colours. The true native type is pure yellow, and flowers whenever the sun shines, from June to September.

**Dyer's wintergreen** (*Genista tinctoria*) Similar to gorse, but smaller (1m tall) and without the prickles.

**Tormentil** (*Potentilla erecta*) Rare in the wild. An extremely pretty flower growing 60cm tall, and blooming in early summer.

**Agrimony** (*Agrimonia eupatoria*) An important medicinal herb, and also a useful dye plant, producing a rich yellow colour. The flowers are small, on spikes about 60cm tall. The leaves are similar to those of meadowsweet, and the fruit have hooks on them, and cling to your socks.

**Stonecrop** (*Sedum acre*) (left) A tiny succulent, a bit like a cactus. Survives the toughest of conditions, produces a brilliant sheet of flowers in early summer and the fleshy leaves turn red in dry periods. The growth of interest in green and brown roofs has made stonecrop extremely popular as a plant for poor thin well-drained soils on exposed rooftops.

**Greater celandine** (*Chelidonium majus*) One of my favourite wildflowers, though it can be a bit straggly and ungainly for some tastes. The leaves are a particularly fresh green, the flowers are pretty too, and the plant will colonise open ground and thrive in the woodland edge. The fruits split to reveal a row of shiny black seeds, each

with a white blob on. This is a waxy material which ants feed on, and in carrying off the seed they help with dispersal. Beware though. The bright yellow sap that oozes out of any broken leaf or stem is a seriously persistent stain and poisonous.

**Yellow toadflax** (*Linaria vulgaris*) (left) A must in the wildlife garden. One of the loveliest of wildflowers, flowering late into the autumn and growing on any soil. A bee plant.

**Globe flower** (*Trollius europaeus*) This elegant plant looks too posh to be a wildflower. Like a giant buttercup with spherical blooms, it grows naturally in wet ground, but seems happy in most garden conditions. There are various shades of yellow and orange available, but I still prefer the simple butter-yellow of the native type.

**Welsh poppy** (*Meconopsis cambrica*) Not native to most of the British Isles of course, but so lovely it should be in everyone's garden. It grows best as an annual, seeding merrily into cracks and crevices, but the odd plant may survive for two or three years. Over the years it has become a signature of early summer in my own garden and I love it.

**Common fleabane** (*Pulicaria dysenterica*) (left) A rich orange-yellow daisy which flowers about 60cm tall.

## GREEN

**Stinking hellebore** (*Helleborus foetidus*) (left) A dramatic, rather sinister plant of chalk or woodlands. Strong leaf shape, dark leathery green leaves, and clusters of handsome green flowers each with a purple margin. The seed pods produce an acrid smell if you crush them. Flowers appear as early as February, and are a useful source of nectar for newly emerged bees.

**Lady's mantle** (*Alchemilla vulgaris*) A perennial which seeds readily into paved areas. The green flowers come in clouds in midsummer, and the leaves are extremely pretty, often holding a droplet of water in the centre, and always looking fresh.

of feathery-leaved stems, and will grow up to 2m tall. The prize for growth, though, must go to the sunflower, and you should have a clump of these friendly giants in your wildlife service station. Seeds planted in April will produce plants as much as 3m tall by August, and the huge plates of florets glisten with nectar day after day. Both bees and butterflies feed on the 'faces', and in autumn you can expect a second performance when the more acrobatic of the garden birds move in and start stripping the seeds. Greenfinches in particular are brilliant at tackling sunflower seed. They perch on top of the stem, seize the striped seed in their tough beaks, spin it round like a can of beans, open up the outer skin and neatly remove the delicious high-energy kernel

Old, dead sunflower stems may be a bit more untidy than you can cope with in your suburban garden, and if so, I suggest you cut the stems once the seed starts to ripen, and hang them upside down in a less prominent spot, where the birds can still get at them easily. Hang them from a swinging wire and you will also reduce the risk of a rat raid.

BELOW You can grow cosmos flowers from seed, but I tend to plant one or two established pot-grown specimens to stay one step ahead of the slugs. These delightful flowers will reach well over a metre tall by midsummer. Deadhead them regularly and they will keep on coming until the first heavy frost.

RIGHT Sunflowers are always fun to grow. The seeds are the food of first choice for very many garden birds, and if you can't leave the sunflowers standing, cut them down and hang the seed heads up as natural feeders.

BELOW RIGHT Poached-egg plant, *Limnanthes douglasii*, is one easy annual that delivers troublefree cheerfulness wherever it grows. The clue to its wildlife value lies in its other common name, bees' butter.

These days it is possible enjoy the benefits of sunflowers on a more modest scale, with hybrids that grow no more than a meter tall, and provided you avoid the double-flowered varieties, and choose nectar-rich ones for the garden you can still enjoy their smiling faces through the summer – though I must say if you have the space, there is nothing quite so spectacular as a flower that towers above your head.

## BEAUTIFUL WEEDS

Finally, you might like to consider growing some of our own colourful native cornfield weeds as annual border flowers. Corncockle, for instance, is every bit as beautiful as the tobacco flowers, though it does not have their perfume, and the seeds are poisonous. Corn marigold is a presentable alternative to accompany the Californian poppies in your yellow border, and of course our own scarlet poppies would be hard to beat for a real splash of colour. Cornflowers are always worth a place somewhere, and pheasant's eye (*Adonis annua*) looks far too exotic to be classified simply as a cornfield weed.

LEFT Sunflowers brighten any garden. It is difficult not to be cheered when you see them smiling down, and they are extremely good for bees and birds.

OPPOSITE Be imaginative with plants. There is no rule that says food and flowers need to be kept apart.

There are vegetables that you can fit into your flower borders, too. I grow broad beans in mine, because I love the perfume, and the bees love the flowers. I grow courgettes because I've found nothing to beat the drama of their big floppy leaves, and their huge yellow flowers. If you have room you might like to grow some of the edible squashes. They are more striking than plain courgettes, and they are suitable for training over low walls and fences. I usually have one or two of the poorer cabbage seedlings planted in the flower borders, well away from the vegetable patch. The theory is that when the cabbages flower, they attract the cabbage white butterflies and they lay their eggs here, instead of fluttering off to infest the real crop. Unfortunately no one seems to have told the butterflies.

## RHS GARDEN HYDE HALL

Created from scratch on unpromising soil in windswept Essex farming countryside, Hyde Hall is an inspiring place to learn about wildlife garden habitats. The wildflower meadows are the most striking feature, and through spring and summer they are glorious. The main garden has been created around the historic manor house at the top of a low hill, and thanks to the protection of hedges and walls it has become a wonderful refuge for fruit and flowers.

Visit at any time of the year and you can observe which flowers or seed heads the birds and insects prefer and, in contrast to the neighbouring farmland, the garden has become an oasis for wildlife. You can hear it in the birdsong, and as a pesticide-free landscape you can see it in the rich diversity of insect life.

Specialist experts and volunteers from Essex Wildlife Trust (www. essexwt.org.uk) work closely with Hyde Hall, and as a result visitors can enjoy an early dawn chorus walk, or a dusk walk to see the bats and barn owls that hunt over the meadows, or spend time in the bird hide overlooking the garden's small lake.

## 10

Growing food and wildlife gardening are natural companions. Attracting helpful wildlife to the garden can increase cropping.

# A WILD KITCHEN GARDEN

THE HUMAN visitors to my garden always seem rather surprised to discover that I grow fruit and vegetables. They assume that would be out of the question with all this wildlife around. In fact, the opposite is true. The pests that attack most gardeners' vegetables are kept under control pretty effectively by the predators from my rich habitats. Far from being a threat to the neighbours' gardens, I probably provide the majority of the ladybirds, hedgehogs and other pest-eaters that clean up their patches – unless, of course, they happen to be into wildlife gardening too, in which case they will have their own.

I must admit I am not a fanatical vegetable grower. I simply do not have the time, but I do love to be able to pick fresh salad leaves or pull up a home-grown carrot in the summer, and despite the boom in pick-your-own soft fruit, I still think the raspberries picked and eaten straight from the garden do have a special flavour. The annual harvest from my one redcurrant bush provides me with a year's supply of jelly, and fresh herbs such as tarragon and chives, marjoram and thyme are so much tastier than the commercially dried equivalent. I also make sure to grow a few edible flowers that can transform a boring salad into something much more special.

## NATURAL CONFIDENCE

Apart from this 'freshness factor', the other important reason for growing your own is the reassurance it gives that for once you do know exactly what you are eating. The unblemished produce you buy in its poly-bags at the supermarket or pick for yourself in the countryside is probably only blemish-free because it is sprayed with pesticides. It is true that commercial practices have become less chemical dependent since the 1980s when I wrote the first edition of *How to Make a Wildlife Garden*. Increased sophistication in the chemicals themselves and the drive from plant breeders to increase natural pest and disease resistance have been transformational since I trained as a horticulturist in the 1960s, but nevertheless unless you buy organic, lots of shop-bought fruit and vegetables will include chemical products that are better avoided. For many of us, grow-your-own is as much about peace of mind as it is about freshness and flavour. Frankly, I heave a little sigh of relief if I find a caterpillar sharing my cauliflower.

LEFT I don't mind fair shares, but when a blackbird shows signs of a raspberry habit, it's time to provide some fruit-net protection.

RIGHT Food growing can be just one more element in a well-managed, wildlife-friendly garden. Here the mini-meadow, the flower border and the sheltering hedgerow all help to improve cropping. The addition of a small garden pond would attract more predators for natural pest control.

BELOW The caterpillars of cabbage white butterflies need to be controlled. The finger and thumb technique is usually adequate in my small scale veg patch, and most of the eggs tend to be laid on nearby nasturtium leaves.

There is something reassuring about a plate of salad that I know has never been sprayed in its life. If the edges of the leaves look a little serrated, then I can smile to myself and know that I'm safe. The garden chemicals industry has done a magnificent job of building up their market. Despite the growing popularity of organic gardening, the increasing availability of 'wildlife friendly' garden products and the increased awareness of food quality, the garden centres still offer all kinds of poisons, presented as a means of giving you more wholesome fruit and vegetables. How crazy can you get? The increased and often indiscriminate use of modern chemicals has done much to upset the balanced environment that my gardening grandparents enjoyed, and of course once you are hooked it's difficult to break the artificial cycle. Once the first spray of the season wipes out your natural predators, you have to keep spraying the wave after wave of fast-recovery pests, since most of them return more rapidly than their predators.

## ORGANIC PRINCIPLES

The alternative to all this dependence on poisonous chemicals is organic gardening. For years this was seen as the domain of the 'nut cutlet' brigade. Now, though,

there is a green revolution going on all over Europe. There are lots of publications dealing with organic gardening techniques, and the charity Garden Organic has a brilliant public demonstration of best practice in their gardens at Ryton in Warwickshire – well worth a visit! For a more exclusive demonstration of organic good practice, the jardin potager at chef Raymond Blanc's Oxfordshire restaurant, or the Prince of Wales' walled fruit and vegetable garden at Highgrove take some beating. There is far greater emphasis on organic techniques in many of the great public parks and gardens around the country, and of course the gardens of the Royal Horticultural Society are among the best examples. Much of the secret of success lies in sustaining high fertility by putting back plenty of organic compost as you crop, and of course the compost is only produced because there is a healthy workforce of fungi and microorganisms available to convert the cabbage stems and lawn clippings. For our purposes, though, I think it is most interesting to concentrate on the way that wildlife gardening can positively help to control pests and improve the quality of your produce.

The first suggestion is that you take a few simple precautions to protect your crops against the more obvious damage. You will attract a lot of birds with your wildlife service station gardening. Although you may know that your generosity ends at pyracantha berries and bruised windfalls, it is fair to assume that the blackbirds will try to extend the menu to raspberries and the bullfinches will love the blackcurrant buds. A netted fruit cage is a simple, harmless way of defining the boundary between wildlife larder and human food crop, and if you have serious problems with pigeons, for example, you can extend the idea to lower netted structures over your cabbages and Brussels sprouts. In my small garden, timing is critical. I do not want permanent structures, but provided I drape fruit netting over my wall-trained cherry and my currant bush, then a week or two of relatively unsightly protection usually guarantees a safe crop.

## PROTECTING YOUR PATCH

There is also a range of intriguing devices for scaring away the larger forms of wildlife without harming them – persuading them to transfer their attention to the allotments down the road, in other words. Human look-alike scarecrows are not likely to be effective. The local birds will already have marked you down as a soft touch and are not likely to be too worried by one of your old jumpers stuffed with straw. The fluttering and clattering kind of scarers are more effective, and I use them among my raspberries. In my garden the birds seem far too preoccupied with the natural food in the woodland edge habitat or on the edge of the pond. They do not seem to show much interest in the crops in my relatively tidy veg patch.

Small mammals can be a problem. Your log pile might just house a rogue woodmouse that develops a taste for newly sown peas, though it has not happened to me yet. There are one or two folk remedies that are worth giving a whirl. Some gardeners used to put great faith in mothballs, but they were banned a good few years ago. Spearmint and caper spurge (*Euphorbia lactea*) are two plants that have a reputation for driving away both mice and moles. There is little scientific evidence to support these folk remedies, but since garden peas do end up sharing the saucepan with mint, it can do no harm to have them living together first.

**BELOW** Companion planted pot marigolds will attract hoverflies and wasps; predators of many of the insects and grubs you may not want in your vegetable patch.

**BOTTOM** Mixing food crops and flowers in the veg patch makes perfect sense, and some crops such as chard, seen here, are decorative enough to hold their own in the flower border.

**RIGHT** In a fruitful year there will generally be more than enough apples to satisfy all appetites.

## COMPANION PLANTING

Having mentioned the idea of growing mint and peas together, it is worth elaborating a little on the idea of companion planting. Years of accumulated knowledge have produced a whole host of suggestions for crop plants which seem in some mysterious way to protect and promote one another, and there are also a number of plant combinations that are thought to be counterproductive. Companion planting used to be dismissed as 'muck and magic' but research is showing that some plants can bring benefits to their neighbours and a great many successful amateur food growers consider it best practice. One particular idea is well worth discussing in detail. There is a great advantage to be gained by growing flowers among your vegetables, and by having a patch or two of 'weeds' close by too. Most people will probably smile at that suggestion, having dreamed for years of the day when there is *not* a mass of weeds in the vegetable patch. What I am suggesting is that they should be positively encouraged – within reason, of course.

There are three reasons for growing flowers among your food plants. Some of them are known to have a chemical influence on the soil or the surrounding air that helps to control or at least suppress some of the pests and diseases. All of them attract pollinating insects, and some of them attract predators such as hoverflies that can be of great benefit in the vegetable patch, and many of them have edible petals that can provide some colourful garnish.

I always grow both French and English pot marigolds (*Tagetes* and *Calendula*) in my small vegetable patch, because they are particularly popular with hoverflies and wasps. Although the adult insects feed on pollen, and the common wasp will gorge itself on ripe fruit too, they are also important predators. Between them they provide impressive biological control of cabbage white caterpillars and many other grubs, larvae and aphids. The various types of wasps and hoverflies operate in different ways. The common wasp collects caterpillars from the vegetable patch, and everywhere else in your garden, and flies off with them to the nest. Here the prey is stored in a larder, and when the wasp eggs themselves hatch, the wasp grubs feed on the accumulated food store. Just stand and watch your cabbage patch for a few minutes in the height of summer; you are sure

to see wasp after wasp patrolling over the leaves, and then suddenly dropping like a stone on to some poor, unsuspecting pest, and buzzing off back to base with their juicy cargo hanging helplessly from their undercarriage. Many of the garden hoverflies produce predatory larvae which kill aphids and other pests, and the ichneumons and braconids lay their eggs inside living caterpillars on your cabbages. The pest continues to munch away for a little while longer, but when the hoverfly larvae themselves hatch, they eat away the host caterpillar from the inside. Not a pretty thought, I know, but these natural predators and parasites are efficient if you give them half a chance, and flowers among your fruit and veg will help to increase their numbers.

The weed patch works in a similar though less clearly understood way. Few if any of the weed species are likely to harbour pests and diseases that attack crop plants, but they may well harbour preferred prey species which attract more predators to the adjacent crop areas. Whatever the reason, if you can grow a patch of weeds, kept separate so that they do not compete with the veg for moisture or food, that does seem to help reduce the problem of vegetable garden pests and diseases.

## SNAIL AND SLUG SOLUTIONS

Slugs and snails can be a menace, particularly to young seedlings in wet weather. A path of coarse bark or sharp gravel around the veg patch seems to put a lot of them off, and in all but the wettest of summers the majority of the many slugs and snails in my own garden do not go near the vegetables. They are far too contented browsing on the fallen leaves and fungi of the woodland edge and the hedge bottom.

One of the most spectacular of all my garden's slugs is the leopard slug. This handsome species is relatively common and I have a thriving population living in my plastic compost bin. Leopard slugs don't feed on living plants, but rather concentrate on dead plant material. Even more importantly the leopard slug is a significant consumer of other slugs, and so it is an entirely helpful member of my garden wildlife community.

If you are lucky, you will have a number of other efficient slug-gobblers to help you. A few minutes standing in the dark listening to a hedgehog chomping and snuffling through the undergrowth will confirm that an enormous number can meet a sticky end that way. Piles of broken snail shells beside a stone or a particular

OPPOSITE Borage and pot-marigold (*Calendula officinalis*) are two of the very best annuals to grow for insects, and the petals of both make any salad extra-special.

BELOW Runner beans are a pretty foolproof way of filling the freezer. The vines will grow to well above head height, and of course the bees are an essential part of the production process.

paving slab are evidence of the song thrush's favourite pastime – snail-bashing. Toads, ground beetles and slow worms are other successful slug hunters. Sadly, all these effective natural predators have become much rarer in the time that I've been gardening. I do still have song thrushes in my inner city neighbourhood. Hedgehogs do still turn up from time to time, and toads spawn in my garden pond, but generally speaking the numbers are down dramatically. The loss of habitat, and the widescale use of chemical pesticides have had a disastrous impact on our wildlife.

If you cannot wait for nature to sort out the slugs, then please don't resort to poisons. The slug pellets may be labelled as 'harmless to hedgehogs', but when the hedgehogs eat the poisoned slugs, that is a different story. One hedgehog can get through dozens of slugs and snails in a night, and the poison quickly builds up to a deadly concentration. Slug killers based on aluminium sulphate or iron phosphate are less environmentally damaging than the more traditional pellets. There are microscopic parasitic nematodes naturally present in soil, and some of these can infect and kill slugs and snails. These nematodes are also available commercially. They

RIGHT Not all slugs are bad. The handsome leopard slug preys on other more troublesome slug species, although will eat vegetable leaves if pushed.

FAR RIGHT Song thrushes seek out and smash snails. Look out for the anvil on a rock or paving slab.

BELOW Toads are like gold dust. Do everything you can to encourage them and they will provide very effective slug control. My toads breed in my pond and overwinter in the damp crevices of my open-jointed stone retaining wall.

arrive in the post and are easy to apply to the soil. They are relatively expensive but they do have a dramatic impact on slug and snail numbers on a localised scale without posing any wider poisoning risk.

There are a great many simple and practical methods of trapping or killing slugs. I know a few people who put down half-grapefruit skins around the edge of their vegetable crops. The slugs gather underneath them, and are then escorted carefully to some distant wilderness. It is no good just tossing them over the fence into next door's garden, however tempting that may be, because these amazing creatures have a effective homing facility, and often will simply slide back under the fence or over the wall when you turn your back.

If you must kill them, slugs are easy to tempt into a sump filled with beer. You can buy fancy plastic devices with roofs on to stop hedgehogs and other slug gourmets getting at the corpses, but a plastic cup sunk into the ground, and protected with a couple of stones will suffice just as well. Keep the rim just proud of the soil level, so that helpful ground beetles do not run the risk of tumbling in by accident. The sweet, sticky liquid seems to be preferable to even the most juicy leaves of lettuces, and once the slugs fall in, they cannot climb out. If the hedgehog does manage to pick up a stomach full of beer-soaked slugs then the worst after-effect it can expect is a hangover. Presumably, when this happens he will be even pricklier than usual the following morning!

## KEEPING IT SIMPLE

There is one final tactic which helps me to grow perfectly respectable fruit and vegetables without needing to spray. I avoid species which are particularly difficult. I generally grow a copper-leaved variety of lettuce, for instance, because the birds simply do not seem tempted by it at all. I grow climbing French beans but generally avoid the dwarf forms. All those tender little beans dangling at ground level are too tempting for the slugs, but when suspended several feet in the air they seem relatively safe. I grow broad beans every year, and pinch out the tops at the first sign of blackfly. I grow wonderful carrots, but sow thinly enough never to need to thin at the seedling stage, and this seems to help them escape attack from carrot fly. That particular pest is also put off by a nearby crop of leeks, and because carrot flies fly close to the ground, a simple enclosure of insect-proof mesh provides almost fool-proof protection. I grow courgettes and tomatoes in pots out of slugs' reach until they are big enough and tough enough to survive the odd bit of casual chewing. I grow winter broccoli because it crops when few pests are around, and I grow lots of rhubarb, Jerusalem artichokes and ruby chard because nothing seems to like eating their leaves. My sandy soil produces clean potatoes unaided, though I appreciate that little black keel slugs can be a problem on wet ground. If I plant broad beans among the spuds they both seem to benefit.

By creating a garden for wildlife you are giving yourself a real advantage in the vegetable-growing stakes. It seems a shame not to make the most of it. Your encouragement of predators such as ladybirds, toads and robins provides you with a resident pesticide squad, and if you choose what you grow wisely, protect against crop damage where practical, and put up with the odd happy little poison-free caterpillar in your salad from time to time, then there is no reason why you and your garden wildlife cannot walk off with the prizes at the local show.

11 |

# BOOSTING WILDLIFE HABITATS

THE COMMONEST positive garden wildlife conservation gesture most people make is to put up a bird feeder. In fact this is just one of a whole host of ways in which your wildlife service station can be made more attractive to the passing trade. The boost to plant life, to pollen and seed supply has already been discussed. Now it is time to think about other ways of creating a super-habitat.

A bird table is a good idea. It gives you an opportunity to attract a wide range of wild creatures to a spot where you can watch them and enjoy their company in comfort. The table itself doesn't need to be sophisticated at all. What matters is the way you use it. You must take the responsibility seriously. Once you begin putting out a supply of food, the birds from a wide area will quickly come to rely on you, and they can suffer if the free hand-outs suddenly stop appearing. It is a good idea to feed at regular times each day. For me, that tends to be just after breakfast. It is convenient as a way of using up the toast crumbs, and in the depths of winter it means the food is there as it gets light, and the birds emerge from another cold night, desperate for life-giving food. Although I am away from the house most

days during the week, this early morning ritual has the added advantage that when I am at home, at the weekend for example, I can enjoy the squabbles that follow throughout the rest of the day.

## FINDING THE RIGHT SPOT

The siting of the bird table is critical. In fact you should be thinking of a 'feeding station' rather than limiting yourself to a table alone. A few garden birds are reluctant to feed high above the ground, and prefer to peck and scratch around at ground level. Hedge sparrows and wrens feed here, for example, and so some open ground around the base of the table is useful if you want to watch.

One advantage of a feeding station is that it helps you study the birds. The first consideration, therefore, should be your convenience. Choose a spot which will give you unrestricted viewing from one or more of your busy windows. My bird table is about 1.5m from the kitchen window and provides some encouragement to do the washing up. It is also important to have a nice, convenient route from the house to the birds. A fifty metre trek down the garden with the birdseed may be fine on a sunny day

in November, but when the snow is one metre thick, you will be grateful for a nice short, paved route, and that will help to encourage you to keep up the regular service when it is most needed.

If you concentrate your wildlife anywhere, the word will quickly get round to the local predators. There was a time when I could depend on spotted flycatchers to swoop down to snatch the small tortoiseshells in mid-flight. Sadly these wonderful migratory birds have disappeared almost entirely from almost all our gardens. Other predators have fared rather better. The cabbages on the vegetable patch become a focus for the wasps' attention once they start to generate a steady production line of caterpillars, and night after night the bats visit my pond – grateful, no doubt, for the concentration of aquatic insect life I have so graciously provided for them. The bird table falls into the same category. It gathers together a regular, noisy concentration of birds and that is bound to arouse the interest of predators. Top of the pecking order in most neighbourhoods is the local domestic cat. You may have the odd sparrowhawk playing out its textbook

Feeding garden birds has been one of the transforming success stories in UK conservation since the 1980s. Feed regularly, provide a variety of different foods and give yourself a clear and comfortable view of nature from your window.

sparrow-snatching role occasionally, but cats are the real menace, and you must take the problem seriously when you take on a bird table. Don't put it too close to potential moggie-cover. Bushes and small trees are fine, so long as they are more than a leap away – perhaps 2m as a minimum. In fact the birds will appreciate a handy branch to fly up to at any sign of danger. I have a substantial twig fixed into a hole in my bird table, and it is surprising how many birds perch there first, before daring to land on the table.

## PREVENTING DISEASE

Another possible hazard you introduce by bringing together a high concentration of birds is the risk of promoting infectious diseases. For this reason, it is advisable to move the station each year, though in a small garden that might be rather difficult. You should also make sure you do not overfeed or allow food to lie uneaten. If there is an accumulation of stale food, that too can cause health problems for the birds, and it is also likely to attract scavengers such as rats. I suspect that this is not the kind of garden wildlife most people are keen to be watching from the kitchen window.

As bird feeding has become much more common in our gardens there have been some serious outbreaks of disease among some of our birds. The steep decline in the number of greenfinches since the turn of the century seems to be one sad example of this problem. Keeping the feeders and the feeding area clean is therefore highly desirable. Hot soapy water and a scrubbing brush will do the trick if you clean up frequently. Tubular seed feeders will need a special bottle brush for cleaning their interiors, and it pays to disinfect more thoroughly towards the end of the summer in anticipation of a busy winter feeding season.

## PREDATOR PRECAUTIONS

If cats are a serious threat to your bird watching, then there are a number of things you can do to help. Keeping a dog, or even better a rather overweight and dopey neutered tom cat yourself is supposed to be the ultimate deterrent, though I must confess I find the prospect of this cure rather unattractive. A large bell around the neck of each of the offending local cats will at least give the birds a bit of warning. An inverted metal cone around the leg of the bird table will make it difficult for the cats to climb up, and an increase in height of just 30cm or so can put it beyond the reach of all but the most athletic of cats. If none of these precautions work, try hanging the table from a branch. It will swing there freely and be far too unstable to carry the cat. Some people swear by the electric cat deterrents which

emit a high-pitched sound which humans can't hear, but which most cats hate. These do work, but some cats seem resistant. Maybe they are just determined – or simply deaf. In my experience their effectiveness seems to fade after a few weeks, which suggests that even the sensitive cats get used to the noise.

## A VARIED DIET

The choice of food you offer will affect the range of birds you see. You need to provide both hard and soft foods. The house sparrows, tits and finches have tough beaks and are happy cracking sunflower seeds and corn, but the insect-eaters with the pointed bills are not likely to feed unless you provide something softer. Bread is not a healthy diet for birds, although they do get through tons of the stuff each winter. One of the most successful developments in the bird food industry has been the commercial production of fat-based products. I have had particular success with the cylindrical fat bars that incorporate dried insects. For years I struggled to persuade my local greater spotted woodpecker to visit. My neighbour just a few doors down had much more success until I tried suspending a fat bar on a long wire just outside my window. Now these wonderful, colourful and exciting birds are daily visitors, and I am always thrilled when I hear their unmistakable *chip-chip* call announcing their imminent arrival. Some people also manage to attract woodpeckers by making a suet log. Both the greater and lesser spotted woodpeckers find a great deal of their natural food by working away with their sharp beaks behind the bark of old silver birch trees. If you can get your hands on a couple of feet of birch log – preferably dead and going rotten – then you can provide a tempting lure easily. Just gouge out a hole or two from the log and fill these with a mixture of soft fat and bird seed. Then hang the log vertically so it swings from a convenient branch. This fascination that woodpeckers have for dead birch logs can be a mixed blessing. A friend of mine made the mistake of

**BELOW LEFT** I'm thrilled to see a greater spotted woodpecker outside my window almost every morning. A large fat bar with dried insects seems to be the secret.

**BELOW** A fieldfare eating rotting apples on my garden lawn is a direct ecological link with its breeding grounds, which could be north of the Arctic circle.

**RIGHT** Different foods suit different birds. Great tits seem to be very fond of suet and seeds.

using silver birch for the leg of his bird table. He was thrilled when the local woodpecker began visiting the table regularly, but not so enchanted when it hopped underneath and pecked the post to bits.

One or two other species have a preference for a particular type of food. Robins are passionate about mature cheddar; goldfinches seem to find niger seed irresistible; blackbirds, fieldfares and redwings are at their most contented pecking away at soft over-ripe apples on the lawn. I pester my local fruit shop for bruised fruit from November onwards.

We had a song thrush at one time that was fond of cherries. It would collect them from the back doorstep, flutter off to a safe spot a few feet away, and then roll the fruit around in the dust with its beak, with exactly the same sideways action it used for slugs. When the cherry was suitably scruffy it would swallow it whole, before hopping back for a second helping.

The wild bird feeding business has become extremely sophisticated since the 1980s. Garden bird surveys have shown that the number of different bird species which can be attracted to artificial feeders has

expanded dramatically – from 18 to over 70 in a ten year period – and there seem to be two reasons for this. One is the tragic loss of natural food, particularly in the farming countryside. There are far fewer weed seeds. Fields of stubble have been replaced by year-round cultivation and no-break cropping, and many of the hedgerows, small woodlands and wetlands have gone. Much more positively, the other great influence on garden bird feeding has been the impressive array of foods now on offer to gardeners. Niger seed, dried raisins, fat bars and even live waxworms and wireworms are all available by mail-order. Garden centres are piled high with sacks and packets of wild bird food and even the supermarkets are stocking a range of products – often displayed uncomfortably close to the cat food. Most impressive of all has been the emergence of sunflower hearts as the food of choice for many birds. In my teens I worked on Saturdays in a pet shop, and in those days sunflower seed was sold as 'parrot seed'. There were two types, one black skinned and the other striped, and they were sold exclusively for caged birds. Sometime in the 1980s an experiment showed that

garden birds would take sunflower seed as readily as the much more common peanuts and the research also showed that the black sunflower seeds were strongly preferred to the striped ones. The house sparrows and other seed eaters selected the black seeds for their higher fat content which delivers more energy for the effort involved. Now, sunflower seed dominates the wild bird food market, and the seeds are de-husked mechanically to improve access for the birds and to reduce the mess in the garden. From time to time over the years I have met people who have bird feeders that are failing to attract the birds. Invariably the miracle cure has been a switch to peeled sunflower hearts. They are expensive, but they have an astonishing success rate.

One of the nice things about the various correspondence I have received over the years has been the discovery that bird populations develop local specialities. Presumably the first great tit to discover the delights that lay beneath the milk bottle top was a hyperactive, gifted fledgling. The trick was obviously spotted by the local competition, and caught on with a vengeance. In the early 1980s, one

LEFT This nesting box for Bluetits has a metal protector to make it more difficult for bigger birds to hack their way in.

BELOW Ring-neck parakeets are an introduced species from Africa and Asia. They are spreading rapidly northwards from South-East England and can take over valuable nesting holes from other species.

RIGHT Most of the bats that visit gardens need more than safe site for roosting and for raising their young. You can't have too many bat boxes in and around your garden.

or two gardeners were reporting greenfinches and siskins on their feeders. Now they are widespread regulars. Goldfinches have joined them and every year new records are being established. One correspondent told me of his local jackdaws hanging on seed feeders, and another has skylarks taking food scattered on the ground. Many gardeners in south east England, Amsterdam and other urban areas now have ring-necked parakeets ripping the blossom from their trees and there are seaside gardens where oystercatchers help to aerate the lawn as they probe for worms.

## A SAFE SPOT TO NEST

Nest boxes are the second most popular technique for habitat boosting. In fact in most urban areas there would be few bluetits and great tits around if it wasn't for the artificial nesting sites that we provide. Many of our popular garden birds would naturally nest inside hollow tree trunks, or the cavities in rotten branches. This is true for tiny little birds like the bluetit, and for relative giants such as the green woodpecker and the tawny owl. Our tidy-mindedness and our

preoccupation with public safety have made sure that there are few dead trees, or even dead branches, permitted in town, and so many of our adopted woodland birds have had to adapt a little. Many species of bats also use the same sort of tree sites to roost, breed and hibernate and their numbers have plummeted alarmingly as we have made more and more of them homeless. Bat boxes are more urgently needed than bird boxes these days, since at least two species of these incredible little flying mammals are faced with imminent extinction, and most of the other native species are in steep decline.

## TYPES OF NEST BOX

There is a lot more to nest boxes than you might think. The actual design of the box greatly influences the choice of resident you are likely to attract, and positioning is all-important too. The simplest boxes to build are little more than a flat, open tray – just an artificial ledge for the bird to build on. A piece of wood 10–15cm square, with a 3cm upstand around the edge, is all you need. Fix this little tray about a meter above the ground on a wall or a fence where

it will be camouflaged by the leaves of climbers, and you may attract nesting robins. Fix it a little higher and you may find that blackbirds or song thrushes will use it. This is a good habitat booster to fix in the space you have provided beyond the curtain of climbers on your garden fence or wall. Back in the 1980s, this kind of nest tray would commonly be adopted by a spotted flycatcher, and I used to delay fixing the one in my garden until the end of April, to reserve the space for this charming little migrant. Spotted flycatchers were a delightful feature of my garden for years, and I used to love watching them, perching on their favourite twig, and swooping out to snap flies and butterflies in mid-air. Sadly, they have now become uncommon. They struggle to make the increasingly arduous journey to and from Africa, and they have also been victims of the pesticide revolution. I miss them.

The same platform design can be used to accommodate swallows. This is another migratory species that has suffered much the same fate, but swallows do still arrive in sufficient numbers to mark the start of summer for many people. These superbly streamlined summer visitors nest inside buildings. In the countryside they fly in and out through an open barn door, and often build their modest little mud nest on a rafter or a beam. They are birds of cow pastures and rural meadows and have always been uncommon in towns, but you may just persuade a pair to join you for the summer if you leave the door of the garden shed permanently ajar, and fix the tray up high in a corner, where the swallows have a clear flight path in and out. If the swallows don't find it then robins, wrens and blackbirds are all possible takers.

Most of the tray-nesting birds will also build in open-fronted boxes. These are little more than a basic tray with three sides and a roof, and they are generally sold by the RSPB and others under the name of robin boxes. They don't need so much camouflage as the open tray, but they too are far better placed on a wall than a tree. A whole range of egg and chick thieves are able to climb or land in trees, and the open-fronted box is vulnerable. On a wall the only predator that is still a serious threat is the magpie. Give your box roof a good overhang and make sure there isn't a perch within reach, otherwise the magpies will have the whole nest out in no time.

**BELOW** Birds such as robins, blackbirds and the increasingly rare spotted flycatchers need open-fronted nesting boxes in shady and well-camouflaged locations. They are especially vulnerable to attacks from magpies, grey squirrels and other predators.

**RIGHT** Barn owls are farmland birds, but if your garden is on the edge of open country then a nesting box may be successful.

If you have the right site available, you might like to put up a bigger version of the robin box. Make the nest tray about 40cm square, and allow for about 30cm of headroom. If you put the box high up inside an empty building – say an old Victorian coach house or a warehouse – and position it close to an opening in the wall, you may be lucky enough to attract barn owls. These are the wonderful creamy white hunters that you occasionally spot flapping like giant moths across a country lane in front of your headlights. Many old barns have been replaced by modern weatherproof (and owl-proof) asbestos hangers these days, and the barn owl needs all the help we can provide.

## POSITIONING YOUR BOXES
If you fix your big box to the outside of the building, rather than the inside, there are a couple of species of bird that may use it. Put it high up – even the top of a twenty-storey tower block isn't too far from the ground – and you have a chance of pulling in a pair of kestrels. These magnificent predators became familiar once they staked out their territory along the

rough verges of the motorways. They can be seen hanging menacingly over the small mammal habitat of urban wasteland, too, living up to their lovely old name of wind-hover, and most of the urban kestrels nest high on buildings. A nest box, with a sprinkling of fine gravel on the floor, provides them with the perfect weatherproof shady ledge. Town pigeons will welcome a big box too, if it is a little lower down.

The Peregrine falcon is a third bird of prey that will make use of a building-based nest tray. These superb aerial hunters almost died out in the UK in the second half of the twentieth century, but laws to protect them, a reduction in indiscriminate pesticide use, and the provision of safe nesting sites has seen a remarkable recovery. Pairs of nesting Peregrines are a feature of town halls, church spires and tower blocks all over the country.

The most familiar nest box is a closed box with a small hole in it. The best material is probably unstained and unpreserved rough cut timber, though you can now buy pre-moulded plastic boxes (which may tend to sweat), and boxes made of a moulded mixture of concrete and sawdust are increasingly popular. There

are waxed-paper boxes, terracotta pot ones and all sorts of weird and wonderfully decorated mini-thatched cottages and half-timbered black and white mock-Tudor boxes. The more subdued the nest box is, the better. The name of the game is camouflage, not neon-lit advertisement.

### THE RIGHT FIT

The size of the hole has a great influence on who moves in. Basically, the bigger it is, the greater will be the range of species that can squeeze in, and what tends to happen is that the biggest bird wins. A tiny hole just 3cm in diameter will leave bluetits with sole possession. Go up 5mm in size and great tits can manage to squeeze through, and the bluetits lose control. A 5cm hole opens up the market to sparrows and robins, and if you go any bigger, you are most likely to finish up housing starlings year after year. Woodpeckers do occasionally nest in large 'tit' boxes, and obviously they are well equipped to hack away until the hole is whatever size they need. They usually reserve this particular performance until the box is already occupied, however, and enlarge

BELOW I have kestrels that nest on the roof of a tower block opposite my house. These wonderful birds of prey take readily to open-fronted nesting boxes, and a scattering of gravel in the bottom seems to make them feel at home.

RIGHT Tawny owls are much more common in leafy residential neighbourhoods. They often nest high up in hollow trees, but in town a nesting box positioned high up on a building can provide a welcome alternative.

the hole with the much more sinister intention of gobbling up the eggs or baby birds. If you have the rather colourful problem of robber woodpeckers in your garden, you can thwart a lot of them by reinforcing the hole with a punched-out metal plate, but despite all that head-banging, woodpeckers are far from stupid, and it won't take them long to work out that they can chop out a perfectly adequate hole of their own through the unprotected wood in the other side of the box. The only effective defence is a box made of cement and sawdust, which is one reason

why they are so widely used elsewhere in Europe.

Most box-nesting birds will adjust the entrance hole a little when they decide to move in. This seems to be a part of their territorial marking procedure. There was a great tit in the garden one year that tapped and pecked away all round the hole for days and days, despite the fact that he could squeeze in and out without any difficulty. Nuthatches prefer a hole which starts off being too large, and they reverse the chipping process by narrowing down the opening with a ring of mud until it is just the right size for them. Treecreepers only seem happy nesting in a special wedge-shaped box that presumably feels like the gap behind a loose piece of peeling bark which would be their more natural nest site choice.

Tawny owls will nest in another, much bigger type of box which is known as an owl 'chimney'. This is a long, square 'tube' of wood, open at the top end and with drainage holes at the bottom. It needs to have internal dimensions of about 20cm by 20cm, and be at least 60cm long, and I'm told it also helps if there is a shovelful of compost in the bottom to make it seem more like a hollow rotting branch. If you fix it

## REMARKABLE SWIFTS

I said that swifts were my most inspiring birds. It is partly their wild disregard for humans that I admire. I share the thrill they seem to be enjoying as they scream in high-speed squadrons over the garden, and I envy their tremendous command of the air. It is the story of their life cycle that captivates me, though. When the two eggs hatch, the parents feed the young with thousands of insects and spiders caught on the wing. In bad weather a pair of parent swifts will travel hundreds of kilometres to hunt for food, which they store in a sticky ball in their throat, and the young have evolved to survive for several days without food during their parents' hunting absences. Eventually the fledglings venture to the mouth of the nest hole, and with all the courage of a first-time parachutist, launch themselves into the air. There is no time for practising. You either fly or you have had it, and amazingly those young birds will not land again for two years.

The only time that swifts land is when they have eggs to lay and young to feed, and it takes two years to reach maturity. In that time the young birds will fly over 800,000 kilometres, nipping over to Hungary or to Denmark for a couple of days of rich feeding if the insects are a bit sparse at home, and climbing thousands of metres up into the sky each evening, to glide effortlessly on the wing, and sleep through the hours of darkness.

The most incredible thing of all is that each year the newly-fledged young birds leave for Africa a couple of weeks ahead of their parents. They find their own way south of the Sahara or beyond the Nile, with no help from Mum, and they then find their own way back to our street the following May. The idea that by spending half an hour one winter evening knocking up a nest box I might be privileged enough to play a small part in that miracle is one of the things that makes attracting wildlife exciting for me. Even if I don't succeed in providing nesting accommodation, I get a great kick out of sharing the midges from my pond and the butterflies from the meadow with long-distance travellers such as swifts, swallows, house martins, chiffchaffs and willow warblers.

securely on top of a sturdy branch, preferably with a slight slope and at least 10m above the ground, you may have the great privilege of being kept awake night after night by lovesick screech owls practicing their horror-movie sound effects outside your bedroom window.

## LONG-DISTANCE VISITORS
Swifts give me more pleasure than any other bird I know. They seem to symbolise everything that is wild and free, and they have an incredible lifestyle. They spend our winter months in central Africa, feeding on flying insects above the forest canopy in the Congo, but they breed in northern Europe, and return with miraculous accuracy to the building where they themselves were hatched. There is colony of swifts in my neighbourhood, and over a period of 25 years I have watched their numbers decline from about 50 pairs in the early 1990s, to the tiny handful of half a dozen birds that still manage to make the 12,000 kilometre round trip. In the first week of May each year I hold my breath and wait to hear the first heart-stopping scream of my first returner. The European swift is one of the wild species that has adopted high

manmade buildings as their primary nesting habitat. They nest in the roof space, and need access through a small entry hole under the eaves or beneath the roof tiles themselves. Improved insulation, the use of roofing felt barriers and a general improvement in building maintenance have rendered many traditional swift nesting sites inaccessible, mine included. I have done something about that. Swifts need something rather similar to an owl chimney on its side, with both ends blocked off and a narrow, 2.5cm slot under the front end for the birds to fly up and in to. I have fixed these under the eaves of the house. At the beginning of August every year the young, newlyfledged swifts flutter all around the house, presumably searching under the eaves for holes which they can return to for egg-laying a couple of years later. In a number of towns and cities, new swift colonies have been successfully established, much against the trend, and one key to their effectiveness has been technological. It seems that when a recording of the sound of swifts is played, ideally from within the roof itself, this is registered by potential colonisers as a sure sign that the building and its boxes are fit for purpose.

House martins have a different approach to nesting. They build their own solid little mud hut, glued tightly to the underside of a windowsill or a roof overhang. They seem to build mostly on new houses, and one probable reason must be the plentiful supply of wet mud to be found on building sites. I get house martins collecting mud from the edge of the pond, but they fly straight past my desirable residence and insist on building above the bay window of the semi down the road. I have put up a number of off-the-peg pre-cast concrete martin boxes over the years. They look convincing to me, and since house martins

**ABOVE** A few artificial nesting cups may help to establish a new colony of house martins at your house. They work best when fixed under the eaves against a white background.

**RIGHT** A sturdy house gives added protection when the hedgehog is hibernating, but a well-built pile of logs and leaves will also do the job.

seem to like building little colonies of mud nests I hoped that, even if they didn't occupy the nest boxes, they might build one or two of their own on the same wall – but so far nothing has happened. I read somewhere that damage to last year's nest is thought to trigger the returning birds' nest-building instinct, so I have snapped a few lumps off my concrete in the hope that the birds might have read the same article, but I have a funny suspicion that they just watch my desperate measures with mild, muddy amusement. The frustrating thing is that the chap down the road, whose house is a veritable holiday camp for house martins, can't stand the mess they make – and keeps knocking the nests off with a stick.

### HOMES FOR CREATURES BIG AND SMALL

Birds aren't the only wild creatures you can persuade to move into artificial homes. You can set up tempting potential residences for a whole host of animals, from large mammals such as the fox and the hedgehog down to tiny creatures like solitary bees and hunting spiders. The secret is to use your imagination. Try and think of yourself as an earwig looking for somewhere to hibernate, or a queen bee on the hunt for a suitable new nest site. Think yourself into the role of a pregnant vixen looking for just the right secluded spot in which to have her litter of cubs. If you can think this way as you build up your wildlife garden, you will find yourself incorporating all kinds of extra 'wildlife opportunities' – little wrinkles in the landscape that you think might appeal to some home-hunting plant or animal.

Urban foxes are well known for living under garden sheds. They need a nice dry, shallow hole which is safe, and which ideally offers at least two exits. If you are putting in a new shed, you have a choice to make. Do you put it on a floor of solid concrete, and rule out any chance of housing foxes, or do you opt for a shed with a timber floor, and set it on foundations of railway sleepers or concrete footings, allowing for a gap beneath the shed which might be adopted?

There are some fanciful designs around for 'hedgehog houses'. They are fun to play about with

if you have time, but you can create a pretty useful hibernating site much more simply by piling three or four substantial logs together so that they create a hedgehog-sized hole, and then covering the whole structure with masses of leaves and dead twigs.

CREATE A DRY-STONE AND EARTH BANK
One useful way of concentrating a variety of mini-homes or niches together in one spot is to build a dry-stone and earth bank. Stack stones randomly

## HOLEY HABITATS

A lot of insects lay their eggs in tiny, narrow holes. Wood wasps make their homes in log piles at the woodland edge, a few beetles are wood-boring by nature, and solitary bees are fascinating little creatures that will occupy other insects' vacated holes. You can simulate this tiny niche by drilling lots of holes in the logs, or in your fence posts, perhaps. Some of the species will also oblige by occupying the holes created when you tie a bundle of drinking straws together and block up one end. Hang your little bundles under ledges and overhangs and wait for the insects to investigate. Custom-built bundles of holes are widely marketed as 'bug-hotels' and it is good to see garden centres and other commercial suppliers taking the habitat needs of such small creatures seriously. However, there is no need

to pay a small fortune for a bundle of hollow straws and sections of bamboo cane. You can easily make your own.

to form a double-sided wall, with a space in the centre. Keep incorporating layers of soil and fill the middle in too. Make sure you leave lots of little holes through the stone facing which lead to bigger gaps in the centre. A whole range of pretty wildflowers favour wall habitats. Herb robert is a favourite of mine – a small member of the cranesbill family with a cut leaf and red stems. Stonecrop (*Sedum acre*) will quickly spread along the earth joints, and cover the stone bank with its little yellow star-shaped flowers in summer. Harebells (*Campanula rotundifolia*), ivy-leaved toadflax and primroses will all thrive, and if it is fairly shady and not too dry, a whole range of lovely native ferns can be persuaded to become established, too.

You will quickly find the creepy-crawly end of the animal world moving into your bank. There are lots of nooks and crannies to hide in, and hunting spiders, woodlice and ants will be there in no time. If you pack one or two of the inner cavities with old nesting material from a mouse cage you will be providing irresistible conditions for queen bumblebees to occupy, and you can create several bee nest sites

elsewhere in the garden, by burying clay plant pots in banks and shrub beds, so that just the hole in the bottom is visible. If more mouse bedding is stuffed inside these pots, you should have bees flying busily in and out of the drainage hole by mid-summer.

## MAKING THE MOST OF A BRICK WALL

If you look closely at old brickwork, you will often discover that it is extensively colonised by all kinds of things. New brickwork takes a long time to acquire its 'hangers-on', but you can speed up the process easily. Take a masonry drill and bore a few holes in the mortar. In no time you will find the entrance to these man-made tunnels decorated by a swirl of gossamer, and a light brush with a feather will bring the resident spider rushing out. Old walls also support lots of the lower forms of plant life, such as algae and liverworts, and in the relatively unpolluted atmosphere of modern towns and cities, we are again beginning to see lots of lichens. You can have an impact on the rate of colonisation if you paint a coat of 'magic mixture' on the surface of the brick. My particular brew is made of a thin flour and milk paste, souped-

LEFT Wild primroses need the shade, but can be encouraged to colonise stone walls and steep banks.

BELOW LEFT The native harebell is a plant that grows particularly well with its roots in the tough conditions of a stone bank.

BELOW Nooks and crannies turn a wall into a wildlife habitat. Use your imagination and almost any building material that comes to hand.

up with just a dash of cow slurry or bottled liquid manure. Initially you will probably be rewarded with nothing more interesting than a crop of dull mould, but within a month or two you will begin to see the surface patterns change, and if you compare treated and untreated walls you will realise how much effect you have had.

BE CREATIVE

There is no end to the ways in which you can enhance the garden habitats. A sheet of old corrugated iron laid out in the mini-meadow will heat up in the sun and could well accommodate slow worms as well as the more predictable centipedes and beetles. A chunk of paving slab in the woodland edge will often be used by ants as a lid to their underground nest. I used a spare corner of butyl pond liner to create a tiny little artificial puddle among the logs. This is now completely overgrown with deadnettle and grasses, but amazingly enough each generation of tiny little frogs that emerges from the main pond seems to head instinctively for the little bit of shady dampness, crossing lawn and meadow to get there.

I have counted as many as forty of these perfect miniatures in an area not much larger than a couple of dinner plates.

Some friends have a small walled yard, with nowhere in which to create a leaf-litter habitat, or anything resembling a woodland edge. They had the bright idea of fixing a panel of several different planks of wood to form a kind of sculpture just an inch or so proud of the wall. Visitors admire this piece of 'modern art' but the real magic of their creation is the colony of bats that roost behind the boarding, and the range of wasps and other wood-boring creatures that are gradually perforating the timber.

Do be inventive. Do think about the way wildlife will use your garden, and if you see some creature making unorthodox use of one of your artificial aids, so much the better. A good many bird nesting boxes are used by hibernating moths, butterflies and bats in the winter. The hole I left in the brickwork of my patio wall, as a 'perfect nesting site for wrens' has been occupied each year by bees, and both bees and wasps will regularly colonise bird nesting boxes. The bark chippings I put down to suppress the weed

BELOW Imagine that you are a small wild creature in search of a safe hiding place. The more shelter you provide, the greater the range of wildlife you will be able to support.

problem have proved tremendously successful as a hunting ground for the perfectly camouflaged hunting spiders. Even the half-brick-sized gap I cursed the builder for leaving under the eaves of the extension has been put to good use. For two years in a row the little cock wren has built there. The first year his mate turned down the accommodation in favour of one of the alternatives he had on offer. The second year, though, she graciously moved in and succeeded in raising a fine brood of six beautiful babies.

**ABOVE** Something as simple as an upturned clay plant pot can provide protection for creatures such as toads.

## AT THE BOTTOM OF THE GARDEN

There is one final habitat booster that should find a place in everybody's garden. That is the compost heap. We all produce mountains of waste greenery every year. Cabbage leaves, potato peel, weed seedlings, the excess waterweed from the pond all make wonderful compost if you allow time for them to rot down. Composting is so much better than burning and binning your green waste. The ideal spot for a compost heap is in a shady corner, out of sight of the house, but reasonably convenient for deliveries of kitchen waste. You need some sort of perforated container – either well-spaced timber planking, or well-staked netting, and the bottom of the heap should rest on the soil. You must make sure plenty of air is able to circulate around the heap, and you may need to protect it against heavy rain with a tarpaulin or a sheet of polythene if the heap is out in the open. The softer material will rot down the fastest. Twiggy material – hedge clippings and rose prunings, for example – is better stacked separately or used to make hibernation habitat. A heap built up through the summer should be turned into sweet-smelling crumbly compost and ready to use the following spring.

The whole business of compost-making relies entirely on the vigorous activity of plant and animal life, and that is what makes a compost heap such a marvellous asset in the wildlife garden. Most of the actual organisms of decay are minute – far too small to be seen with the naked eye – but you can tell they are at work by the way they generate heat, and on a chilly morning you may see wisps of steam rising from a well-constructed compost heap. There are larger decomposers too. If you pull back the top layer of your heap you will find a network of white filaments of fungal mycelia, and you will also see a whole host of different creepy-crawlies. Some of them, most noticeably the bright red little worms, are living directly on the dead plant material, and breaking it down to a size that the smaller microorganisms can cope with, but there will be lots of predators in your compost heap, too. There will be beetles and centipedes, and a number of other fast-moving wriggly creatures, eating up the smaller organisms of decay and feeding on any bits of animal remains that you add to the heap.

With so much going on, it is not surprising to find that the compost heap becomes an important 'fast food section' of your service station wildlife garden. Some of the bigger creatures may spend almost the whole time there. You are likely to have a fat, contented toad or two living in the moist warmth of the heap, gorging themselves on some of the hardworking slugs, and your resident hedgehog may move into the compost corner too, at least for the

BELOW Reptiles such as grass snakes and slow worms are surprisingly common in gardens, and they particularly welcome the warm, damp interior of a compost heap.

RIGHT A well organised heap of twigs and other woody garden waste will provide excellent habitat and gradually decompose to form usable compost.

summer, starting each evening's ramble with a tasty compost-grown snack before moving off around the rest of the garden.

## COMPOST HEAP INHABITANTS

The heat generated by the compost heap is an important feature of the habitat. It speeds up the rate of decomposition, but it also provides ideal conditions for one or two of our more delicate wild animals to breed in. Slow worms in particular like to give birth to their tiny babies in the warmth of a compost heap, and grass snakes often lay their eggs there. Both of these creatures are perfectly harmless and marvellous additions to your wildlife garden. The grass snakes may get through a few of your frogs and toads, and being spectacular swimmers they can also catch small fish occasionally, but the slow worm has a diet made up mainly of slugs and worms, and does nothing but good. Both of these creatures are persecuted in the wild, largely by people who simply think all 'snakes' are deadly poisonous. If you build a compost heap, put in a pond, leave some of the lawn a little longer and stack the odd log pile around in your shrubbery, you will be providing the ideal habitat for slow worms and grass snakes to visit and to stay, and your garden will become a safe sanctuary for two increasingly rare and handsome wild creatures. If your patch is too small for the relative untidiness of a traditional compost heap, then don't despair. On a trip to Sweden many years ago I learned that composting can be a much more tightly contained activity. For dealing with kitchen waste, rather than the bulkier garden generated waste, a wormery is ideal. Worms work in the dark, with much less need for ventilation than a traditional garden compost heap,

so it is possible to carry out your waste reduction in a smart plastic container, and worm bins seem to be a feature of almost every Scandinavian balcony and patio garden. I have had a big worm bin for almost thirty years. It takes all my kitchen waste, and the occasional harvest of surplus slime and vegetation from my garden pond. It never smells. It is entirely trouble free and it looks respectable.

## PRECIOUS PEAT

There is one particularly compelling reason to compost. You will generate your own alternative to peat for mulching the flower beds. The peat which we can buy in plastic sacks from DIY stores and garden centres is all excavated from endangered wildlife habitat. Peat bogs are among our most precious wildlife communities, and anything that gardeners can do to save them must be worth the effort. In the years since I made my first wildlife garden at Chelsea Flower Show, back in the mid-1980s, the horticultural industry has been persuaded to take alternatives to peat-based composts much more seriously. Many local councils now compost

municipal green waste, and there are a great many peat substitutes available to buy. This continues to be a successful environmental campaign, and home composting is an ideal way in which almost every gardener can make a difference.

Our native bluebell offers intense colour, delicate form and the most intoxicating perfume. They are the stars of my own wildlife garden every May.

11

# PROPAGATING NATIVE PLANTS

NATIVE PLANTS are the basic ingredients which turn your garden into a rich habitat for wildlife. The choice of species is enormous. Hundreds of different types of wildflowers, shrubs and trees grow wild in our countryside. Some of them are common, and some are extremely rare. Since I first began writing about wildlife gardening, many of the most attractive native plants have become widely available and can be bought off the shelf in garden centres. The growing public interest in them has created a market and the horticultural nursery trade has responded enthusiastically. Nevertheless if you want a garden full of wildflowers it makes good sense to grow some of them yourself.

It has always been possible to buy native trees and shrubs without too much trouble. Species like hazel, silver birch and beech have been grown commercially for years and even the less garden-suitable native shrubs such as field maple, wild rose and goat willow have been grown on a vast scale for planting on motorway embankments, countryside projects and in the more enlightened of local authorities' parks. Often you will find that these 'native' trees and shrubs

are in fact imported, and therefore not ideal for habitat creation. Wholesale nurseries in the UK will often buy in plants directly from Holland, Germany or eastern Europe. Even when the plants are home-grown, the nursery often uses imported seed, so your 'English alder', your elderberry or your silver birch could well be a European subspecies. In the 1990s, over 60 per cent of all 'English' oaks were grown from acorns harvested in Eastern Europe. Do ask your nursery sales manager for home-grown plants from indigenous seed stock. If enough people ask, and then explain the significance of native plants for nature conservation, eventually the nursery industry will get the message and supply the goods.

## BUYING FROM NURSERIES

There are a growing number of nurseries which specialise in growing native wildflowers. They are mostly fairly small, and some of them are extremely good. In the early days I had to buy most of my pot-grown wildflowers from nurseries in Somerset and Nottinghamshire, but it has gradually become possible to source the plants much more locally.

This is important because there are subtle genetic variations in our native wildflowers, determined by local conditions, and it is good to avoid mixing regional variations if at all possible. The seeds of wildflowers are increasingly easy to come by, but again foreign stock is widespread. This can be a serious problem, as the foreign strain of some of our wildflowers is much more vigorous than the native type, and if we start sprinkling the super-seedlings around our towns and villages, some of the plants are certain to escape. In the worst cases, such introductions could well overwhelm the indigenous stock or weaken their natural resistance to local pests and diseases. The more responsible seed houses are particular about this point. They go to great pains to obtain seed from truly native wildflowers wherever they can, and if it proves impossible and they have to resort to a foreign seed source, then they make this clear, both in their catalogues and on the packets. There is not much risk in a town garden in the heart of the city, but if your wildlife garden is in a rural village, or even the leafy suburbs, do try and restrict your seed purchases exclusively to native stock.

Most of the specialist nurseries will ship seeds and pot-grown seedlings through the post, so it is worth sending off for the catalogues or checking them out online. There is a short list of recommended seed suppliers and specialist wildflower nurseries at the back of the book.

GROW YOUR OWN

Of course, packets of seed and nursery-grown potted plants are the easy way – but however conscientious your suppliers are, the best way to stock your wildlife garden is by growing your own plants, using the seed of wild plants which are not just native to your country, but native to your own local landscape. These are truly indigenous plants, and they will be intimately locked into the local climate, soil type and the indigenous wildlife. Ideally, local wildflowers, trees and shrubs should be the source of your wildlife garden plants, but you must *never* dig up any wild plant and move it to your garden, however common it might seem to be. Wild plants are protected by the law, and that law is there for a good reason. Digging up wild plants will eventually lead to their

LEFT Simple snowdrops are an ideal addition to your carpet of spring woodland wildflowers. The bulbs are best transplanted in the green, just after the flowers have faded.

BELOW It has become relatively easy to buy nursery-grown wildflowers such as these cowslips.

RIGHT This is the seed head of field scabious, one of the many wildflowers now available in garden centres.

disappearance in the wild. As a wildlife gardener your aim should be to provide an *extra* habitat, not simply to rob one in order to create another.

Fortunately, it is easy to grow new plants without harming the parent plant growing in the wild. The simple secret is to collect seed, or in a few cases to take a cutting or two. For a number of especially rare wildflowers it is illegal to remove any part of these plants, and that includes the seeds. Obviously when a colony becomes small it needs all the seed each plant produces, in order to maintain its own numbers. As a general rule, you should not collect your propagation material from plants which are growing on their own. Try and find a big, healthy colony of the wildflower or shrub, and collect seed or cuttings from there. That way you are much less likely to do any harm. Collect the smallest amount of seed you can, and once you have taken seed from the wild, do make sure you use it. It is a terrible waste to pick seed and then leave it unsown. One useful development in recent years has been the harvesting of wildflower seeds by conservation organisations such as the Wildlife Trusts. Many of them are using their best established nature reserves as a source of seeds for establishing new habitats. The *Jubilee Meadows* programme, started as a partnership between HRH the Prince of Wales and the network of County Wildlife Trusts is a particularly successful example.

As wildlife gardens become more popular, there will be less and less need to collect seed and cuttings from the wild. Wildlife gardeners are increasingly able to exchange seed – and whole plants for that matter – and when such plant exchanges become commonplace those wildflowers will definitely be safe from extinction.

## SOURCING YOUR WILDFLOWER SEED

When it comes to collecting, do avoid raiding the special habitats. You don't need to plant rare wildflowers at all. There are some common ones which make wonderfully colourful border flowers such as yellow toadflax, purple toadflax, knapweed, hawkweed, and ox-eye daisy. A lot of these you can find growing on urban wasteland. I have collected most of the wild seed for my flower garden from plants growing in the brick rubble and abandoned

BELOW However tempting, please, never dig up plants from the wild. Thanks to seed houses and plant nurseries there is no need, and it's against the law.

BOTTOM Knapweed, or hardhead, is a tough meadow wildflower that often grows on uncut road verges. Harvesting a single seed head will enable you to start your own colony.

LEFT Yellow rattle is one wildflower that really helps if you are planning to create a mini-meadow. Once established, it suppresses the grasses and gives the wildflowers a better chance.

LEFT BELOW For the edge of the pond, flowering rush is a magnificent choice.

grassland of a few urban wild spaces close to home.

You do need to go to the appropriate wild habitat in order to collect seed of the more specialised wildflowers, of course. Again, you should avoid nature reserves at all costs, and don't take from small pockets of habitat, either. Most of my wetland species have been grown from seed collected along a weedy stretch of derelict canal in the Black Country. Flag iris, flowering rush, burr reed, water plantain, lesser spearwort and water mint all grow there in abundance, and the seed heads are easy to get at. The greater spearwort and ragged robin came from a patch of canal-side marshland which was unfortunately being tipped on, and I think that is perhaps the one time when it is permissible to dig up a whole plant. You must get permission from the owners first, though, and you should also contact your County Wildlife Trust, to tell them what you plan to do. If the plants are about to be destroyed completely, then it seems silly not to transplant them, but do make sure there is nothing you can do to stop the development first. The best place for wild plants to grow is the place where they have always grown. Your garden should be seen as second best.

If it is seed of meadow plants you need, you may find that your local County Wildlife Trust is harvesting meadow nature reserves, and selling seed to the public. Alternatively, see if you can find a local road verge that has plenty of wildflowers. Since highway authorities began to economise by mowing verges less frequently, some of the green reservations and embankments have begun to blossom. On the deeper soils you will tend to find fairly vigorous wildflowers such as teasels, cow parsley and thistle, but on the poorer thinner soils, there is often a whole kaleidoscope of colourful meadow flowers. On one local patch of steep embankment I have collected seed of ox-eye daisy, knapweed, yellow rattle, lady's bedstraw, yarrow, purple vetch, field scabious, wild carrot, meadow buttercup and bird's-foot trefoil, as well as several of the prettier dwarf grasses. This little roadside community must have arrived as seed in a lorry load of soil when the road was first built, and despite my selective harvesting, the spread of wildflowers grows bigger every year.

Another obvious place to collect meadow flower seed ought to be the local park. The green revolution has been slow to take off, but some park keepers are beginning to manage their green deserts as meadows once again. In the future I hope there will be great summer seed-gathering parties, with lots of eager wildlife gardeners harvesting a couple of cowslip seed heads here, or a fritillary seed there. For the time being, though, we must restrict our seed gathering to the more common wildflowers on those accessible bits of grassland that have somehow escaped the mower and the herbicide.

**LEFT, TOP AND ABOVE**
Some seed heads are spectacular. The seeds of meadow cranesbill are flicked into pastures new from these enchanting seed heads, yellow flag iris scatters its big brown floating seeds into water for dispersal, and carrot flowers curl in on themselves to form ideal protection for ladybirds.

BELOW Meadowsweet's seed head may not be much to look at, but it appeals to flocks of seed eaters.

BOTTOM By contrast the large, perfectly formed clock of goat's beard is an architectural masterpiece, seen here among yellow rattle and knapweed in a late summer meadow.

## FINDING WOODLAND WILDFLOWERS

Woodland wildflowers are rather more difficult. Flowery woodlands are now sadly few and far between, and they all obviously belong to somebody. It isn't advisable simply to crash into the nearest wood and start snipping away at the bluebell seed pods. I suggest that first of all you contact both the local Parks Department and the County Wildlife Trust, and ask them if they manage any woodlands where you might be allowed to collect a little seed. Look out, too, for rich old hedgerows. You may not find primroses or wood anemones there, but you can often find the less choosy species such as campion, bluebell and foxglove, and you will be able to tell easily whether or not the hedgerow community can stand the loss of a few dozen seeds.

## TREES AND SHRUBS FROM SEED

You can grow trees and shrubs from seed, too, and huge numbers of people now treat this personally. I was involved in launching the *Trees of Time and Place* campaign around the turn of the millennium. Many thousands of people gathered seeds from a tree that

had been special to them in the last century, grew a seedling, and planted it for the future. Although it may seem easier and quicker to root a cutting, seed propagation is better, because it gives you a bit of variety among the resulting plants, and that makes your habitat look more natural. You may be tempted to take cuttings from a hawthorn bush because it has a particularly heavy crop of fruit each year, or because you like the pink tint in its May blossom — but if you take cuttings, every one of the resulting plants will be identical, and you will lose the interest that seedling variation brings. Hawthorn cuttings are also surprisingly difficult to propagate.

The general rule with the seeds of most species seems to be to collect them when they have just reached ripeness, and to sow them straight away. Certainly that is the case with acorns, for example, and it also seems to help with the germination of a number of notoriously difficult wildflowers.

## GERMINATION

Where the seed is enclosed in a fleshy fruit, the presence of the flesh often builds up an inhibiting factor in the seed it contains, and for a number of plants that inbuilt resistance to germination is 'unlocked' when the fruit is digested by a bird or a mammal, and the stripped seed is then excreted. Hawthorn, for example, is a difficult seed to germinate until it has been part digested by a bird. If you are propagating from fleshy fruit — and the common examples would be bramble, elderberry, rose hip, hawthorn, rowan, cherry, crab apple, sloe, yew, honeysuckle and guelder rose — extract the seed from the fruit pulp as soon as you can. For a small number of seedlings you can do that easily by squeezing the individual

fruit until the seeds pop out. For larger quantities you can use a fruit juice extractor, in which case most of the tough little seeds will survive. Alternatively the juicier, edible fruits can be used to make wine or jelly, and the seed can then be extracted by drying the resulting pulp. I can't think of a better excuse for making elderberry or blackberry wine. No one will believe you simply did it for the seeds!

A great many seeds do incorporate a delaying mechanism which can stop them germinating for several years in some cases. Sometimes this inhibition is caused by chemicals, as seems to be the case with the pulp fruit seeds, and sometimes there is simply a tough coating around the seeds which has to be penetrated by moisture before germination can take place.

## TOUGHER SEEDS

If the seed looks tough, or if you have experienced difficulty in the past, it is well worth encouraging more rapid germination by using various techniques known collectively as stratifying. The easiest stratification method of all I described earlier in the book. Simply sow the seed in a mixture of sand and grit in a pot or box. Put this outside in a cold, exposed position and let the worst of the icy winter weather break down the barriers. As an alternative, where seeds have a particularly tough outer skin you can try physically damaging this by rubbing the seeds between sheets of sandpaper, so that the shiny surface is scratched. Alternatively, for big seeds such as some of the vetches, you can nick each seed with a penknife, or scrape away a groove with a nail file. This is a technique that has always been used by gardeners to trigger the germination of tough-skinned sweet pea seeds. A dilute acid is a useful way of breaking the inhibition, though you have to be careful not to overdo it. The easiest weak acid for most of us to use is vinegar. There are one or two plant species that need high temperatures rather than low ones to help them germinate. These are the plants that often seem to colonise burnt areas. Gorse is a good example, and its shiny pea-like seeds are notoriously difficult to germinate. You can immerse the seeds in hot water, but I think it is more fun to put the seed in a twist of newspaper, and then set fire to it. Foresters use the same technique for preparing the seed of lodgepole pine (*Pinus contorta*), a North American

BELOW Yew's seeds and foliage are both poisonous, which is one reason they were grown in churchyards away from livestock. The soft sticky fruits are a favourite with thrushes, and they excrete the poisonous seeds without harm.

RIGHT Although the early white blossom on the bare twigs is beautiful, and sloe gin is undoubtedly a bonus, blackthorn spreads rapidly and is very difficult to control.

RIGHT BELOW Crab apples come in various shapes, sizes and fruit colours, but I love the wild crab of hedgerows.

OPPOSITE It is hard to believe that this germinating acorn could grow into a giant oak tree that could live for many hundreds of years.

ABOVE *Viburnum opulus*, the guelder rose. There are a number of attractive native shrubs that bear heavy crops of autumn fruits.

pioneer of ground cleared by forest fires, and many of the wonderful garden plants that originate in the burned fynbos landscapes of the South African Cape are propagated in the same way.

POTTING ON

Sowing and growing-on is just the same for wild plants as for anything else. In order to germinate, all seed needs adequate air, moisture and warmth. A peat free compost mixed with plenty of sand and grit, shallow sowing and light watering from below will satisfy that requirement. Once germination has taken place, high humidity is important, to stop the delicate little seedlings drying out. A polythene bag supported as a mini-greenhouse over the top of the pot of seedlings is usually all that is needed, and plenty of light is essential if the seedlings are not to grow straggly and weak. Woodland species will benefit from a bit less light than meadow and wasteland species. Wetland wildflowers will obviously need much more water, and a little leaf mould seems to help with woodland species, too. Patience is an important ingredient in this. Many seeds need a period of cold before they will germinate and even then it may be several seasons before some of the seed germinates. Don't throw the pots away in disgust.

## TAKING CUTTINGS

You may decide to propagate one or two plants vegetatively. Perhaps you have found a particularly sweet and juicy crop of blackberries, and you don't want to run the risk of producing a tasteless, seedy offspring from seed. Perhaps you only want one or two plants and simply don't fancy the fiddling about with seed propagation. Since different plants vary in their requirements I suggest that you consult the RHS website for precise advice. Most of the climbers, shrubs and trees are best grown from softwood cuttings. Wait until mid-June, choose a vigorous, non-flowering side shoot, peel it off the main stem, take off the lower leaves, and stick it peeled end down into the side of a pot of gritty soil. Put a poly bag over the top to keep the air humid, and stand the pot in a saucer out of the sun so you can keep the compost moist, but not wet. The cutting should produce roots within a week or two, and once it shows signs of growing, pot it on, or plant it out.

**BELOW LEFT** If you are harvesting seed such as this yellow rattle, use a paper bag. Plastic is likely to suffocate and rot the seeds.

**BELOW RIGHT** When rooted cuttings and seedlings are large enough to handle, plant them out or move them into bigger pots.

## LAYERING

For climbers and more straggly shrubs, you might try layering. Instead of taking the cutting from the parent plant, bend a healthy growing stem right over, anchor the tip of the shoot to the soil, and leave it there until it roots. Once the tip produces a new plantlet you can cut through the old stem and transplant the new offspring. This is a good way of propagating honeysuckle, wild rose and blackberry.

## DIVIDE AND MULTIPLY

Once you have clumps of wildflowers established in your wildlife garden, you can help many of them

to multiply quickly by digging them up, dividing them and replanting the plantlets. The procedure is described clearly in every book about herbaceous borders. Some clumps will be easy to split. Primroses can be teased into smaller plants with fingers and thumbs, and the waterside plants tend to be easy to split. For the bigger, toughest clumps, lift them in late summer or early spring, and force the whole mass of roots apart by using a couple of garden forks. I find it helps to soak the plant in a bucket of water to soften the soil, and so long as you replant immediately, the divided clumps will benefit much from being split up and spread out every few years.

## YOUR SELF-SEEDING GARDEN

If your habitats are working, once the various appropriate wildflowers are established, you will probably find your garden is generating a mass of seedlings for other people to use. In only its second season I was able to collect dozens of seedlings from my woodland edge and my marsh habitat. Once you begin to recognise the leaf shape of seedlings such as meadowsweet, ragged robin, pink campion, primrose and violet, you will be able to make good use of them,

**BELOW LEFT** Scrambling plants such as this clematis, brambles and honeysuckle can be propagated by pinning down a stem until it grows new roots.

**BELOW RIGHT** In early summer I split the larger clumps of primroses, space out and replant most of them and give a few away to friends.

instead of simply pulling them out as weeds. Perhaps one of the most useful things you could do for nature conservation is to pot up a range of your garden-grown wildflower seedlings each year, and offer them to your local County Wildlife Trust. They will be able to sell them to other would-be wildlife gardeners, and your efforts will kill three birds with one stone. You will avoid being overrun, the wildflowers will be established in yet another safe patch of garden and the Trust will raise some cash to help with other important aspects of nature conservation.

## 12

Much of our wildlife is mobile and needs a network of interconnected habitats. For example, hawker dragonflies will breed and spend their early years in a pond, but the adults will hunt over meadows and along the sheltering habitat of hedgerows.

# A RICH TAPESTRY OF WILDLIFE

SO FAR I have tended to talk about the wild plants and animals as if they are locked into one habitat or another. In fact, so far as the animals in your wildlife garden are concerned, the interchange *between* habitats is critical too. Build your pond in the centre of a sea of tarmac, and the variety of wildlife it could support would be extremely limited. The snails would be okay, and one or two of the long-distance flying insects would make it backwards and forwards across the wasteland, but the frogs and the newts, the toads and the less adventurous migratory insects would be lost. They need much more than the pond itself if they are to survive and complete their life cycles.

## A RANGE OF HABITATS

In the short term you may be able to rely on borrowing wildlife from outside your garden, but it is important to work towards providing a variety of different habitats of your own, which will complement one another. Watch your resident robin for a few minutes. He will spend most of his time in the woodland edge or the hedgerow, with his chestnut-brown back camouflaging him against the leaf shade. His song will tell you where to look. The minute you appear with your garden fork he will be down at your feet, head cocked on one side, waiting to pounce on anything that wriggles as you begin to dig. Watch for a little while, and sooner or later you will see him flutter over to the pond for a drink, or nip across to the compost heap for a quick dig around after mini-beasts. When it comes to the breeding season the robin will patrol his territory aggressively, singing at the top of his voice, and again the woodland edge will provide a useful song perch, but for nest sites the robin needs dense undergrowth, and the hedge bottom and the climber-covered fence become important. Generally speaking, a pair of robins will occupy about a half hectare of suburban gardens, but without the range of habitats I have just described, they may need to push out the boundaries, and you might have to share your robins with dozens of your neighbours.

By contrast, wrens and dunnocks are far less adventurous, and seem hardly ever to stray from the hedge bottom and the woodland edge. Blackbirds are woodland birds, and certainly they spend a great

LEFT Robins are birds of woodland glades and disturbed ground, so they will have been associated with humans for millennia. No wonder they are so fearless.

BELOW Muntjac deer are relatively recent incomers to Britain, but their ability to creep through suburbia by night has meant that they are now remarkably common garden visitors.

RIGHT Foxes have found sanctuary in the parks and gardens of suburbia. They will cover a sizable territory and are well adapted to travel around the habitat networks of towns and cities.

deal of time scratching around amongst the leaf litter of the woodland edge, but they also like to feed on the lawn area. I watch them pacing attentively from one spot to the next listening intently, and then stabbing with their beaks and dragging out another poor unsuspecting earthworm. Song thrushes hunt for snails among the ivy and the woodland edge undergrowth, but usually brings them out into the sunshine to smash the shell on a makeshift anvil. In the nesting season the pond becomes a crucial part of their total environment, since songthrushes line their nests with mud.

## LONG-DISTANCE TRAVELLERS

Some of the big dragonflies that visit the pond to breed and lay their eggs travel around a good deal. The hawkers are probably the most spectacular, and they eat hundreds of small insects every day. Although the nymph spends all of its two or three years in the water, munching its way through tadpoles all spring and summer, the adult hunts by flying mainly along the woodland edge and the more overgrown hedgerows. In fact, it is presumably this widespread

hunting which brings hawkers into contact with new ponds so quickly. Even when they are jerking around a half--metre or so above my pond, they constantly sweep off over the meadow to snatch up a fly or midge that catches their eye. I have even seen the brown hawker catch a cabbage white butterfly on the wing, and then retire to a twig of the nearby apple tree, nip off the white wings which flutter to the ground, and then chew its way through the body.

## INCREASING DIVERSITY

When I first created each of my wildlife gardens I was amazed by the amount of wildlife that arrived almost immediately, and it just keeps getting better. My notebook confirms it, of course, but just a casual glance out of the window at any time of the year leaves me in no doubt that the garden is full of life. Obviously, it is the big creatures that you notice first, and one of my biggest visitors has been a muntjac deer. This is tiny by deer standards, in fact much the same size as a fox, but it is a bit of a shock to glance out and see a beautiful wild creature wandering nervously along the 'woodland edge'. In fact, muntjac deer have now become so common in the suburbs of southern Britain that they are beginning to cause some gardeners problems. They were originally imported from China to the grounds of Woburn Abbey by the Duke of Bedford in 1900, but inevitably a few escaped and they have gradually spread.

Muntjac are secretive as a rule, but you may well have seen one in the car headlights and taken it for a fox which had lost its tail. Our visitor only stayed long enough to eat the flowers off every one of my precious clumps of bluebells, and then left. Another favourite food, particularly in early spring, is the succulent little red shoots on rose bushes. I already knew there was a muntjac about because a local gardener had thoughtfully brought me a jam jar full of 'strange droppings' to identify. The last thing I want to do is solicit parcels of droppings from all over the place, but it is often the only evidence you have that some unusual creature has passed through your garden, and on this occasion I was able to impress my enquirer with a rapid identification. Believe it not, there is an excellent book on the subject, and although muntjac itself is not included, the droppings are just like a smaller version of those produced by fallow deer.

You might not think that something as big as a muntjac could possibly pass unnoticed through your neighbourhood, but this is where the wildlife corridors are so important. This little deer generally clings to the overgrown areas and seems to have no difficulty travelling undetected along railway cuttings, canal embankments and old hedge lines. Muntjac make a noise when they are disturbed – a sort of short, sharp bark — and their alternative name is the barking deer.

## LISTENING IN

With a few of your wild visitors it may be the sound, rather than the sight, that gives them away. Certainly that is the way I discovered that we had a visiting lesser spotted woodpecker, for instance. It has a high-pitched piping call which is unmistakable once you know it. It is also the call of the greater spotted woodpecker that prompts me to look up from my desk as this spectacular bird arrives at my fat bar bird feeder. The foxes give themselves away by calling too. The blood-curdling scream of a vixen is unforgettable, and again these marvellous mammals are experts at passing through suburbia almost unnoticed. Unlike the muntjac, foxes are mainly nocturnal, and escape a lot of human attention by operating after dark, but in hard winters particularly, or when they have cubs to feed, they can often be seen loping home with a guilty look after a hard night of scavenging. Urban foxes are extremely inventive so far as daytime hideaways are concerned. They lie up on shed roofs,

BELOW Hedgehogs need to move around their territory on a nightly basis. Make sure you leave gaps for them in fences and walls at ground level.

RIGHT Weasels are rare these days, but where they occur they rarely stray far from the habitat edges of hedges, walls and ditches.

RIGHT BELOW Badgers have huge territories and your garden may be en route from woodland to park, allotment to cemetery to railway embankment.

in drain culverts and under brambles. The prize for artistic presentation, though, must surely go to the wily old dog-fox who slept each day stretched lazily across a raft of *Clematis montana* in the garden of a friend of mine. The clematis had grown up and over an old hawthorn tree, and produced a solid tangle of twisted stems. The fox had no difficulty in climbing the tree, and was invisible from below, though you did get a lovely view of him, with his orange coat contrasting beautifully with the pink of the flowers, if you looked down from a bedroom window. If you don't see or hear your foxy visitors, you may well smell them. Foxes mark their territory with a powerful, musky scent, and if you have a marking post in your garden you will certainly know about it.

## TRAVERSING BARRIERS

There are a number of other British predatory mammals that inhabit wildlife gardens. I have devoted a good deal of space to the hedgehog already, and this endearing, bumbling little creature does find his way into some urban gardens. Hedgehogs are extremely agile climbers, and seem capable of scaling high brick walls with scarcely a pause for breath. They clamber up like a giant clockwork toy, roll up for protection and then drop softly down on the other side. They also have an amazing ability to squeeze through small holes. If your garden wall or fence looks to be too much of a challenge for a mountaineering hedgehog to tackle, try cutting a small hole, say 10cm square, at ground level: it will become a thoroughfare for small creatures and will save your hedgehog a bit of time. The recent fashion for replacing garden hedges with fences has caused hedgehogs some problems. This is

particularly the case where a horizontal concrete strip is fitted to the bottom of the fence panel, since this does serve as a barrier to hedgehogs on the move.

Badgers are still pretty rare in gardens, although their protective legislation has boosted their numbers dramatically since the turn of the century, and they are penetrating ever more deeply into suburbia. They do need extensive territory, and not many gardens are big enough to cope with the upheaval of an expansive badger set – garden visitors tend to travel in from wilder landscape nearby. Badgers do have a number of smaller predatory relatives though, and some of these may well turn up from time to time.

The weasel is tiny – about 20cm from nose to tail – and inquisitive. It streaks across open spaces, close to the ground, and will occasionally stop, sit up on its haunches and inspect you. The stoat is rather bigger – perhaps 35cm long – and it moves differently, with a bounding gait. It tends to be less active during daylight. Both mustelids are vicious little carnivores, hunting along the hedge bottom and over the stone bank for voles and mice, and weasels are capable of climbing up trees and entering nest boxes to catch

the young birds. In hard weather you may even see them scramble up and take food from the bird table. These fascinating animals need plenty of cover, and just like the hedgehogs, they definitely prefer to travel along hedgerows and other ecological corridors.

Squirrels are the other large mammals you are likely to have visit you. Although they are always shown in cuddly poses, gnawing away at hazelnuts, they do eat a wide range of things. Most of us are never likely to see red squirrels, of course, because they are now confined to a few localised colonies, but grey squirrels are common. They have become expert at breaking open bird feeders and a whole industry has sprung up to provide squirrel-proof bird feeders. You can also buy a bird-proof squirrel feeder – a box with a hinged lid and a see-through Perspex front which gives squirrels their own exclusive supply of food, and diverts their attention from the bird feeders. Squirrels can be a real problem in spring, when they sometimes turn their attention to young birds in their nests, and they will also take eggs. They cause serious problems for foresters and park-keepers, as squirrels damage the young twigs of broadleaved trees by gnawing away at the bark.

Generally speaking, grey squirrels will only use your garden in its service station capacity, and build their tree-top drays or nest bundles in a clump of trees where there is rather more space.

ABOVE One mammal that needs no introduction, the grey squirrel is the ultimate wildlife garden opportunist.

## SEEDS AND SPORES

The more mobile a species is, the more chance you have of enjoying a visit. It isn't just animals that move around, of course, and perhaps the most extensive of travellers are the fungi. They colonise by producing millions of tiny spores which are easily transported in the air, and form part of the aerial plankton, along with pollen grains and a few species of small animals. Fungi live by digesting dead material. Your wildlife garden will contain a good deal of dead vegetable matter, from logs to lettuce leaves, and while many of the fungi are specific, their spores are so numerous that if you provide a suitable habitat you are likely to be colonised. Certainly you can expect some spectacular toadstools on your logs in autumn, and if you have used chopped bark or shredded wood as a mulch you can expect to see crowds of colourful toadstools popping up all over the place. You may be lucky, and have a delicious species such as the pale yellow chanterelle growing under the birch trees of your woodland edge, but for the most part, garden fungi are likely to be better for looking at than eating. Many of the most spectacular toadstools belong to fungi that only seem to thrive in ancient habitats, but one or two of the rarest are fungi of new landscapes. There are quarries, for instance, with brand new landscapes sporting extremely unusual species, and on a large brick-strewn National Car Park site in the centre of Birmingham a rare 'morel' suddenly

**BELOW LEFT, BELOW RIGHT AND TOP RIGHT** Fascinating, beautiful and intriguing, some poisonous and some delicious. Don't overlook the various fungi in your garden; they may surprise you.

appeared a year or two ago, much to the surprise of the man on the gate. He wasn't used to queues of bobble-hatted botanists paying to visit his car park to photograph fungi.

Some of the flowering plants are surprisingly mobile, too. There are a number which spread by producing seeds with wings or parachutes, and they can blow in, but they mostly have tiny seeds with relatively little in the way of an energy store, and they need open, cultivated soil if they are to colonise. Plants like sow thistle (*Sonchus* spp), hawkweed (*Hieracium umbellatum*), groundsel (*Senecio vulgaris*) and willowherb (*Epilobium* spp) will certainly keep up a constant bombardment, but will only establish themselves in the vegetable patch or other patches of loose soil. Some other species may simply appear once the habitat is right. I have hedge mustard in my garden which now fills the woodland edge habitat with handsome white flowers, and there is white deadnettle, too. Both these plants were probably always around, but my change of circumstances has suited them both well and they have thrived.

RIGHT Rosebay willowherb may have a startling beauty when its seed head is captured in a photograph, but the sight of thousands of the little parachutists landing in your veg patch is probably taking wildlife gardening a step too far.

BELOW Garlic mustard is a woodland wildflower that seems to arrive as if by magic – and to stay.

OPPOSITE Burdock disperses its seed by hooking onto passing animal fur – or socks, or scarves, or almost anything. Great fun to throw at unsuspecting school friends.

## SEED CARRIERS

Other species must be brought in by birds and animals. Goose grass or cleavers (*Galium aparine*) is a good example of a plant whose seeds cling to the fur of passing foxes and dogs. Burdock (*Arctium lappa*) travels the same way, though here it is a whole fruit containing several big black seeds which is transported. A burdock plant has sprung up in my garden, and I am happy as it is excellent for butterflies in August, and then attracts flocks of seed-eating birds in the autumn and winter.

Birds also act as agents for introducing a good many new plants into the garden. Plant birch or alder through a mulch of chopped bark, and fairly soon you will begin to see seedlings of hawthorn, bramble and dog rose popping up. You will probably find seedlings of garden shrubs such as mahonia, berberis and cotoneaster, too. This is the result of birds roosting in your saplings, after having gorged themselves on berries from elsewhere. The seed passes through the bird unharmed, and you finish up with a new seedling. You may find oak trees springing up if there are large oaks in the neighbourhood. These are clear evidence that you have a jay active in your garden, picking up acorns and bringing them to be buried in your woodland edge. Squirrels also bury hazelnuts, and I remember being thrilled one year to discover hazel seedlings appearing all over the far end of the garden. I thought at first that this was the work of an absent-minded hoarding squirrel, but then remembered that for a week or two after Christmas two years before, I had used a bowl of hazelnuts as ammunition for throwing at the local cats. These little seedlings had come back to haunt me.

## SMALL BUT SIGNIFICANT

As your wildlife garden develops, I promise you will see far more birds, you will hear more scuffles and squeaks from small mammals if you venture out after dark, and you will even look on new types of weeds as 'firsts' for the species list. The astounding success of wildlife gardening, though, is at the creepy-crawly end of the business. The increase in the variety and number of insects, spiders and other invertebrates is astonishing. Every time I walk through my garden I seem to discover another little creature I have never

seen before. My hazel has wonderful shiny shield bugs on it, the birch leaves are decorated in midsummer with the lively larvae of the birch sawfly, each one of which springs to attention by standing on its head as you approach. Lift a log and there is a mass of spectacular beetles and other fast-moving mini-beasts scattering for cover. If I sit and watch a patch of marigolds for a minute or two, numerous different species of bees, wasps and wasp look-alikes will visit. Peer down among the grasses of the meadow, and there are spiders galore, some of them beautifully camouflaged to blend in among the green and gold of the mini-jungle.

Many of these mini-beasts are cleverly disguised, and you need to spend time sitting and concentrating on a small patch of the garden before you notice them. There are crab spiders that change colour to suit their setting, and sit among the creamy flowers of the cow parsley tribe, legs outstretched, almost invisible and ready to pounce. Many of the caterpillars are subtly marked, and disappear into their habitat. Some of the moth caterpillars look exactly like snapped-off twigs, and stand motionless if you approach them.

## TYPES OF BEE

**Bumblebees** There are dozens of different species of bumblebees in Europe, and gardens are an important habitat for many. Their hairy bodies are distinctive although the colour pattern varies from species to species. Bumblebees need dry holes in which to nest. Some may occupy bird boxes, whilst others prefer abandoned mouse holes in long grass. Grow plenty of flowers for pollen and nectar and the bumblebees will benefit.

**Honeybees** form large colonies of as many as 6,000 individuals and they have been domesticated to produce honey and beeswax for thousands of years. Most of the honey bees in your garden are likely to be from local hives, but wild honeybees do nest in hollow trees and other cavities. Pollen from particular flowers such as heather, lavender or lime trees lends the honey distinctive flavours.

**Solitary bees** are varied and make up the great majority of bee species that visit gardens. Many are in serious trouble and wildlife gardens can help them. Some tunnel into soft soil while others lay eggs in hollow plant stems or holes in stonework and mortar. Build a 'bee hotel' with lengths of cane, hollow plant stems and drinking straws, try to leave a sandy bank undisturbed through the summer and keep your eyes peeled. These are very important pollinators.

Others, like the poplar hawkmoth and the orange tip caterpillars are just the same green as their food plants, and blend in perfectly. There are others, of course, which adopt the opposite strategy and stand out like sore thumbs. These gaudy little creatures are usually poisonous or unpalatable, and their markings warn off the wisest of the local birds.

## FOOD CHAINS

All of these wild plants and animals depend on one another for survival. The blackbird that helps to

establish the new bramble seedling may well be back a couple of years later to collect its fruity reward, or it may visit the first spring after transplanting, to pick off caterpillars to feed to its young. The fungi that have their spores spread by browsing slugs are at the same time helping break down the dead wood to a state where the slugs themselves can feed on it. They in turn provide food for the hedgehogs which may have hibernated there when the logs were less rotten.

Remember that native plants and rotting vegetable matter are the basic materials of wildlife gardening. Place them in their appropriate habitat setting, and then watch carefully. The animal life will move in and colonise the habitat, and as the garden matures your resident web of native wildlife will become more and more intertwined, and will provide you with increased enjoyment from your wildlife garden.

LEFT Some garden predators are cleverly camouflaged. This crab spider lurks almost invisible in the centre of an umbelliferous flower head until a fly lands within grabbing distance.

ABOVE The cunningly camouflaged caterpillar of a poplar hawkmoth is easily mistaken for a rolled-up leaf.

## 13

Ladybirds make excellent subjects for detailed study, even in the smallest of gardens. There is so much we still don't know about some of our most familiar wildlife.

# STUDYING GARDEN WILDLIFE

THE LAST thing I want to do is to make people take their garden wildlife terribly seriously. The wildlife in my own garden is an immense source of *pleasure* to me. I enjoy the company of songbirds, and the spectacle of bats and dragonflies. It also gives me a great deal of satisfaction to know that I am, genuinely, making a difference to the survival chances of a whole range of wild plants and animals.

If you do want to use your garden for more serious study, though, there is a great need to learn more about the habits and characteristics of even our most familiar wildlife. You will get an extra level of enjoyment out of learning some of the secrets of your resident plants and animals, and you may well discover something which even the most learned of experts have overlooked. You can begin modestly enough by doing no more than keeping a diary. Having changed your garden, or created a whole set of brand new wildlife habitats, you should find it interesting simply to keep a record of the way the wildlife community develops. If you are a methodical, precise sort of person, you may want to measure the growth of your trees, or the spread of your original clumps of wildflowers, and you may want to combine your wildlife observations with a detailed record of the weather. I'm afraid my records don't stretch that far, but I am interested in building up a picture of the rate of colonisation, and noting population changes. All I do is to spend as much time as I can sitting quietly in the garden, or moving slowly around the paths – looking. Each time I spot something new I make an entry in my notebook – nothing elaborate you understand, just time, date and what it is I have spotted. Of course, some of the things I've noticed for the first time could well have been around for ages, but there is a general picture building up of the way the diversity of wildlife is increasing as each habitat becomes more mature.

This simple diary already makes fascinating reading – for me at least. It jogs my memory about all sorts of exciting discoveries I have made, and the act of writing up each observation is useful too, in that it forces me to check the names of things, and I learn a lot that way. The pond provided the most constant stream of new entries in the first couple of years, with whirligig beetles and pond skaters arriving almost instantly,

and great diving beetles turning up in great numbers in the second summer. I've noted more and more birds using the pond for both drinking and bathing, with much more of the splashing taking place in the cold of the winter than in the warmth of summer. The meadow has a lengthy list of resident plants, with the seeded area producing many of its prettiest flowers in the second, rather than the first season. The meadow's insect life has developed almost as dramatically as the pond's although I must admit that I find it much more difficult to identify meadow creepy-crawlies – there are just so many different kinds of beetles, spiders and 'little black flies'.

## OBSERVING CHANGE

The list of garden birds grows longer all the time, with most of the later additions visiting the woodland edge. I think the lesser spotted woodpecker is probably the most exciting so far, though I must admit I smiled a little the day I was able to add a noisy, cream-coloured parakeet to the list. By the time that the quarter-acre garden that I filmed for *Bluetits and Bumblebees* was just two years old, I had

recorded 40 different species of wild bird visiting it. The list of breeding birds is much shorter, of course, but even that is pleasing. Robins, wrens, bluetits, great tits, song thrushes, blackbirds and greenfinches are all nesting regularly.

Some exciting birds have passed through on migration. Early one November morning I disturbed a woodcock skulking in the undergrowth. These relatively rare game birds migrate south each autumn, and generally fly at night. The moonlight reflected in my pond was apparently enough to tempt the woodcock down at dawn.

Enjoying three different gardens, over a period of 30 years, I have also been able to spot some trends, Hedgehogs were frequent visitors in the early days. Now I am lucky to see a hedgehog in my garden more than once or twice each year. The general number and variety of butterflies has dropped dramatically, but the bees and ladybirds seem to be surviving well. Most striking of all has been the change in bird visitors. The spotted flycatcher was once a summer certainty. Now it has disappeared completely. The swifts that used to scream around my

LEFT Bats visit my garden on warm summer evenings, but after more than 25 years of enjoyment and observation I still don't know where they roost.

BELOW Twice in my life I have disturbed a woodcock in my urban garden. These astonishing birds migrate at night, and clearly my woodland glade with a wildlife pond works for them. Keep watching. You never know what may turn up.

roof by the score are now reduced to single figures. By contrast some species have hung on valiantly. I can usually hear two competing song thrushes in my inner city dawn chorus and robins remain constant companions, despite the attention of a dozen local cats. Most striking of all has been the return of one or two of our most colourful birds, thanks largely to the increase in sophisticated bird feeding. Bullfinches and goldfinches were in serious trouble in the 1980s. Thirty years later they are an almost daily occurrence in my garden. Nuthatches and greater spotted woodpeckers both visit daily, and clearly see my feeding station as a reliable source of food. Most surprising of all, I also see goldcrests frequently. These exquisite, tiny birds seem to have benefitted enormously from the Leyland cypress forest that has spread across suburbia in the past half century. The dense evergreen foliage of these ornamental conifers seems to suit these tiny birds particularly well.

## USING YOUR OBSERVATIONS

Of course these simple observations teach you things which help you improve your wildlife garden. You

will quickly learn that the small birds are unlikely to use a nest box that is exposed to full sun. They seem to know that a shady box is less likely to overheat the fledglings later in the spring. I am particularly interested in insects, and my notes about the flowers that insects feed on are helping me to improve the nectar service station year by year. The Royal Horticultural Society has been making a more professional academic study of pollinating insects on plots of garden flowers and native plants in their research gardens at RHS Garden Wisley, and as a consequence of all that learning over several decades, it has become far easier to maximise the wildlife benefit of the planting that we do. That wealth of experience is also reflected in the nursery catalogues and garden centres, where plants are often displayed as 'wildlife-friendly'.

Once you have settled into the habit of recording things you notice, why not make a special study of one particular aspect of the wildlife you observe? Here the choice is endless. Just choose a subject that seems to be throwing up some interesting, general observations, and begin to keep more detailed records. The dragonflies on my pond are a case in

ABOVE Volunteers play a vital role in adding to our knowledge, as here, in the *Plants for Bugs* research centre at RHS Garden Wisley.

OPPOSITE The *Big Garden Birdwatch* has become a world class model of citizen science, and the unique scale of so many observations means that the population fluctuation of species such as this tiny goldcrest can be tracked year after year.

LEFT Wildlife studies in your garden give you the luxury of time and comfort. Watch dragonflies such as this broad bodied chaser for the whole of a lazy summer's afternoon, or go back to bed after you've experienced a 4am dawn chorus.

point. The first year, I was more than satisfied simply spotting each new species as it turned up, making a note of its antics, and using a reference book to sort out which species was which. I learned, for instance, that the broad bodied chaser (*Libellula depressa*) arrived early in the summer, and had disappeared by mid-July. By contrast, the relatively enormous brown hawkers (*Aeshna grandis*) visited the pond regularly until well into September, and the common darter, (*Sympetrum striolatum*) seemed to come and go for short spells all through the summer.

As the second summer went by, I began to take more of an interest in the different ways in which the various species of dragonflies mate, and more particularly the varied and apparently specific sites they choose for egg-laying. The hawkers seem to prefer to lay their eggs on the damp logs of my marsh-side causeway, whilst the golden female of the chaser bobs along, placing her eggs individually on plants just below the water surface. The darter does likewise, but with this species, the male and female bob along in tandem. I have also discovered that when the hawker nymphs eventually crawl out

of the pond, they climb up the stem of a water plant to shed their casing. The chasers, on the other hand, leave the pond and crawl to nearby meadow or shrubbery before they metamorphose.

## FOOD HABITS

I mentioned food preferences for garden butterflies in Chapter 8. Birds are even easier to observe, and you can carry out an interesting study by watching your bird table closely. Make a note of which birds are the first to land after you put the food out. Which are the most aggressive birds, and do the same ones always dominate the pecking order? Do any of the species prefer to feed on the ground? Is there a pattern to the number of times any particular bird looks up in between pecks? Which birds carry their food away from the table to eat it? I am certain that as you watch the birds, you will notice other aspects of the bird table activity that you will want to know more about, and you can simply start another set of detailed records. If this idea appeals, you might enjoy participating in the British Trust for Ornithology's *Garden Bird Census*. The address is at the back of this book. If such detailed and methodical study does not appeal you can still contribute by joining the hundreds of thousands of other gardeners who join in with special surveys such as butterfly, hedgehog or bumblebee counts, or the amazingly successful *Big Garden Bird Watch*. That annual survey regularly attracts half a million participants on the chosen weekend towards the end of March, and the knowledge gained is greatly valued in scientific circles.

## BEHAVIOURAL PATTERNS

One of the nice things about noting down your wildlife observations is that you can begin to discover

LEFT Set up simple experiments. This mix of materials will help to identify the nesting preferences of your garden birds.

OPPOSITE Make time and space to enjoy the habitats that you've created. Settle into a secluded seat and let the wildlife come to you.

patterns of behaviour, and to predict when certain things will happen. If you do keep a note of weather conditions, for instance, then you may be able to tell when you can expect your first visit from winter migrants such as redwings and fieldfares. They usually turn up the day after heavy snowfalls and autumn gales in the North Sea. If you hear the announcement on the shipping forecast, you can have a pile of apples sitting on the lawn to greet them, and increase your chances of a visit even more.

Your records will tell you where the various birds nest, and it is interesting to build up a picture of when they begin to nest each year, too. Some species will start as early as February some years, but others don't even arrive here for the summer until May. Most species are choosy about nest sites. I have already suggested that sunny nest boxes are unpopular, and you will remember that the height of nesting varies from species to species, too. You might like to run a simple experiment to see what building materials each bird prefers. You can do this by analysing the old nests, of course, by pulling them to bits to see what they are made of. I have great fun

each year hanging up a bag of various suitable nesting materials, and watching the birds flying in to collect them. Some species are perfectly happy pulling their lengths of wool, old oak leaves or feathers from a net hanging in the apple tree. Others simply won't use that source at all, but are prepared to tug away at the goodies if they are put in a similar net, but anchored to the ground. The song thrush and the house martins both use mud in their building, and the edge of the pond is a useful source of suitable sticky stuff for both of them. I have known my local song thrush take three weeks to complete the nest building, so there is plenty of opportunity to enjoy watching the process.

Most breeding birds are extremely territorial, and when the season begins, you will notice that birds which tolerated one another happily in the struggle of winter suddenly become aggressive. It is interesting to work out a map of territories for your garden and the area around it. The best way to begin this study is to get up early on a couple of mornings, after you know the nesting season has begun. If you can manage to be out in the garden about an hour before dawn – and in late April that probably means before 4am –

then you should have the mind-blowing experience of hearing the dawn chorus from the beginning. Just close your eyes, and count on your fingers as you hear each new voice join in the chorus. You will soon run out of fingers, and I promise you that even in the depths of the city you will be amazed by the volume, and the beauty of the sounds. If you have a portable tape-recorder (or a smart-phone) it is worth taping your dawn chorus, so that you can listen to it at a more civilised hour, and try to work out who all the performers are. These days there are apps to download to your smart phone, that can help you to identify the individual species, but for the territory project that is unnecessary. You simply need to listen carefully and make a note whenever you hear the same birdsong coming from two or more places.

## BATTLE CRIES

I find the dawn chorus so enchanting that back in 1987 I launched *International Dawn Chorus Day*. This began as a simple way for me to share a special experience with friends living many miles apart.

The idea has grown over the years, and on the first Sunday in May many thousands of people rise before dawn to share in the magic. I have participated in international dawn chorus day in places as varied as Vancouver, Amsterdam and Israel's Golan Heights, but my downtown Wolverhampton wildlife garden still takes some beating.

The dawn chorus isn't a great, happy choir of chummy feathered friends, all showing how glad they are to be alive. It is a battle in sound. Each male bird is sitting firmly in his nesting territory, and shouting for all he is worth that he is a highly desirable mate, and that this is his patch! Woe betide any other breeding male of the same species who dares to try to move in. When you hear two different great tits piping away, each one is telling the other to stick to his own territory, and that helps you to work out just how many breeding pairs, how many territories there are around your garden. Most years I have the pleasure of hearing stereo song thrushes. The two cock thrushes sit each morning and evening on the topmost branch of their respective trees, one in the

garden next door and the other two doors away on the other side. They sing away at one another, with me marvelling at the liquid sounds as I crouch sleepily in the middle. The thing that I find particularly interesting is that my garden pond appears to be in a sort of no-man's-land right on the boundary of the two territories. While the cock birds sing to tell the competition who is boss, their mates meet at the watering hole, collect a beak full of mud and wet leaves each, and then flying off in opposite directions to carry on with the construction work.

Most of the time there is no obvious boundary line on the ground, just some invisible zone that both birds recognise. Sometimes, though, you can see that a boundary is formed by a hedge or a building. I have known three pairs of bluetits all nest within my garden. Each pair occupied a different nest box, but the house provided a dividing lump which conveniently kept the territorial birds apart. There was one pair on each side of the house, and the third was right down at the opposite end of the garden, nesting in a box on the fence.

It was listening that led me to discover the wren nesting in a hole under the eaves of my office, and this noisy little bird leaves you in no doubt about its territorial rights. I also discovered a robin nesting in a nest box with an oversized hole at the far end of the garden, by sitting and listening carefully. If you want to see a dramatic demonstration of territorial behaviour, try intruding into the local robin's stamping ground. Stick up a dummy robin – a brown mitten with a piece of red cloth fixed to the front will do, or one of those life-sized Christmas decorations. Within minutes the resident cock robin will be beating the stuffing out of the impostor. Do take the dummy away once you have seen the performance, though, otherwise the real robin could become distressed.

Having observed how possessive and territorial nesting birds are, you can probably realise that the bird table could be a bit of a handicap in the breeding season. If there are lots of different birds flying in for their daily snack, this will upset the birds nesting close by, and they are likely to move out. If the garden is big enough, keep nest boxes at least 20m away from the bird table and give the nesting birds a clear line of flight that avoids the feeding station.

LEFT A wildlife garden will stimulate all the senses and emphasise the changing seasons. Don't miss dawn chorus day on the first Sunday in May, and learn to recognise the song of stars such as this common wren.

RIGHT For me, wildlife gardening has never been about rarities or list-ticking. Nevertheless, gardens do provide habitat for some surprising species. This is a bloody-nosed beetle, and with a name like that you just want to find out more about it.

## LEARNING FROM MINI-BEASTS

The best guide to the health of a habitat lies in the happiness of its creepy-crawlies. You will see lots of them around in the garden, of course. Turn over a log, the centipedes wriggle away, and the woodlice rush around in all directions desperately trying to escape the sunlight. Dozens of little black hunting spiders decorate the surface of the bark mulch in the sunny shrub border in midsummer, and there are holes bitten out of almost every leaf in the wildlife garden. If you want more than just a passing acquaintance with your mini-beasts, it is easy to trap them. Concentrate particularly on the ones that roam around at ground level at first. If you can build up a picture of the variety and number of creatures living in different parts of your garden, it will give you a clearer idea of how well your various habitats are working. All you need is a set of miniature mammoth traps. Most of the beetles, millipedes and other crawling creatures move around without much concern for the road ahead. If you put a hole in their path, then the odds are they will fall in. You can come along later and see what you have caught. Choose a number of different

habitats around the wildlife garden – the close-mown lawn, a patch of rough meadow, the vegetable garden, somewhere in the woodland edge – select as many different types of mini-environment as you can. Then dig a hole in each location just the right size to take a smooth-sided plastic cup. Drop a cup into each hole, put something juicy and delicious in the bottom of each to act as bait (an old, green piece of liver is irresistible) and put a flat stone over the top, propped on a pebble, to keep the rain out. Leave the traps no longer than twelve hours, and when you lift off the lid, you will find all kinds of little creatures have fallen in and been unable to clamber out. Trap for several days and nights and you should get a good picture of the mini-beasts there are around. You can refine the experiment by noting which animals are nocturnal, for instance, and only appear in the night-time traps. You can also see if there is a preference for different food by varying the bait.

There is one great problem with pitfall trapping. The trapped mini-beasts have a tendency to eat one another. You are likely to have your results biased by finding one big, fat, rather smug-looking spider in the bottom of each cup, and nothing else. You can reduce the problem by inspecting the traps more frequently, before the big boys get too hungry, or you can pickle the catch immediately each creature drops in by putting a splash of water and washing up liquid  in the bottom of each cup. That helps to improve your scientific results, but it doesn't do a lot for the poor unfortunate wildlife. When you have finished your observations, do remember to take the cups away and fill in the hole – otherwise the mini-beast trap will carry on working until it fills up with mini-corpses.

Your pitfall traps will almost certainly show you clearly how much more activity there is in your wildlife garden after dark than there is in daylight. The birds and butterflies may be active in sunshine, but most garden wildlife works on the night shift. You must find time to go into your garden after dark, and see what you come across. You'll be surprised how much activity there is among nocturnal mammals, if you have a fall of snow in the late evening. By the following morning the garden will be crisscrossed by dozens of animal tracks. Most of them will be cats,

I'm afraid, but if you study them carefully, looking at the precise pattern of the pawmarks, you are likely to find a fox track or two. Foxes are far more common than most people realise, and they thrive in urban territories with an abundance of discarded fast food.

NIGHT-TIME NOISES

You get a good idea of the amount of night-time wildlife activity there is in your garden simply by listening. Choose a warm evening, or wrap up well, and tuck yourself into the woodland edge. Try and select a spot where the breeze is blowing off the garden and into your face. It is fairly obvious that animals which move around in the dark are likely to have particularly sensitive noses, and if the breeze is blowing from you towards them, they will smell you and know you are around much sooner. Now, just sit quietly and listen. Nothing much will happen for a few minutes, though you may hear that fox of yours screaming somewhere in the distance, or an owl calling across the neighbourhood. As you settle in, and your eyes and ears become accustomed to the dark, you will begin to hear the garden come

OPPOSITE Get yourself a
good torch. Your wildlife
garden is a whole new world
after dark.

LEFT Without the odd night-
time safari you could miss
out on some of our most
spectacular garden wildlife,
like this swallow-tail moth.

the odd night stretched out on the lawn, under the stars. If you're not terribly brave, you can do what I do and sleep on a camp bed in a sleeping bag. That way most of the creatures of the night can pass right under you, and you need never know. It must be a bit disconcerting to wake up from dreams of nightingales and moonlight to discover a hedgehog snuffling his way across your stomach.

## FASCINATING MOTHS

I think the most beautiful creatures of the night are the moths. I know there are some people who hate them, but I think they are fascinating. They have suffered from pollution and habitat destruction in recent years like everything else, but we still do have a fantastic variety of moths around, and in a good wildlife garden you can expect to find a great many different kinds. Many of the most spectacular ones are attracted to lights and I have seen some amazing, beautiful creatures simply by leaving on the kitchen light and popping in from time to time through the evening to check on who has turned up. I remember the swallow-tail moth. This is a beautiful, lemon-yellow insect which only flies for a couple of weeks each July or August. The wing shape is unusual, and we had three on the kitchen window in one evening. The range of moths reduces as you travel north, and my garden is at the limit of the range for a few species which are fairly common in the softer south. The most spectacular of the ones that has visited us is the red underwing. It is big – perhaps 5cm across the wings – and it adopts the same strategy for survival as the tiger moths. Its underwings are a brilliant crimson as the name suggests, and obvious when it is flying or stretched out against the window. When

to life. It will start with a tiny scuffle somewhere a few feet away, but pretty soon you will have squeaks and scuffles going on all around you, and you will be amazed at the amount of secret activity there is in your mini-habitats. The night noises vary with the time of year. In spring you may be lucky enough to have the song of a nightingale for company, or at least a lovesick blackbird or robin, kept awake by the glow of a streetlight. In late March and early April you will have the amazing racket of amorous frogs, shouting out for females to come and join them in the deep end. Late summer nights are alive with the sound of young animals. A whole family of hedgehogs may snuffle through the garden, or you may hear what sounds like dozens of mice or voles scampering around, playing amongst the dead leaves under the hedge. If there is someone in your family who is good with electronics, get a microphone rigged up in the garden, and connect it to some headphones in the bedroom. You can then share in all the scuffles and snuffles of the night-time garden without aggravating your arthritis or freezing to death. If you are brave, you can do what a friend of mine does and spend threatened, though, this beautiful creature drops to the ground and closes its wings. The overwings are beautifully marked with a dusty brown and grey pattern, and the moth is perfectly camouflaged against most dark backgrounds.

There have been even bigger moths at the kitchen window, from time to time. There are several species of hawkmoth which are common in gardens, and so far we have been visited by the poplar, the lime and the elephant hawkmoths. These are spectacular creatures, and their caterpillars are enormous. I'm pleased to say that as far as moths are concerned the rich habitat parts of our wildlife garden work particularly well, and I have found elephant hawkmoth caterpillars feeding on the leaves of the rosebay willowherb, and the caterpillar of poplar hawkmoths munching away at the pussy willow leaves.

## ATTRACTING MOTHS

You can do better than rely on chance meetings at the kitchen window. Many of the service station nectar flowers are important for night-flying moths, and a quick tour of inspection with a powerful torch on warm, overcast summer evenings will show you which are the most popular. Three of the summer flowers in my garden are streets ahead of the rest. The first is evening primrose (*Oenothera biennis*) and its big, lemon-yellow flowers are usually surrounded by moths from dusk onwards. Secondly, there are the tobacco plants (*Nicotiana affinis*). The paler ones seem best, and of course the perfume of both these lovely flowers should be a clear indication that they are likely to be good moth plants. The third winner is honeysuckle. The hawkmoths in particular seem to love it, and the long, trumpet-like flowers are perfectly suited to pollination by moths.

There is a third way of attracting night-flying moths to your service station, apart from bright lights and perfumed flowers. This is a technique known as sugaring. Moths are attracted by sweet, sugary smells. If you paint a suitably sickly-sweet mixture on a tree trunk or a fence post, then on a good evening you can be lucky and attract a whole range of night-flying insects. There are lots of 'magic' recipes, but most of them contain beer, molasses and pulped overripe fruit. I usually include a drop or two of rosewater or

OPPOSITE A bright light and a warm muggy summer's evening are all you need for a memorable few hours of moth watching. Try it with an expert if you can. Most wildlife trusts, Buglife and Butterfly Conservation hold moth watching events.

BELOW So much magic to discover. This red underwing is perfectly camouflaged, until it flashes its petticoats.

orange-blossom water, too. The technique seems to work particularly well on the south and east coasts of England, where migratory moths arrive exhausted and ravenous from the darkness of their cross-channel journey. Elsewhere results are usually pretty disappointing, but it is worth trying sugaring alongside a bright light, particularly if you can do so for several warm nights in succession. The combined pulling power may just give you a pleasant surprise.

The range of moths you are likely to find visiting your garden is enormous, and an awful lot of them look confusingly similar. If you ever get the chance, join the local experts around their mercury vapour lamp, and let them show you a few of the ones which are easy to recognise. You will be surprised how quickly you learn to identify thirty or forty of the more dramatic ones, and it will help you begin to realise how varied the different families of moths can be. My neighbours and I have enjoyed community moth evenings on many summer evenings. On one particularly memorable July evening, the TV gardener Charlie Dimmock joined us, and we filmed the whole event. Charlie was captivated by the beauty of the elephant hawkmoths, pepper moths and silver Ys, and the evening was made complete by an aerial bat display and two tawny owls calling long and loud to each other.

The wildlife which shares your garden can give enormous pleasure. The more carefully you study it, the more time you find to sit quietly and watch or listen, the more delighted you will be by all the evidence of the way your habitats are working. If you can take the trouble to keep notes, take photographs or make sketches, your knowledge will increase year by year, and as more and more people study the wildlife on their doorsteps, the detailed things we learn should help us produce more and more successful new habitats for wildlife. This in turn should also help us appreciate the damage we can doing to our environment without even thinking.

14 |

# OVER THE GARDEN WALL

AS YOUR wildlife garden gets better and better, and you learn more and more about the range of animals that use it as a service station, you will, I hope, develop a keen interest in the wildlife potential of your whole neighbourhood. I hope that your garden wildlife will encourage you first of all to wonder where it all comes from, then to play an active part in protecting the exciting wild spaces that generate your garden visitors, and finally to persuade the people who manage the 'green deserts' in your area to adopt your ideas, and create rich habitat parks, school grounds and traffic islands.

All those small tortoiseshell butterflies on the buddleia, for example: where *do* they find unsprayed nettles on which to lay their eggs? The bright yellow brimstone that is such a welcome visitor in early spring: where *did* it hibernate all winter? Is there a mass of overgrown ivy nearby and more important, where on earth will it find a bush of alder buckthorn for its caterpillars? If you don't fight to save a place for the nettles, or to stop the chopping down of the last local patch of old woodland, then the property speculators, the road builders and your over-tidy neighbours will win, the habitat will disappear, and no matter how carefully you tend your buddleia, your garden will have fewer and fewer visiting butterflies.

One of the most useful things you can do to help your local wildlife, is to spend a few of those long, dark winter evenings studying a map of your local area. When I first took an interest in my neighbourhood I had to rely on the occasional aerial photograph or the view from nearby tall buildings if I wanted to catch a view of the local vegetation patterns. Now, satellite imagery on the internet has improved the situation enormously. By punching in your postcode to a website such as Google Earth, it is instantly possible to explore every corner of your local living landscape. Aim to produce a habitat plan of your area which tells you where your wildlife visitors are coming from.

## HIDDEN HABITATS

Some of the key contributing habitats will be easy to identify. For instance you may have a patch of woodland or a park nearby. Others will not be so obvious, and this is where satellite images and aerial

photos can give you some real surprises. You may never have realised that the rows of grand Georgian houses round the corner are in fact enclosing a huge area of land containing big old trees, hedgerows, ponds – in fact a hectare or so of secret landscape that is good for wildlife. You probably hadn't realised just how much of the old railway siding had become overgrown with bramble and silver birch since the goods yard closed forty or fifty years ago. An aerial photo will show you these things instantly, and it will also help you pick out the wildlife corridor network. You will be able to see where an old hedge and ditch boundary survives between the individual back-to-back gardens of two adjacent housing estates. You will see how important the railway lines are, snaking through houses and factories with their ribbon of scrub and grassland habitat, and connecting the overgrown goods yard to the school playing field.

## MAPPING YOUR WILDLIFE NETWORK

Once you begin to build up the picture, I suggest you do a bit of footwork, and record something of the quality of the green space on your map. At its simplest level, there are basically two kinds of green landscape. There is the rough, tangled, overgrown wildscape which is so good for a whole mass of wild plants and animals, and then there is the smooth, neat, tidy, clinical green desert, which does almost nothing for nature conservation, and little for people either. Your task is to conserve the first category and work to improve the second. Pin up your new, unique neighbourhood habitat map on the wall and keep relating your wildlife garden to it. Each time a new species drops in, either as a casual customer or as a permanent resident, have a good look at the map and try to work out where he or she has come from. I think I now know where my regularly visiting nuthatch breeds. There are one or two big old trees with suitable dead branches in the grounds of a big house about a quarter of a mile away, and he seems to fly in from that general direction. I'm sure our wandering foxes have us on their route because the dustbins of the Cantonese restaurant round the corner provide such rich pickings. The aerial photo has shown me that there are several garden ponds within a few hundred metres of here, and I imagine

LEFT You may not have room for stinging nettles or forest-sized trees in your garden, but they will be somewhere close at hand to provide food and shelter for exciting garden visitors.

BELOW Take a look around your local neighbourhood to see how your garden benefits from the wider wildlife habitat network.

the frogs that laid their spawn in my new pool were caught short on their return journey to one or other of these. The smaller dragonflies and water boatmen probably came from there too, though there is a canal a kilometre away, and certainly that is well within the flying capability of the large hawker dragonflies and the diving beetles.

A kestrel hovers over my small garden occasionally. There is not much rough grassland in this bit of town, but there are one or two big traffic islands, a number of overgrown allotments, and a particularly sad patch of greenbelt farmland not far away which has been bought by a housing developer and then abandoned in the hope of changing its planning status. I imagine my kestrel hunts over all these patches of wild land, and sees my tiny patch as yet another potential source of voles and beetles.

BAT BEHAVIOUR

As I have said before, I don't know where my bats come from. It may be the same old trees that I think the nuthatch uses, but of course the bats arrive after dark, and so I can't tie them down to a direction of

travel. In fact, bats seem to appear by magic. Suddenly you see one flit across a patch of open sky, and then disappear against the dark background of trees or buildings. It may be that my bats use the same roof spaces as visiting swifts. There are certainly a number of big Edwardian gables to choose from close by, and bats do move around of course. Pipistrelles spend a lot of their year roosting in individual nooks and crannies all over the place, but then all the females from a wide area will gather together into one hot, sun-drenched nursery roost, where they give birth and then each raises its own baby. They gather together again for the winter, and this time they choose a different spot to hibernate, preferring a roof space or a hollow tree which is shaded and as cold as can be. Bat boxes can increase the safe options for these creatures, but you will have the greatest success if you provide several in different locations and with varying aspects to suit the seasonal preferences.

## BEGINNING WITH BUTTERFLIES

You can begin extending your circle of wildlife interest simply by thinking about the garden butterflies. As

BELOW LEFT Once your appetite is whetted, you may want to learn more about particular groups of plants or animals. There are all kinds of special interest naturalists groups. The Dragonfly Society is a good example.

BELOW There is good news and bad news. Gardeners have been unable to help the white-letter hairstreak. Its food plant is the English elm tree, so Dutch elm disease has been its undoing.

each individual appears, look up its larval food plant – a few common examples are given in the panel on page 23 – and then plot the options for egg-laying on your map. There will be no end of choice for the troublesome large white – all those neat little rows of cabbages, sprouts and cauliflowers to choose from – but how many of them are free from pesticides? Nettles are probably in reasonable supply too, so the spring crop of small tortoiseshells and peacocks will be okay, but is there a particular patch anywhere that gets cut down in June, and then springs up again to provide the soft young shoots so necessary for the second, summer brood of caterpillars, and for the annual egg-laying of the weary migrant red admirals and painted ladies that arrive from Africa and southern Europe to breed in mid-July?

The common blue butterfly bred in my garden, once I had provided a few black medick plants in the meadow, but there aren't many patches of poor wasteland around here, and I think the original colonising blues probably lived as caterpillars on the leaves of a sheet of bird's-foot trefoil I have discovered

LEFT Grey herons nest in tree top colonies well away from most gardens. Never-theless, you may well have a visit in the frog mating season.

decorating the abandoned coal yard of the nearby railway station. I have holly blues here, too, and they lay their autumn eggs on my ivy flowers, but I think the spring brood is raised on the flowers of a huge holly tree in the front garden of a house a few doors away. The speckled woods could well have been breeding on the couch grass in the shade of the council's shrub beds before they discovered the few coarse grasses growing in the dappled shade of my woodland edge habitat, but the white-letter hairstreak is not so lucky. It needs mature, healthy elm trees for its egg-laying, and since Dutch elm disease devastated this part of the country, these beautiful insects have disappeared completely from my list of garden visitors.

## BIRD WATCHING

The butterflies are easy. They are simple to identify as adults, and their larval food plants are well documented. You could try the same sort of exercise with the garden birds. You know that you have far more customers at your bird table in the winter than you could ever hope to provide nesting sites for in your wildlife garden, so where do they all breed? A few

of them will stake out territories in your neighbours' gardens, of course – blackbirds in the pyracantha next door, dunnocks in the privet hedge across the road and the goldcrests have erect conifers galore to choose from, since one third of all the trees in urban Britain are thought to be Leyland or Lawson's cypress. Some of the bird table winter visitors fly miles away to breed. The siskins, the redwings, the bramblings and the fieldfares don't need to find a nesting site anywhere near your garden. But what about all those greenfinches? Where is the most likely patch of bushes for them to build in? Where does the cock wren find the four or five safe holes it needs to provide an adequate choice of nests for his fickle mate to select from? If a great, ungainly grey heron flaps down to snatch a frog from your pond, how far has it flown from the noisy chatter of its communal heronry? Will the hollow tree used by the tawny owls last year for breeding still be there next spring, when they have need of it again?

You can have a lot of fun speculating about your wildlife garden's links with its surroundings. Draw up the ideal slug-rich circuit for your hedgehogs. Keep one ear open for reports of frogs and toads from surprised, pondless neighbours. Work out the extent of the empire ruled by the noisy magpies which build their thorny-roofed nest high in the poplar on the far side of the playing field.

## UNEXPECTED VISITORS

A most spectacular insect passed through our garden one summer. It was a good 8cm long, and a frantic thumb through my insect book told me that it was a giant ichneumon fly (*Rhyssa persuasoria*). This amazing creature has a long, sharp, thread-like spike at its back end. This is what makes it look so colossal, and it uses this ovipositor to drill down through the bark of pine trees, and lay its eggs in the larvae of the pine sawfly, known as the horntail (*Uroceras gigas*). Goodness knows how it can tell exactly where to drill. I racked my brain to try and think of a pine plantation within range of my garden, and then realised that this spectacular visitor was, in fact, much more likely to have emerged from the soft, pine woodwork of a new conservatory being built a few houses away. I often wonder if she ever managed to find another confused bourgeois suburban wood wasp to mate with, and where on earth she could find a pine tree, complete with horntail larvae, in which to lay her eggs.

## TAKING ACTION

Once you begin to see your wildlife garden in the context of its surrounding landscape, I hope you will be galvanised into action. Perhaps you will suddenly realise what an impact the new superstore has had, in being built on the best bit of bramble-covered wasteland in the area. You might start getting angry when the railway company chooses the height of the

The common frog is now uncommon in the farming countryside. Wildlife gardens and artificial ponds are making a huge difference in the towns.

nesting season to cut down and burn all the railway embankment scrub, or when local volunteers choose April every year for an annual spring clean, litter-picking through vulnerable wildlife habitat. Hopefully, you will no longer think it such a good idea for the council to spray all the nettles and long grass in the area. When the politicians press for 'maximum new development on brownfield land' then you, at least, will realise that some brownfields are green indeed, and richer by far in wildlife than the alternative rural green fields. The untidy bits of land are the last safe sanctuary for so many of our wild plants and animals,

# CATERPILLAR PLANTS FOR GARDEN BUTTERFLIES

**Hop** (*Humulus lupulus*) (top right) for the comma.

**Black medick** (*Medicago lupulina*) or **bird's-foot trefoil** (*Lutus corniculatus*) (right) for the common blue, the green hairstreak and the clouded yellow.

**Couch grass** (*Agropyron repens*) and cock's foot grass particularly in dappled shade, for the speckled wood, the ringlet and the gatekeeper.

**Annual meadow grass** (*Poa annua*) for the wall brown and the meadow brown.

**Goat's tail grass**, **soft creeping grass** and **hop-grass** for the small skipper.

**Ivy and holly flowers** for the alternative generations of the holly blue.

**Sheep's sorrel** (*Rumex acetosella*) or **dock** (*Rumex obtusifolius*) for the small copper.

**Stinging nettles** (*Urtica dioica*) (right) for the red admiral, small tortoiseshell, peacock, comma and painted lady.

**Hedge mustard** (*Sisymbrium officinale*) for the large white, small white, green-veined white, and orange tip.

**Broom** (*Cytisus scoparius*) for the green hairstreak.

**Lady's smock** (*Cardamine pratensis*) for the orange tip and the green-veined white.

**Sweet rocket** (*Hesperis matronalis*) and **honesty** (*Lunaria annua*) for the orange tip.

**Nasturtium** (*Tropaeolum majus*) for the large white.

**Buckthorn** (*Rhamnus cathartica*) for the brimstone.

The moths are mostly just as specific in their food plant requirements as the butterfly larvae. A good many feed on meadow grasses, and **goat willow** (*Salix caprea*) (left) is particularly useful since it is suitable for some of the more spectacular garden moths' caterpillars.

and yet largely through ignorance, the nature-loving public press continually for neater, tidier landscapes.

If we are to cling on to our wild spaces in towns and villages, then we have to change their image, and we need to take care of them. That task is becoming easier year by year, as word gets round that wildlife lives there. You can speed up the educational process through the work you do in your garden. Show people your habitat map, and choose a few simple examples to explain the corridor idea, and the need for wild places. Talk particularly to your local councillors. So often a habitat is wrecked by well-meaning decision-makers who think they are doing the best thing. If you don't bother to explain the situation, then you must share the blame for the destruction.

Do show your habitat map to the officers in the local authority planning department, too. Until recently, wildlife enthusiasts were dismissed as eccentric or nutty, but planners are now beginning to incorporate ecological principles into their own plans, and they will certainly understand your mapping approach. In fact, an increasing number of local authorities now have official strategy plans for

BELOW Once you realise that your wildlife garden is a service station for the surrounding habitat network, you need to take a greater interest in the fortunes of the neighbouring landscape. A nearby brownfield site may be the source of many of your garden birds and butterflies.

RIGHT Historic cemeteries such as Nunhead in South London are beginning to be valued for the wildlife sanctuaries they have become.

nature conservation, which are based on the kind of information you have to offer. Contact with the planning department has a two-way benefit. They will appreciate the detailed information you are able to provide, and in turn they will be able to keep you informed about any applications they receive which could mean destruction of important wildlife sites. You may have to learn the emerging planner-speak terms such as 'green infrastructure' and 'ecosystem services', but what matters is the fact that there is now a real appetite for making green habitat networks an official element in the local landscapes where we live and work.

## JOINING FORCES

However welcoming your local planners may be, they are obviously going to prefer to deal with *representatives* of interested groups, rather than dozens of individuals, and since you are almost certainly going to have people with similar ideas to your own living close by, it is definitely worth trying to group together. There may be a suitable club or society already meeting in the area. National conservation organisations such as the Royal Society of Wildlife Trusts and the RSPB have local groups in many towns and cities, and you can simply feed your ideas into the nearest one. If no suitable group exists, why not start one? It is easy enough to arrange a meeting, perhaps show a few photos of local sites, put up your map, and then form a committee from the keenest of the people who turn up.

You can also boost your support, and increase your chances of success considerably by encouraging the local schools to become involved. Children are the prime users of many of the wilder sites. They will often know which is the best pond for newts, or where the kestrels nest. Again there is an increasing interest in outdoor teaching of environmental education and various conservation charities work hard to link local wildlife into the curriculum. You should try to see your local wildlife group as a force for education and persuasion, rather than a fighting force. Build up the information you have about the wild spaces in your area, and try to establish a regular system of consultation with the planners. I have been involved in a charitable trust called the Urban Wildlife

Trust since it was first formed in the late 1970s. Over the years we have carried out detailed surveys of a great deal of our urban open space, we have helped the local authorities prepare policy documents by providing them with detailed information, and our volunteers and professional staff try to visit the site of every planning application in the region. Perhaps most important of all, we have helped make nature conservation 'respectable'. Many councillors had a sympathy for wildlife, but until we became organised they seemed embarrassed to declare their interest, for fear of being labelled unrepresentative. At least they can now say that they represent us as well as the wildlife in their constituency.

Having an organised group of sympathisers is extremely useful when you come up against the inevitable threat to a site. The shape of our environment is determined by the amount of influence and pressure directed at the decision-making elected representatives by a whole range of lobby groups. The property speculators will be telling councillors that their new warehouse development will create jobs. The highway lobby will be stressing the immense importance of lopping a minute or two off the journey to work. Urban wildspace will be labelled brownfield land by those who wish to keep new housing off the rural greenfield sites. You and your friends have to join in the debate. You have to convince the politicians that woodlands tomorrow are more important than warehouses today, and it certainly helps if you can claim to represent the views of a large number of members. It also helps if you can back up your understandably emotional claims with some firm, scientific evidence, collected over several years – so don't wait till there is a crisis before you form your green action group. In fact, in my experience the politicians and their advisers are generally much more impressed by the dedication and commitment of a long-established survey team than they are by the long list of obscure Latin names they may be able to produce.

PLANNING YOUR ARGUMENT
This book is not intended as a campaign manual, but there are three tactics in particular which I find powerful in arguing for conservation of wild green

OPPOSITE Tadpoles and cleavers should be a feature of every childhood. Sadly, few children have the opportunity to roam, so wildlife gardens, natural school grounds and study areas in public parks now play a vital role in introducing children to the natural world.

RIGHT When making the case for nature on the doorstep it helps to begin with colourful butterflies and familiar garden favourites such as lavender.

space, rather than habitat destruction. The first is the importance of wildlife, and wild spaces, to children. Even the most hardened of pro-development politicians was a child once, and all of them had a favourite wild space where they built dens, caught tadpoles and had adventures. It pays to remind them that the site under discussion is one of the few that remain, and that for the children of today and tomorrow it may offer the only chance of an escape to nature.

The second tactic relates to the health benefits of access to nature. Year after year more evidence emerges to show that close contact with nature and gentle exercise in green leafy surroundings make a positive contribution to public health and well-being. Scientists have measured significant reduction in stress levels within just four minutes of escaping into a leafy park or garden, and healthy living is an important item on every local politician's agenda.

The third tactic arises naturally out of your survey work. Sites for development tend almost always to be treated in isolation. The developers or their architect will have drawn a thick black line around the site boundary, and the decision-makers may be oblivious of the way the individual site fits into its surrounding landscape. You can show that the site is, in fact, a vital link in the green network, and use your now famous map to explain how a seemingly modest little supermarket, drainage scheme or car park will effectively ruin the extended habitat network, weaken the green infrastructure and therefore reduce the chances of survival for a whole range of attractive and popular furry and feathered friends. Hedgehogs, kingfishers, owls and butterflies are all likely to receive universal support. You need to tread warily as you enthuse about foxes, grass snakes and dragonflies, and however fond you are of slugs and brown rats, I strongly advise you to save your enthusiasm for internal meetings only. Remember that one person's small mammal is another person's vermin.

## GREEN DESERTS

Once you have reached the stage where the wild, unofficial spaces of the neighbourhood are being taken seriously, then you should think about turning your attention to the green deserts. There is so much potential for habitat creation in towns. There is a huge area of land committed to amenity and recreation, and there is also a vast financial commitment to planting, mowing, draining and generally manipulating the land. Despite all this commitment, most results are pitifully disappointing. Millions of trees are planted every year along the roadsides, in parks and elsewhere. An unhealthy proportion of them are exotic species, the majority of them fail to survive the first few years, and few are planted as part of a long term woodland development programme.

Vast fleets of mowing machines tear up and down throughout the summer, scalping the urban savannah and producing boring, uniform green grasslands where nothing is encouraged to flower, and few people would dream of walking for enjoyment except to empty their dogs. The cost of all this intensive wildlife suppression is enormous: hundreds of millions of pounds spent uncreatively year after year. If just 10 per cent of our municipal grassland was managed more imaginatively, almost every town dweller could have cowslips, skylarks and meadow brown butterflies to enjoy within a few minutes' walk from home.

The way our green deserts are being managed is changing. Slowly, one or two of the more progressive parks departments are beginning to develop their parks and gardens as living landscapes suitable for wildlife *and* people. They are often discouraged, though, by the tidy-minded lobby who write and complain that the wildflower meadow experiment is simply an excuse for cutting down on mowing, or that the more naturalistic tree and shrub planting adopted as a means of initiating new woodland looks a mess in the first few seasons, or that it harbours muggers. It is up to you to counter those arguments. If you want a richer environment, with more birdsong and butterflies, then you have to lend your support to those park-keepers who are having a go at making their spaces more wildlife-friendly. If you are a little hesitant, just remember that the habitat suppressors and destroyers are lobbying from a purely selfish point of view. When you shout for the rich, green, leafy alternative, you are lobbying not only for yourself, but for the children of tomorrow, and of course for the wildlife that will live in your new, improved habitats. If we all shout loudly enough, we can perhaps stop solving the problems of bad drainage and enjoy the delights of wetland habitats; we can stop simply planting trees, and begin to manage new woodland. Our urban grasslands can replace the wildflower meadows we have destroyed in the countryside, and urban green space can take over from rural nature reserves as a far more extensive sanctuary for our natural heritage.

OPPOSITE A meadow in the heart of town, however small, will have far greater scope than distant countryside for inspiring the local community.

LEFT Make the most of the magical moments. Watching a dragonfly stretching its wings for the first time is an unforgettable experience.

## TIME FOR CHANGE

If all this talk of environmental lobbies strikes you as being a bit of a green revolution, then you are right. We don't have time or space left for back-tracking compromise. Remember the statistics. Ninety-eight per cent of our meadows destroyed in 50 years. Ten per cent of our Sites of Special Scientific Interest being damaged every year. Spectacular species of butterflies, dragonflies, wildflowers, bats – all threatened with immediate extinction. Remember that the revolution begins with *you* and it can start in your garden.

Wildlife gardens have already saved the frog, the toad and the newt. Our bird population is enhanced dramatically by service station wildlife gardens which provide a lifeline every winter. Your garden, however small it is, can make a real difference. Boost the service station with extra pollen, nectar, seeds, water and you will help the wildlife that lives in the wild spaces beyond the garden fence. Create real habitats – a pond; a marsh; a mini-meadow; a woodland edge – and you will have more and more wild species moving in to share your wildlife garden, to live there, breed there and survive there. Persuade your neighbours to adopt the ideas in this book, and you will soon find yourself living in a wildlife wonderland. New, exciting things will happen every day, right on your doorstep, and as your enthusiasm grows, and your circle of nature-loving friends becomes bigger and bigger, you will have no difficulty at all in finding the energy to save more and more places in your neighbourhood for you and your local wildlife to enjoy.

# PART IV

# USEFUL ADDRESSES

## CONSERVATION ORGANIZATIONS

**Bat Conservation Trust**
5th floor, Quadrant House, 250
Kennington Lane, London SE11 5RD;
0345 1300 228
www.bats.org.uk

**Botanical Society of the British Isles**, c/o The Natural History Museum, Cromwell Road, South Kensington, London, SW7 5BD: 020 7942 5000

**British Dragonfly Society**, c/o
Natural England, Parkside Court, Hall Park Way, Telford, Shropshire, TF3 4LR; 0208 2256800;
www.british-dragonflies.org.uk

**British Herpetological Society**
(reptiles and amphibians) 11 Strathmore Place, Montrose, Angus, DD10 8LQ;
www.thebhs.org

**British Trust for Ornithology**,
The Nunnery, Thetford, Norfolk, IP24 2PU; 01842 750050; www.bto.org

**Buglife,** Bug House, Ham Lane, Orton Waterville, Peterborough, Cambs, PE2 5UU; 01733 201210; www.buglife.org.uk

**Bumblebee Conservation Trust**
Beta Centre, Stirling University Innovation Park, Stirling, FK9 4NF; 01786 594128
www.bumblebeeconservation.org

**Butterfly Conservation**, Manor Yard, East Lulworth, Wareham, Dorset, BH20 5QP; 01929 400209;
www.butterfly-conservation.org

**The Conservation Foundation**,
1 Kensington Gore, London, SW7 2AR;

020 75913111;
www.conservationfoundation.co.uk

**Field Studies Council** Preston Montford, Montford Bridge, Shrewsbury Shropshire SY4 1HW; 01743 852100
www.field-studies-council.org

**Froglife**, 1 Loxley; Werrington; Peterborough; PE4 5BW; 01733 602102; www.froglife.org

**Garden Organic** Ryton Gardens, Wolston Lane, Coventry, Warwickshire, CV8 3LG; 024 76303 517;
www.gardenorganic.org.uk

**The Hardy Plant Society**
15 Basepoint Business Centre, Crab Apple Way, Evesham, Worcester, WR11 1GP; 01386 710317;
www.hardy-plant.org.uk

**International Dawn Chorus Day**
c/o The Wildlife Trust for Birmingham and the Black Country; 16 Greenfield Crescent, Edgbaston, Birmingham, B15 3AU; 0121 4541199; www.idcd.info

**Landlife Wildflowers** National Wildflower Centre, Court Hey Park, Liverpool, Merseyside L16 3NA; 0151 7371819; www.wildflower.org.uk

**Mammal Society** 18 St John's Church Road, London, E9 6EJ;
www.mammal.org.uk

**The National Gardens Scheme Yellow Book**, Hatchlands Park, East Clandon, Guildford, Surrey, GU4 7RT; 01483 211535; www.ngs.org.uk

**The National Trust** Heelis, Kemble Drive, Swindon, Wiltshire, SN2 2NA;

0344 8001895; www.nationaltrust.org.uk

**Plantlife** 14 Rollestone Street, Salisbury, Wiltshire, SP1 1DX; 01722 342730;
www.plantlife.org.uk

**Royal Entomological Society** The Mansion House, Chiswell Green Lane St Albans, AL2 3NS; 01727 899387;
www.royensoc.co.uk

**Royal Horticultural Society**,
80 Vincent Square, London SW1P 2PE; 020 3176 5800; www.rhs.org.uk

**Royal Society for the Protection of Birds** The Lodge, Sandy, Bedfordshire, SG19 2DL; 01767 693690;
www.rspb.org.uk

**The Scottish Wildlife Trust**,
Cramond House, off Cramond Glebe Road, Edinburgh, EH4 6NS; 0131 312 7765; www.swt.org.uk

**The Wildfowl and Wetlands Trust**
Slimbridge, Gloucestershire, GL2 7BT; 01453 891900; www.wwt.org.uk

**The Wildlife Trust** The Kiln, Waterside, Mather Road, Newark NG24 1WT; 01636 677711;
www.wildlifetrusts.org

**The Woodland Trust**, Autumn Park, Dysart Road, Grantham, Lincolnshire NG31 6LL; 01476 581111;
www.woodland-trust.org.uk

**Wildlife Gardening Forum  c/o**
17 Honey Lane, Cholsey, Oxon OX10 9NL; 07923 473907

**Wildlife Watch** The Kiln, Waterside, Mather Road, Newark, NG24 1WT; 01636 670000; watch@wildlifetrusts.org

WILDLIFE FOOD SUPPLIERS

www.vinehousefarm.co.uk
www.gardenwildlifedirect.co.uk
www.birdfood.co.uk
http://shopping.rspb.org.uk/bird-food.html
www.arkwildlife.co.uk
www.haiths.com
www.britishbirdfood.co.uk

WILDFLOWER SEED SUPPLIERS

www.wildflower.org.uk
www.johnchamberswildflowers.co.uk
www.bostonseeds.com
www.meadowmania.co.uk
www.wildseed.co.uk
www.nickys-nursery.co.uk

NURSERY-GROWN WILDFLOWER
PLANTS

www.naturescape.co.uk
www.reallywildflowers.co.uk
www.heritagewildflowers.co.uk

# GARDEN SHOWS

At the time when the first edition of *How to Make a Wildlife Garden* was published, back in the mid 1980s, *The RHS Chelsea Flower Show* was already world famous, but it was the only great horticultural event in the RHS calendar. Thirty odd years later there is a programme of several spectacular regional shows every year, including Tatton Park in the north west, Gardeners' World Live and Malvern Autumn Show in the Midlands, Cardiff in South Wales, and the enormous annual show at Hampton Court. Each of the RHS gardens also hosts its own annual show.

I will always have a soft spot for Chelsea. I have been visiting most years since my days as a horticulture student, and in 1985 I helped to break the formality mould when I made the very first wildlife garden. I also made a big wildlife garden at the first Gardeners' World Live show in Birmingham's National Exhibition Centre.

Over the years the shows have really embraced the idea of gardening with wildlife. The individual show gardens have become very much more naturalistic, with soft edged ponds, flowers chosen for their pollination potential, frequent displays of native plants, and even the occasional daisy in the otherwise immaculate lawns. There is always plenty to inspire the wildlife gardener, particularly when it comes to plant combinations, but there are also increasing numbers of 'bee hotels', nesting boxes and hibernation log piles in the show gardens

The sales areas have also become increasingly nature orientated. Of course there is no shortage of pesticide and weedkiller displays, but every year there are more bird feeders, pond liners, nesting boxes, observation cameras and other aids to gardening with wildlife. Nurseries now highlight those plants and seeds that are particularly helpful in attracting pollinators or seed eaters. Pond liners and circulation pumps for 'natural' wetlands have become much more popular and there are even companies selling optical instruments and other high value products to enhance wildlife enjoyment.

A day spent at an RHS show will almost always generate new ideas for your own wildlife garden, and the more encouragement we wildlife gardeners provide, the greater will be the response from exhibitors in catering for our particular environmental interests.
**www.rhs.org.uk/shows-events/rhs-chelsea-flower-show**

# INDEX

Page numbers in *italics* indicate a caption to an illustration. Page numbers in **bold** indicate text in a box. Many entries are categorised under specific headings, i.e. 'birds' and 'insects' (with separate headings for bees/butterflies/moths/spiders).

## A

adding flowers to grasses 108–9
algae 202
    *see also* ponds: algae
    management
amphibians and reptiles
    frogs 37, 115, 135, 203–4, 243, 249, 251, *252*
    grass snakes *206*, 206
    newts 42, 45–6, 62, 135, 136
    slow worms 185, 203, *206*, 206
    toads 135, 136, 185, *186*, 187, *205*, 206, 251
annuals 88–91, 167–73
    half-hardy 168–9
    hardy 169–72
    from seed 88–91
Arnhem (Netherlands) 122

## B

badgers *224*, 225
bark, chopped 59, 61, 204

Barn Elms (London) 116
bats 143, 190, 195, *235*
    bat boxes *40*, 41, *194*, 250
    behaviour 249–50
    decline in numbers 12
    natterer 143
    pipistrelle *17*, 143, 250
beer used against slugs 185–6
bees *15*, **15**, 91, *143*, 144, 157, 160, *163*, *166*, 169, 172, 229
    bumblebees *91*, *148*, 151, **154**, *156*, 202, **230**
    collecting nectar 89
    herbs for 163
    honey *163*, 164–5, **230**
    leafcutter 64, 65–6, 167
    recording 234
    solitary **230**
biennials 168
birds 41–2
    bird tables *28*, 29, 37, 41, 45, *190*, 237, 240
        cleanliness **191**
    blackbird 11, *26*, 55, 63, 80, 82, 88, **166**, *180*, 181, *196*, 221–2, 230–1, 251
    brambling 251
    bullfinch 96, 158, 160, 161, 181
    buzzard 18
    census 237
    coaltit 45
    colonisation of wildflowers or

        trees 20
    corncrake 93–4
    dawn chorus 239
    dunnock 55, 221, 251
    fieldfare 31, *192*, 238
    finch 21, 41, 55, 80, **154**, *163*, 191
    flycatcher
        pied 86
        spotted 190, 195, *196*, 234
    food for 237
        choices 191–4, 237
        peanuts *189*
        sunflower seeds 193
    garden warbler 29, *31*
    goldcrest *235*, *237*, 251
    goldfinch *40*, *144*, *150*, 151, **154**, 161, 192, 194, *235*
    greenfinch 161, 172, **191**, 194, 251
    grey heron 251, *251*
    hedges for 78
    housemartin 116, *117*, 200, *200*, 238
    jackdaw 194
    jay 66, 228–9
    kestrel 18, 93, 94, 196–7, *198*, 249
    kingfisher 18, *247*
    lapwing 94
    magpie 251
    migration 116

nest boxes 29, 41, 44, *45*, 194–9, 238, *238*
nuthatch 45, 198, 235, 248
osprey 14
owl
    barn 196, *196*
    tawny 18, 194, *198*, 198–9, 251
oystercatcher 194
parakeet 234
    ring-neck *194*
    rose-ringed 194
peregrine falcon 197
pigeon 181, 196–7
    wood 55
recording 234–5
red kite 14, 18
redpoll *64*, 66
redwing 31, *32*, *80*, 192, 238, 251
robin 55, 187, 192, *196*, 196, 197, 221, *222*, 235, 240
sandmartin 116
seagulls 116
seed carrying 228
siskin 31, *32*, 66, 194, 251
skylark 93, *95*, 194
song thrush 222, 235, 238, 239–40
sparrow 157, 161, 197
    house 33, 191, 193
sparrowhawk 190
starling 31, 37, 115, **166**, 197
swallow 116, 195–6
swift 18, 116, **199**, 199–200, 234–5
thrush **166**
    song *45*, 55, *182*, 185, *186*, 192
tits 161, 191
    bluetit 29, 45, 167, 194, *194*, 194, 197, 240
    great *13*, 45, *192*, 193, 197, 198
    long-tailed 55
treecreeper 198
watching 251
water for *118*, 234
waxwing *54*

willow warbler 116
woodcock 234, *235*
woodpecker 45, 197–8
    greater spotted *192*, 192, 224, 235
    green 194
    lesser spotted 224, 234
wren 55, 63, *83*, 204, 221, 240, *241*, 251
Blanc, Raymond 181
British Trust for Ornithology's Garden Bird Census 237
brownfield sites *15*, *254*, 256
Buglife and Butterfly Conservation *245*
bulbs for meadows 105
butterflies 41, 169, 172, *257*
    blue
        common 93, 151, 250–1, **253**
        holly 251, **253**
    brimstone 82, 156, 158, 247, **253**
    brown
        meadow 93, **253**
        wall 54, **253**
    caterpillar plants for **253**
    climbers for 82
    clouded yellow **253**
    comma *54*, **253**
    copper 98
        small 97, 151, 164, **253**
    fritillary 46
        marsh 97
    gatekeeper 54, 87–8, **253**
    hairstreak
        green **253**
        white letter *250*, 251
    hedgerows for 79
    herbs for 163
    homes for 204
    orange tip 35, 79, 99, 158, *158*, **159**, *159*, 229–30, **253**
    painted lady *11*, 29, *31*, 250, **253**
    peacock 87–8, 156, 250, **253**
    recording 234, 250–1
    red admiral 160, *164*, 250, **253**

    ringlet **253**
    skipper 98, 151
        small **253**
    speckled wood 54, 87–8, 251, **253**
    tortoiseshell 156, 158, 247, 250
        small **253**
    white
        cabbage *88*, 91, *180*, 183, 222
        green-veined **253**
        large **253**
        small **253**
    for woodland edge 54

## C

canals *17*, 18
cats 190, 191
cemeteries *254*
centipedes 206, 241
Chelsea Flower Show 22, 23
chemicals 179, 180, 185
clay puddling **122**
climbers (*general*) 41, 81–91
    for woodland edge 72
    exotic **87**
companion planting *182*, 183–4
compost heaps 39, 61, *61*, 99, 181, 205–7
cornfield *40*
corridors see linkages for wildlife
cottage gardens 142–77
    for nectar and seed **146**
councils, talking to 254–5
cuttings 211, 218

## D

Dawn Chorus Day 239
deadheading 169
diary keeping 233
digging up plants 210–11
Dimmock, Charlie 245
disturbed ground for wildflowers 43–4
division 218–19
dogs 191

dormice 86
drainage 46, 106

**E**

earthworms 39
ecotone *53*
emergents 128
environment, disappearing wildlife
        in 12

**F**

farming
        bee population and **15**
        land management 15–16, 193
fens destruction 13
fish 117, 135–6
        salmon 14
        sticklebacks 136
        tench 136
floods 117–18, 119
food chains 63–4, 230–1
fountains, bubbler 43
foxes 18, 37, 63, 201, 222, 248
fungi *59*, 59–60, 226, *227*, 231
        chanterelle 226
        in compost heap 206
        invasive **60**
        toadstools 226

**G**

galls 67
Game Conservancy 135
garden shows 261
gardens for wildlife
        planning 35–47
        role 22–3, 24–33
        top ten ingredients for **32**
grasses *107*, *108*, 214
grassland destruction 13
gravel pits 116
Great Dixter *144*, 144

**H**

habitat mapping 247–9
habitat restoration 16, 42

Harlow Carr **74–5**
haymaking 110
heather moorland 16
heathland destruction 13
hedgehogs 26, 37, *37*, 41–2, 63,
        79, 184, 185, 186, *200*, 206, *224*,
        224–5, 231, 243, *243*, 251
        boxes for *200*, 201
        decline in numbers 12
        recording 234
hedgerows 37, 76–81, *80*
        destruction 13, 77
        planting 79–81
        *see also* trees and shrubs
herbs (*general*) 161–5, 179
Highgrove 181
honey fungus (*Armillaria mellea*) **60**
Hyde Hall **176–7**

**I**

insects 27–9
        ants 66, **170**, 202, 203
        aphids 29, 167
        beetles 61, *91*, 91, *163*, 185,
                206
                bloody nosed *241*
                diving 115, 127, *128*, *134*,
                        134
                great diving 234
                lesser stag beetle 62, *62*
                soldier **154**, *164*, 165
                whirligig 42, 134, 233
        birch sawfly 229
        blackfly 29, 86
        brachonids 184
        carrot flies 186
        damselflies 42, *45*, 115, 119, *132*, 134
                banded agrion *132*
                larvae 134
        dragonflies 37, 42, 46, 115, 134, 237,
                249, *250*, 259
                broad bodied darter *237*, 237
                common sympetrum 237
                extinction of species 12
                hawker *7*, *17*, *221*, 222, 249
                hawker, brown 237
                Southern hawker *88*
                turquoise darter 131

gall wasp 70
grassland 93
homes for 204
hotels 42, *64*, **201**, 204–5
hoverflies 161, *163*, 169, *170*, *182*,
        183
ichneumon 184
        giant (*Ryssa persuasoria*) 251
lacewings 86
ladybirds *28*, 29, 86, 152, 157, 187,
        234
larvae 64, 86
leaf-eating 64–6
leaf-miners **170**
leatherjackets 39
mayflies 116
in meadows 234
midges 116
pine sawfly/horntail (*Vroceras gigas*)
        252
pollination by 236
pond skaters 42, 115, 134, 233
scorpion fly 86
shield bugs 67, 229
sticklebacks 18
wasps *182*, *183*, 190, 204, 229
        wood 62
water boarmen 249
wood wasps **201**, 252
in woodland 61–3
woodlice 202
*see also* bees; butterflies; moths;
        spiders

**J**

Jekyll, Gertrude 144
Jubilee Meadows 212

**K**

kitchen garden 178–87

**L**

land management by farmers 15–16
lawns 36, 37–9, 92–113
        meadows from 41
        weeds 95

layering 218
leaf-litter *78, 79*, 204
Lewis, Pam 40
lichens 202–3
linkages for wildlife 13–14, *17*, 18–20, 77, 220–31, 248
liverworts 202
living walls *84*, **84**
Lloyd, Christopher 144
lobbying 16–17, 256–7
logs for wildlife *32, 41, 59*, 59, 60, 61, 182, 192, *200*
London Wetlands Trust *117*

## M

marshland 43, 131–4
plants for **133**
meadows **15**, 37–9, *92*, 92–113
  bulbs 105
  creation 43–4
  destruction 13
  haymaking 110
  to help with food cropping *180*
  insects in 234
  low fertility 40
  mowing patterns 94–9, 100–1, 107–8, 109–10
  in parks *93*, 214
  plotting out 104–5
  seed bed preparation 106–7
  spring flowers for **96**
  styles 99–101
  summer flowers for **97**
  urban *259*
  watering 109–10
mice *182*, 243
millponds 118–19
mink 19
mires: destruction 13
moorland 16
moths 152, 243–5
  attracting 244–5
  buff-tipped *13*
  caterpillar plants for **253**
  caterpillars 65, 97, 229
  crimson burnet **154**
  hawk *84*, 229–30, 244

elephant hawk **155**, 244, 245
  lime 18
  homes for 204
  mullein 152, *153*
  pepper 245
  red underwing 243–4, *245*
  silver Y 245
  swallow-tail *243*, 243
Mountain, Mary 144
mowers 110
mulching 59, 61, 99
muntjac deer *222*, 223–4

## N

nematodes 185
night-time wildlife 11
North Meadow (Wiltshire) 100, *101*
nurseries 209–10

## O

organic gardening 180–1
otters 14, *15*
outdoor rooms 36–7
oxygenators 127

## P

parks 21–2, 45, 46, 52, *257*, *258*
  meadows in *93*, 214
paths through meadows *107*
patio *7*, 36
peat bogs 16, 207
pitfall trapping 241–2
planting on 104
Plantlife 98
Plants for Bugs 236
playing fields 21–2
pollination **15**
ponds *7, 37*, 37, 42, 114–39
  algae management **126**, 127, 137
  edges *213*
  fish 135–6
  liners 120, 122–3
  maintenance 136–7
  making 123–6

mapping in neighbourhood 248
  numbers in gardens 45–6
  plants for 124, **127**, **129**, **130**
    ones to avoid **131**
    *see also* marshland
  pre-formed 126
  puddling **122**
  recycled sink *43*
  seating *121*
  siting 119–22
  snails *43*
  straw for 135
  topping up 136–7
  waterproofing 122–3
potting on 217–18
propagating 208–19
public areas 21–2

## R

railway lines 248, *249*
rainwater runoff 117–18
rats **191**
record keeping 233
reptiles *see* amphibians and reptiles
Robinson, William 144
rooftop gardens 94, *95*
Rosemoor **138–9**
Royal Horticultural Society 22–3, 144, 181, 236
Royal Society of Wildlife Trusts 255
RSPB 16, 17, 255
Ryton 181

## S

salt marshes 16
satellite images 247–8
school grounds *257*
scything 110
seating 24, 36, *103, 121, 238*
seeds 41, 66, 101–4, 144, *153*, 157, 161, *214*
  collecting 211
  self-seeding 219
  trees and shrubs from 215–18
sheepwalks destruction 13

shrews *62*
shrubberies 51, 66–7
shrubs *see* trees and shrubs
Sites of Special Scientific Interest
   259
slugs 62, 184–6, 206, 231
      keel 187
      leopard 184, *186*
Smith, Geoffrey 160
snails *43*, 82, 184–6, *186*, 222
      pond 134, *134*, 137
societies to join 255, 260–1
soil
      fertility 39–41, 99, 105–6
      topsoil stripping 99, 106
spiders 62, *62–3*, 202, 229
      black hunting 241
      crab *231*
      homes for 204
squirrels 225–6, *226*, 229
Sticky Wicket *37*, 40, 99
stoats 225
stratifying 216–17
streams 13, 122
stress, wildlife for 11
strimmers 110
studying wildlife 232–45
sugaring 244–5

**T**

toadstools 60
trees and shrubs 165–7
      buying 209
      choices 39
      colonisation 20
      coppicing 51–2, *53*, **57**
      cuttings 216, 218
      division 218–19
      exotic species 257
      layering 218
      for nectar, pollen or fruit **166**
      ponds and 121
      privet 80, 167
      protection in streets 16–17
      from seed 215–16
      for small-medium garden
      **56–7**
      not recommended **57**

   for woodland 55–8
Trees of Time and Place 215–16

**U**

unwanted weeds 59, 107
urban conservation 17–18
urban drainage 46
urban habitats 20–1, **21**
Urban Wildlife Trust 255–6

**V**

vegetables and fruit 36, 175, 178–87
      apples *182*
      blackcurrants 181
      broad beans 175, 186
      broccoli 187
      butterflies and 250
      cabbages 175, 181, 183–4
      carrots *164*, 186
      chard *182*, 187
      courgettes 187
      crop protection 181–2
      French beans 89, 186
      growing before meadow
      planting 106
      leeks 186
      lettuce 186
      potatoes 187
      raspberries *180*, 181, 182
      rhubarb 187
      runner beans *88, 89, 185*
      salad crops 180
      squashes 175
      tomatoes 187
voles 243

**W**

wasteland 21
water management 119
      water provision *40*, 42–3, 44
*see also* ponds
water voles 12, *13*
weasels *78, 224*, 225
weed control 24
wetlands 21, *21*, 114–39
      destruction 13

miniature **125**
wildflowers
      for the cultivated cornfield
            weed patch **102**
      for the flower border
            blue **149**
            green **171**
            mauve, purple and pink
            **154–5**
            white **159**
            yellow **170–1**
      for the hedge-bottom 79
      for ponds **124**, **127**
      for spring meadow **96**
      for summer meadow **97**
      for woodland edge 53–4,
            **68–9**, 70–2, 215
Wildfowl and Wetland Trust 116
wildlife garden plants 41, 202
Wildlife Trusts 16, 17, 52, 98, 211–12,
      213, 219, 255
window boxes *36*
Wisley *22*, **112**
woodland 26
      canopy 55–8
      destruction 13, 51–2
      edges 39, 50–75, 215
      in garden 35–6
      glade 24–6, 29, 36
      layers 54–8, 66
Woodland Trust 52
woodlice 241
worms 206, 207

# PLANT INDEX

## FLOWERS, CLIMBERS AND GRASSES

aconite 70
agrimony (*Agrimonia eupatoria*) **170**
alkanet
    green (*Pentaglottis sempervirens*) **69**, *149*
alkanet (*Anchusa capensis*) **147**
alyssum
    golden (*Aurinia saxatilis*) *146*, **146**
    sweet (*Lobularia maritima*) **147**
    white 168–9
angelica (*Angelica archangelica*) **147**, *152*, *153*, 162
arabis, white (*Arabis alpina* subsp. *caucasica*) **146**
aubrieta (*Aubrieta deltoidea*) **146**
bell bindweed 72
bellflower
    clustered (*Campanula glomerata*) **147**
    clustered (*Campanula glomerata*)) **149**
    great (*Campanula latifolia*) **149**
    nettle-leaved (*Campanula trachelium*) **69**, 71, **149**
betony (*Stachys officinalis*) *155*, **155**
bird's foot trefoil (*Lutus comiculatus*) 214, 251, **253**
bistort
    amphibious (*Polygonum amphibium*) **124**, 128
    common (*Persicaria bistorta*) **147**
black medick (*Medicago lupulina*) **253**
blanket weed 127, 137
blue lace flower (*Trachymene coerulea*) **147**
bluebell (*Hyacinthoides non-scripta*) *12*, *13*, 13, 58, **68**, 70, 71, **149**, *208*, 215, 223

bog bean (*Menyanthes trifoliata*) 128, **129**
borage *143*, *144*, *163*, *164*, *185*
brooklime/water veronica (*Veronica beccabunga*) **130**, 132
bryony, white 72, *73*
bugle (*Ajuga reptans*) **96**, 132, **133**, **146**, **149**
burdock (*Arctium lappa*) 19, 228
    lesser (*Arctium minus*) **154**
burr-reed 213
buttercup, meadow (*Ranunculus acris*) **97**, 98, **133**, 214
campion 215
    bladder (*Silene vulgaris*) **159**
    pink 71, *103*, *110*
    red (*Silene dioica*) **68**, **155**
    white (*Silene alba*) 71, **159**
canary creeper (*Tropaeolum peregrinum*) 91
candytuft (*Iberis amara*) **147**, 169
caper spurge (*Euphorbia lactea*) 182
carrot, wild *214*, 214
cat's ears (*Hypochaeris radicata*) 95, **96**, 98
celandine 66
    greater (*Chelidonum majus*) **69**, 71, **170–1**
    lesser (*Ranunculus ficaria*) **69**, 72
cherry pie (*Heliotropium arborescens*) **147**, 168
chicory (*Cichorium intybus*) **147**, **149**, 161, 162–3, *163*
chives 163
Christmas rose (*Helleborus niger*) *146*, **146**
clarkia 169
*Clematis*
    *C. alpina* 83
    *C. montana* 224
    wild (old man's beard) 72, *73*, 218, *219*
cock's foot 99
codlins and cream/hairy willowherb

(*Epilobium hirsutum*) **133**, 134
common bent (*Agrostis tenuis*) 108
*Convolvulus tricolor* 169
corn marigold (*Glebionis segetum*) **102**, **170**
corncockle (*Agrostemma githago*) 43, 47, **102**, **147**, **155**, 173
cornfield 173
cornflower (*Centaurea cyanus*) 15, **102**, **146**, **149**
cosmos (*Cosmos bipinnatus*) **147**, 156, 169, 172, *172*
couch grass (*Agropyron repens*) **253**
cow parsley 99, 213
cowslip see *under* primrose
cranesbill (*Geranium* spp) **146**, 163
    meadow (*Geranium pratense*) 109, *109*, **149**, 160, *214*
    wood (*Geranium sylvaticum*) **155**
creeping jenny (*Lysimachia nummularia*) 132, **133**
crocus 157
    spring (*Crocus chrysanthus* and hybrids) **146**
cuckoo pint/lords and ladies (*Arum maculatum*) **68**, 79
cup-and-saucer (*Cobaea scandens*) *91*, 91
daffodil, wild (*Narcissus pseudo-narcissus*) **68**, 70, 105
dahlia 156
daisy (*Bellis perennis*) 37, 95, **96**, 98
dandelion (*Taraxacum officinale*) **96**
deadnettle
    red (*Lamium purpureum*) **68**, 71, 79, **102**, **154**
    white (*Lamium album*) **68**, 71, 79, **159**, 227
devil's bit scabious (*Succisa pratensis*) **97**, **149**
dock (*Rumex obtusifolia*) **253**
duck potato (*Sagittaria latifolia*) **131**
duckweed (*Lemna*) **131**
dyers wintergreen (*Genista tinctoria*)

98, **170**

elephant's ears (*Bergenia cordifolia*) **146**

evening primrose (*Oenothera biennis*) **147**, 152–3, *163*, 244

fairy fern (*Azolla*) 128

fanwort (*Caboma caroliniana*) **131**

fennel, common (*Foeniculum vulgare*) **147**, *162*, *163*

ferns 202

field scabious (*Knautia arvensis*) **97**, 100, *211*

fleabane (*Erigeron* spp) **146**
    common (*Pulicaria dysenterica*) **171**, *171*

forget-me-not (*Myositis* spp) **146**, 168, 169
    water (*Myositis scorpioides*) *47*, 125, **130**, *132*
    wood (*Myositis sylvatica*) **149**

foxglove (*Digitalis purpurea*) *51*, **68**, 71, **147**, **154**, 215

frogbit (*Hydrocharis morus-ranae*) **131**

garlic mustard/Jack-by-the-hedge (*Alliaria petiolata*) **69**, 79, *159*, **159**, *228*

globe artichoke (*Cyanara scolymus*) 161, *163*

globe flower (*Trollius europaeus*) **171**

globe thistle (*Echinops ritro*) **147**, *160*, 161

goat's beard (*Tragopogon pratensis*) **97**, *215*

goat's tail grass **253**

golden rod (*Solidago canadensis* ) **147**, 161

goosegrass/cleavers (*Galium aparine*) 19, 228

gourds *91*

grape hyacinth (*Muscari armeniacum*) **146**, 156, *158*

grass of Parnassus (*Parnassia palustris*) 132

ground elder 72

groundsel (*Senecio vulgaris*) 227

hardhead (*Centaurea nigra*) **97**, **154**, *212*

harebell (*Campanula rotundifolia*) **97**,

149, 202, *203*

hawkweed (*Hieracium umbellatum*) 212, 227

hedge mustard (*Sisymbrium officinale*) 227, **253**

hedge woundwort (*Stachys sylvatica*) **69**

hellebore, stinking (*Helleborus foetidus*) **68–9**, *171*, **171**

hemp agrimony (*Eupatorium cannabinum*) **133**, 134, **147**, **154**

herb robert (*Geranium robertianum*) **68**, *68*, 72, **155**, 202

Himalayan balsam 19

hollyhock (*Alcea rosea*) **147**, *147*, *150*

honesty (*Lunaria annua*) **146**, 157, *158*

honeysuckle 72, *73*, *84*, 85–6, 86, **87**, 216, *218*, *219*, 244

hop (*Humulus lupulus*) **253**

hop-grass **253**

hornwort (*Certaophyllum demersum*) **127**

hyacinth, water (*Eichhornia crassipes*) **131**

hydrangea 83

iris
    flag 213, *214*
    stinking (*Iris foetidissima*) **69**
    yellow (*Iris pseudacorus*) **130**, 131

ivy 81–3, 247, **253**

Jacob's ladder (*Polemonium caeruleum*) **147**

Japanese knotweed 19

knapweed (*Centaurea scabiosa*) 39, **97**, 98, **154**, *212*, 212, *214*, *215*

lady's bedstraw (*Galium verum*) 39, **97**, *109*, 109, *214*

lady's mantle (*Alchemilla vulgaris*) **171**

lady's smock/cuckoo flower (*Cardamine pratense*) 35, 39, 99, *132*, **253**

larkspur 169

lavatera, tree (*Lavatera olbia*) **147**

lavender 28, 164, *257*

lemon balm 165

Lenten rose (*Helleborus orientalis*) **146**

leopard's-bane (*Doronicum x excelsum*) **146**

lettuce, water (*Pistia stratiotes*) **131**

lily-of-the-valley (*Convallaria majalis*) **68**, 70

loosestrife 125
    purple (*Lythrum salicaria*) *133*, **133**, 134, **147**, **155**
    yellow (*Lythrum vulgaris*) **147**

lovage 162

love-in-a-puff (*Cardiospermum halicacabum*) 91

mallow, pink 160

marigold (*Calendula/Tagetes*) 169, *182*, *185*, 229

marjoram (*Origanum vulgare*) **147**, **154**, 164

marsh marigold (*Caltha palustris*) 43, 125, *133*, **133**

marsh woundwort (*Stachys palustris*) *133*

masterwort (*Astrantia major*) **159**

mayweed
    pineapple (*Matricaria discoidea*) **102**
    scentless (*Matricaria maritima*) **159**

meadow clary 100

meadow foxtail (*Alopecuris pratensis*) 108

meadow grass
    annual (*Poa annua*) **253**
    smooth (*Poa pratense*) 108

meadow saffron 105

meadowsweet (*Filipendula ulmaria*) **133**, 134, *215*

Michaelmas daisy (*Aster/ Symphyotrichum* spp) **147**, 158–60, *160*

mignonette (*Reseda odorata*) **147**

milkmaids/lad'ys smock (*Cardamine pratensis*) **96**

mint 165
    water (*Mentha aquatica*) **130**, 131, 213

mullein, giant (*Verbascum*

bombyciferum) 152, *153*

musk mallow (*Malva moschata*) **97**, 100, **147**, **155**

nasturtium (*Tropaeolum majus*) *88*, *89–91*, **147**, **253**

nettles (*Urtica dioica*) 247, 249, 250, **253**

night-flowering catchfly (*Silene noctiflora*) **155**

orchids, common spotted *98*

orpine (*Sedum telephium*) **147**

ox-eye daisy/moonpenny (*Leucanthemum vulgare*) *97*, 108, **170**, *212*, 214

oxlip (*Primula elatior*) 70

parrot's feather (*Myriophyllum aquaticum*) **131**

parsley 165

pennywort, water (*Hydrocotyle ranunculoides*) **131**

petunia 168

pheasant's eye (*Adonis annua*) 173

phlox (*Phlox paniculata*) **147**

pigmyweed, New Zealand (*Craddula helmsii*) **131**

plantain 95, 98
  hoary (*Plantago media*) 108
  water (*Alisma plantago-aquatica*) **130**, *131*, 213

poached egg plant/bees' butter (*Limnanthes douglasii*) **146**, 169, *172*

polyanthus *see* primrose

pondweed 128
  broadleaved (*Potamogeton natans*) **124**
  Canadian (*Elodea canadensis*) 127, **131**
  curly (*Potamogeton crispus*) **127**

poppy
  Californian (*Eschscholtzia californica*) **147**, *168*, *169*, *173*
  common (*Papaver rhoeas*) 44, **147**, *173*
  large-flowered 160
  Oriental (*Papaver orientale*) **147**

Welsh (*Meconopsis cambrica*) 169

poppy (*Papaver rhoeas*) **102**

poppy, Welsh (*Meconopsis cambrica*) *103*, **171**

primrose family (*Primula* spp) **146**, 168
  cowslip (*Primula veris*) 39, **96**, 101, *101*, 103, 108, **170**, *211*
  oxlip (*Primula elatior*) **170**
  primrose (*Primula vulgaris*) 58, 66, **68**, 70, *70*, **170**, 202, *212*, 215, 219, *219*

primrose, water (*Ludwigia*) **131**

purple top (*Verbena bonariensis*) **147**, *156*

ragged robin (*Lychnis flos-cuculi*) 43, *46*, 119, 132, **133**, **146**, 213

ragwort (*Senecio jacobaea*) **170**

ramsons/wild garlic (*Allium ursinum*) **69**, 70

red clover *98*

red fescue (*Festuca rubra*) 108

red hot poker 156

reed
  burr (*Sparganium erectum*) **129**, 131
  common (*Phragmites communis*)) 128
  common (*Phragmites communis*) **131**

reed sweet-grass (*Glyceria maxima*) 131, **131**

reedmace
  greater/bulrush (*Typha latifolia*) 128, **131**
  lesser (*Typha angustifolia*) 128, **129**

rockrose (*Helianthemum nummularium*) **170**

rose 223
  dog (*Rosa canina*) 66, 67
  wild 209, 218

rose campion (*Lychnis coronaria*) 161

rosemary *164*, 164

rough hawkbit (*Leontodon hispidus*) **96**, *170*

rush, flowering (*Butomus umbellatus*)

125, **129**, 131, *213*, 213

ryegrass 108

saffron, meadow (*Colchicum autumnale*) **147**

sage 165

sainfoin (*Onobrychis viciifolia*) **155**, *155*

salad burnet (*Sanguisorba minor*) **96**, *107*, **133**

sanicle (*Sanicula europaea*) **159**

scabious 39
  field (*Knautia arvensis*) **154**, 214
  small (*Scabiosa columbaria*) **147**

scarlet pimpernel (*Anagallis arvensis*) **102**

seakale (*Crambe maritima*) **159**

self-heal (*Prunella vulgaris*) 95, **96**, **149**

Shasta daisy (*Leucanthemum* x *superbum*) **146**

sheep's sorrel (*Rumex acetosella*) **253**

snake's head fritillary (*Fritillaria meleagris*) **96**, 100, *101*, 101, 105

snapdragon (*Antirrhinum majus*) **147**, *156*, 156, 168

sneezewort (*Achillea ptarmica*) *159*, **159**

snowdrop (*Galanthus nivalis*) **68**, 70, 156, *211*

soapwort (*Saponaria officinalis*) *154*, **155**

soft creeping grass **253**

soldiers and sailors (*Pulmonaria saccharata*) **146**

solomon's seal (*Polygonatum multiflorum*) 68, **68**, 71

sorrel
  common (*Rumex acetosa*) 108–9
  sheep's (*Rumex acetosella*) **97**, 97

spearmint (*Menta spicata*) **147**, 182

spearwort
  greater (*Ranunculus lingua*) **129**, 131, **131**, 213
  lesser (*Ranunculus flammula*) **130**, 132, 213

speedwell
> garden (*Veronica longifolia*) **147**, *147*
> germander (*Veronica chamaedrys*) 95, 98, 108, **149**

spider flower (*Cleome hassleriana*) **147**, *156*

St John's wort, perforate (*Hypericum perforatum*) 97, **97**

stitchwort
> greater (*Stellaria holostea*) **159**
> lesser (*Stellaria graminea*) **96**, 99

stonecrop (*Sedum acre*) **170**, *170*, 202

strawberry, wild (*Fragaria vesca*) 69, **69**, 70

sunflower (*Helianthus annuus*) **147**, *172*, 172–3, *175*

sweet bergamot (*Monarda didyma*) **146**, *146*

sweet pea 216

sweet rocket/dame's violet (*Hesperis matronalis*) **146**, 158, **253**

sweet vernal grass (*Anthoxanthum odoratum*) 108

sweet William (*Dianthus barbatus*) *146*, **146**, 168

sweet woodruff (*Galium odoratum*) **68**, 70

tansy (*Tanacetum vulgare*) 163, *170*, **170**

teasel (*Dipsacus fullonum*) **147**, *148*, 148–51, *150*, **154**, 213

thistle 19, 213
> sow (*Sonchus* spp) 227
> spear (*Cirsium vulgare*) **154**

thrift/sea pink (*Armeria maritima*) **146**, **154**

thyme, wild (*Thymus serpyllum*) **154**

timothy (*Phleum pratense*) 108

toadflax
> ivy-leaved 202, *203*
> purple 212
> yellow (*Linaria vulgaris*) *171*, **171**, 212

tobacco plant (*Nicotiana longsdorfii*) **147**, *156*, 168, 244

tormentil (*Potentilla erecta*) **170**

valerian, red (*Centranthus ruber*) **147**

vetch 216
> purple 214

violet, common (*Viola riviniana*) **68**, 70

viper's bugloss (*Echium vulgare*) **147**, **149**

Virginia creeper 83

Virginia stock 169

wallflower (*Erysimum cheiri*) **146**, 168

water avens (*Geum rivale*) **146**

water crowfoot (*Ranunculus aquatilis*) **124**, **127**

water fern (*Azolla filiculoides*) **131**

water milfoil, spiked (*Myriophyllum spicatum*) **127**

water soldier (*Stratiotes aliodes*) **131**

water starwort (*Callitriche* spp) **127**

waterlily (*Nymphaea*) 128
> fringed (*Nymphaea peltata*) **124**
> white (*Nymphaea alba*) **124**
> yellow (*Nuphar lutea*) **131**

waterweed, curly (*Lagarosiphon major*) **131**

willow herb (*Epilobium* spp) 227
> rosebay (*Epilobium angustifolium*) 19, *155*, **155**, 228

winter aconite (*Eranthis hyemalis*) **146**, 156

wood anemone (*Anemone nemorosa*) **69**, *69*, 70, 71–2, **159**, *159*, 215

woody nightshade (*Solanum dulcamara*) 72, **154**

woundwort
> hedge (*Stachys sylvatica*) 78, 79, **154**
> marsh (*Stachys palustris*) **133**

yarrow (*Achillea filipendulina/ millefolium*) 97, 98, 101, **147**, *160*, 160–1, 214

yellow archangel (*Lamium galeobdolon*) **68**, **170**

yellow rattle (*Rhinanthus minor*) 96, **96**, 108, *213*, 214, *215*

Yorkshire fog (*Holcus lanatus*) 108

**TREES AND SHRUBS**

alder (*Alnus glutinosa*) **56**, 67, 117, 228

alder buckthorn 247

*Amelanchier canadensis* **166**

apple trees *31*

ash (*Fraxinus excelsior*) 19, **57**

aspen poplar (*Populus tremula*) **56–7**

azalea 67

beech (*Fagus sylvatica*) **57**, 81, 209

berberis 67, 167, 228

birch (*Betula* spp) 228

bird cherry (*Prunus padum*) 58, 67

blackberry/bramble *54*, 87–8, 216, 218, *219*, 228

blackthorn/sloe 81, 216, *217*

box 81

broom (*Cytisus scoparius/C. praecox*) *166*, 167, **253**

buckthorn (*Rhamnus cathartieus*) **253**

*Buddleja* 165–7, 247
> *B. davidii 164*, 165–7
> *B. globosa 164*

*Ceanothus* **87**

cherry 216

*Cotoneaster* 67, **87**, 167, 228
> *C. frigida* **166**
> *C. horizontalis* **166**

crab apple (*Malus sylvestris*) 39, **56**, 216, *217*

dogwood 80, 81

downy birch (*Betula pubescens*) **56**

elderberry 216

elm (*Ulmus procera*) **57**, 59, 60

field maple 39, 67, 80, 209

flowering currant 167

goat willow (*Salix caprea*) 19, 209, **253**

gorse 216

guelder rose (*Viburnum opulus*) 80, 216, *217*

hawthorn (*Crataegus monogyna*) 39, **56**, 67, 80, *80*, 81, 216, 228

hazel 58, 67, 209, 229

holly 80, **253**

honeysuckle (*Lonicera fragrantissima*) **166**

hornbeam (*Carpinus betulus*) **57**

horse chestnut (*Aesculus hippocastanum*) **57**

ivy *83*

Japanese cherry (*Prunus japonica*) **57**

Japanese quince (*Chaenomeles japonica*) *166*, **166**, 167

lilac 167

lime, small-leaved (*Tilia cordata*) **57**, 58

*Mahonia* spp 167, 228

mock orange 67, 167

Norway maple (*Acer platanoides*) **57**

oak

American red (*Quercus rubra*) 64

English (*Quercus robur/ petraea*) **56–7**, 64, 209, 215, *217*, 228

holm (*Quercus ilex*) 64

Turkey (*Quercus cerris*) 64

Oregon grape (*Mahonia* spp) **166**

*Osmanthus* x *burkwoodii* **166**

*Pyracantha* **87**, **166**, 167

rose 167

dog (*Rosa canina*) 80, 228

wild 216

rowan (*Sorbus aucuparia*) **56**, 58, 67, 216

silver birch (*Betula pendula*) 19, *53*, **56**, *59*, 67, 209

sweet chestnut (*Castanea sativa*) **57**

sycamore (*Acer pseudoplatanus*) 19, **57**

tree of heaven (*Ailanthus alata*) **57**

*Viburnum* 167

*V. bodnantense* **166**

*V. tinus* **166**, *166*

wild cherry/gean (*Prunus avium*) **57**, 67

willow 117

white (*Salix alba*) **57**

yew 81, 216, *217*

# ACKNOWLEDGMENTS

I am especially grateful to the Royal Horticultural Society. By commissioning this new edition of *How to Make a Wildlife Garden* they have reminded me just how far the idea of wildlife gardening has come since 1985. At last I feel "legitimate"!

The patient professionalism of Helen Griffin and Laura Nicolson at Frances Lincoln helped me to make sure that the new edition remained a labour of love. The wildlife in my own small garden continues to surprise and delight me, and over the years a great many gardeners have shared their own garden wildlife experiences with me.

Finally I am grateful to my Mother. At the time of writing she is almost 97, still living in the home I grew up in, and still fascinated by the birds outside her window, the first primroses of spring and the way her garden reflects all the subtleties of our changing seasons.

# PICTURE CREDITS

**Alamy:** birdpix p180t; Andrew Darrington p45tl, 64bl, 85, 245; Anna Stowe Botanica p120–121; Anne Gilbert p162t; Annette Lepple p142; Arterra Picture Library p82, 109, 190, 238; blickwinkel p187, 200; Clynt Garnham p150–151; David Chapman p89b; david tipling p15t, 78br Ernie Janes p156t; Gary K Smith p38, 108; Gary K Smith p38; Graham Hush p107t; Guy Bell p28b; John Glover p42, 67, 87, 123, 157t&b; Kevin Freeborn p145; Les Stocker p27t; marks flowers p185; Martin Hughes-Jones p144; Michael Hawkridge p100; Natural Visions p134; Nature Picture Library p234, 256; Nik Taylor Wildlife p188; Papilio p54; Philip Jones p206; REDA &&CO srl p90; Richard Becker p71; Richard Bowden p175; Robert Brook p14; Stephen Wanstall p163; steve young p27b; Tony Rolls p72

**Brett Westwood** p64tl

**Chris Baines:** p7, 22, 34, 118

**Clare Dinham/Buglife:** (Tata Steelworks) p20, (Lucite, Teesside) p254

**Dom Greves/Butterfly Conservation**: p244

**GAP Photos:** p218br; Abigail Rex p178; BBC Magazines Ltd p219bl; David Dixon - The Garden House p8–9; Gary Smith p181; Howard Rice p80, 114; J S Sira p53; Jonathan Buckley p218l, 219br; Mark Bolton p78t, 103; Matt Anker - Design: Charlotte Murrell p25; Matt Anker - Designer: Ian Hammond. Sponsor: Squires Garden Centres p104–105; Nicola Stocken - Dial Park p26

**Getty:** Diane Cook And Len Jenshel p94

**Chris Harris/Plantlife:** Coronation Meadow at Joan's Hill Farm Reserve, CM for Herefordshire p98–99

**RHS Images:** Andrew Halstead p230bl, 253br; Carol Sheppard p23, 44, 92, 111, 112–113, 211t; Georgi Mabee p236b; Graham Titchmarsh p153t; Jacquie Gray p152; Jason Ingram p140–141; Lee Beel p74–75, 176–177; Mark Bolton p91, 138–139; Mike Sleigh p57bl; Neil Hepworth p87, 160, 196, 201, 204tr, 205, 207, 224; Philippa Gibson p107b; Rob Christiaans p95; Tim Graham p76; Tim Sandall p40, 64r, 125, 184, 204tb, 210; Wendy Wesley p83

**Richard Bowler** p242

**Shutterstock:** 9548315445 p202t; Abi Warner 117t; ajt p217ml; Alba Casals Mitja 117b; AlekseyKarpenko p32t; Alexandra Thompson p18–19; allylondon p251; Andrea Mangoni p62t Andreas Altenburger p6b; Andrew Darby Photography p167t; Andrew Halstead p195; Anest p186t; Ania Klara p147r; Anna Grigorjeva p253bl; Anton Kozyrev p97r; Antonina Potapenko p58; Arjuna Kodisinghe p182b; Armando Frazao p69m; Armin Staudt p146bl; Atiwich Kaewchum p235; Bildagentur Zoonar GmbH p73b, 133b, p230rb; Birute Vijeikiene p167b; Biteki p149; Brian Maudsley p161t; btwcapture p28t; Bukvareva p214bl; Carmen Rieb 102t; Chris Moody p241; chrisbrignell p17; Christopher Elwell p222t; Cmspic p15b; Czesznak Zsolt p37b; dabjola p133t; daizuoxin p172; Dale Stephens p150t; Dave Head p47t; davemhuntphotography p186b; Digoarpi p217t; Dirk Ercken p137; Dmytro Pylypenko p191; DutchScenery p204bl; EMJAY SMITH 159m; epsylon_lyrae p180t; Erni p31t, 56b, 81, 183, 198t, 199, 240, 246 Eugene Sergeev p84–85; fdenb p40b; flaviano fabrizi p154; foto-zone p73t; FotograFFF p227tr; GaryFM p45bl; Gertjan Hooijer p136; Giedriius p2; Graeme Dawes p130m; Grigorii Pisotskii p171t; Gts p164b; gubernat p212b; gudak 159t; HartmutMorgenthal p155m; Henrik Larsson p16, 52; hfuchs p259; HildaWeges Photography p130b; hjochen p171b; Horst Lieber p68t; Ian Grainger p41, 165, 228t; Ian Schofield p5b, p13l; IanRedding p220, 243; Igor Semenov p128; iliuta goean p213b; Irina Falkanfal p193; Ivan Smuk p63; Ivonne Wierink p257; Jiri Vaclavek p89t; Joe Gough 106; Jojoo64 p215t, 248tl; JSvideos p48–49; Karel Gallas p173t; kay roxby p115; Kerioak - Christine Nichols p212t; kgb224 p45tr; Korovina Daria p230rm; Krzysztof Slusarczyk p129; kukuruxa p50; lcrms p201b; Leonid Ikan p55; LianeM p4b, 173b; lkordela p158t; Lollo p30; M. Cornelius p61; Manfred Ruckszio p124m, 153b, 253tr; manfredxy p29; Marcel Derweduwen p164t; Mariia Tagirova p31bl; MarjanCermelj p211b; Mark Graves p249; Mark Medcalf p197; Mark Yuill p255; markh p88; MarkMirror p1, 46, 68b, 69t, 159b, 170t, 250b; Martin Fowler p47b, 56t, 60, 101, 102b, 128t, 128m, 130t, 133m, 155t, 213t, 227bl, 232; Matteo photos p4t; matteo sani p143; Matthew Dixon p12; Matthijs Wetterauw p214t; Maxal Tamor p166b, 228b; Michael Meshcheryakov p225t; Mikhail hoboton Popov p239; mitzy p131; Monakhova Irina p156b; mr_coffee p148; Mylmages - Micha p5t; Nacho Such p194b; Nadezhda Nesterova p229; Nadezhda Shoshina p132t; Natalia Paklina p57tl; Nataliia Melnychuk p217b; neil hardwick p32; Nigel Dowsett p13br; nuwatphoto p147l; Padmayogini p258; Paul Reeves Photography p223; Paul Wishart p70; Pavel Pecherskii p170b; Pelagey p96m; Peter Raymond Llewellyn p166t, 215b; Peter Schwarz p96b; Peter Turner Photography p59, 208; Philip Bird LRPS CPAGB p252; PHOTO FUN p216; photoiconix p79; photowind p237; Poly Liss p158b; Rena Kuljovska p69b; Roxana Bashyrova p66t&b; RubinowaDama p116; Rudmer Zwerver p62b; ruewi p214br; Ruta Saulyte-Laurinaviciene p169; Ruud Morijn Photographer p203; S.Cooper Digital p119; Sally Wallis p161l; SanderMeertinsPhotography p10, 132b; Sara Borbala Balogh p37t; Sarah Marchant p162b, 217mr; scubaluna p127; Sergey Lavrentev p230rt; Sergey Panikratov p96t; Sonja M p182t; Stanislav Duben p198; Stephan Morris p222b; Stephen Farhall p253mr; Steve Meese p226; Stockr p124t; Stocksnapper p155b; Sue Robinson p194t, 248tr; Svetlana0187 p168b; Taina Sohlman p97l; Tamara Kulikova p202b; Teresa Kasprzycka p231; TheDutchMouse p260; Tom linster p192t; Tomasz Czadowski p227br; Torsten Dietrich p57tr; TTphoto p33; V. J. Matthew p146tr; Vahan Abrahamyan p146br; Valerijs Vahrusevs p135; Vitalii Hulai p250t; Vitaly Ilyasov p 65, 236t; vladimir salman p124b; Volodymyr Burdiak p225b; weintel p146t; Wim Verhagen p171m; wishmaster_yz p43; woodygraphs p36; Yakov Oskanov p192

**Steven Wooster:** p39